D1600498

JANE AUSTEN AND THE ROMANTIC POETS

Jane Austen

– and the –

Romantic
Poets

WILLIAM DERESIEWICZ

COLUMBIA UNIVERSITY PRESS
NEW YORK

Columbia University Press
Publishers Since 1893
New York   Chichester, West Sussex
Copyright © 2004 Columbia University Press
All rights reserved

Columbia University Press wishes to express its appreciation for
assistance given by Yale University toward the cost of publishing
this book.

Library of Congress Cataloging-in-Publication Data

Deresiewicz, William, 1964–
Jane Austen and the romatic poets / William Deresiewicz.
p. cm.
Includes bibliographical references and index.
ISBN 0–231–13414–2 (alk. paper)
1. Austen, Jane, 1775–1817—Knowledge—Literature.
2. English poetry—19th century—History and criticism.
3. Austen, Jane, 1775–1817—Criticism and interpretation.
4. Influence (Literary, artistic, etc.) 5. Romanticism—
Great Britian. I. Title.

PR4038.L5D47   2004
823'.7—dc22   2004058253

For Jill

Contents

Acknowledgments

My first thanks must go to Karl Kroeber, who displayed unfailing wisdom, wit, and patience during my seemingly interminable stay in graduate school. I entered my first course with him convinced that nineteenth-century British fiction was the last field I would want to specialize in and left it unable to imagine how I could study anything else. Although my student days seem distant now, I would also like to take this opportunity to thank some of the others whose inspiration and guidance most importantly shaped me during those years: Adele Siegel, Paul McNeil, Edward Tayler, Tobi Tobias, Michael Seidel, Julie Peters, Andrew Delbanco, and Kathy Eden.

Neither graduate school nor an untenured professorship are experiences one can sanely survive without the friendship of fellow students and colleagues. Among the most cherished of these friends have been Morgan Brill, Piotr Siemion, Paul Vita, Gaura Narayan, Renee Tursi, Pericles Lewis, Chris Miller, Amy Hungerford, Nigel Alderman, and Wes Davis. A special thanks to Blakey Vermeule, coach, confidant, and co-conspirator through many a lunch and late-night phone call, and to George Fayen, equal parts mentor and friend, unsurpassed model of pedagogic excellence to generations of students and colleagues.

This project began as a little idea that flew into my ear one day while I was teaching a seminar on Jane Austen in the spring of 1999. Thanks to the students who shared their love of Austen with me that term. Thanks also to the colleagues without whose support and feedback this book would not be what it is. Linda Peterson, Paul Fry, Joe Bizup, Mary Floyd-Wilson, and Michael Thurston offered acute criticisms at the proposal stage. Ruth Yeazell and David Bromwich read the entire manuscript with generous minds and probing eyes, and offered savvy advice about publication as well. Thanks also to the readers for Columbia University Press, who helped me to imagine an audience unbiased by personal association.

The editors and staff of the Press—Jennifer Crewe, Kerri Sullivan, and Juree Sondker—have been a dream to work with. A special thanks to James Shapiro, for championing the manuscript at a crucial point in its travels through the publishing maze, and to Clare Howell, for very generously donating her indexing services. Thanks also to the Frederick W. Hilles Publication Fund of Yale University for helping defray production costs.

The bulk of this book was written during a year's leave in India. Thanks to Yale University for the Morse Fellowship that made the leave possible, and thanks also to the friends who kept me supplied with library books, printer paper, ant traps, and other necessities from across the sea: Clare Howell, Karin Roffman, Ravit Reichman, and my sister, Ellen Schwartz.

My largest debts are to my parents, who made it all possible, and to my wife, Aleeza Jill Nussbaum, who makes it all worth doing in the first place.

JANE AUSTEN AND THE ROMANTIC POETS

CHAPTER ONE

Introduction

———————————————————————————

The long interval that elapsed between the completion of *Northanger Abbey* in 1798, and the commencement of *Mansfield Park* in 1811, may sufficiently account for any difference of style which may be perceived between her three earlier and her three later productions . . . [I]n her last three works are to be found . . . a deeper insight into the delicate anatomy of the human heart, marking the difference between the brilliant girl and the mature woman.

—J. E. Austen-Leigh, *A Memoir of Jane Austen*[1]

Jane Austen's nephew may have gotten his dates slightly wrong,[2] but he was the first to identify one of the most striking facts about his aunt's work. Though her six novels were published within about six years of one another, the last three represent manifestly greater artistic achievements than do the first. While that much has been a critical commonplace since the days of Austen-Leigh, it has never been anything more than a commonplace—often noted, scarcely ever discussed.[3] Early phase and major phase, as I will call them: *Northanger Abbey, Sense and Sensibility, Pride and Prejudice*; *Mansfield Park, Emma, Persuasion*. The former brilliant, cutting, breathtakingly assured, the latter something still more: deeper, denser, more complex, more confounding. Their incontestably great artistic merits notwithstanding, the novels of the early phase are essentially straightforward marriage plots, intricately designed but morally and emotionally unambiguous. In the major phase, Austen discards her allegiance to reason and resolution to emerge as an explorer of uncharted and disturbingly equivocal regions of selfhood and relatedness. From a maker of marriages, she becomes an investigator into "the delicate anatomy of the human heart."

What accounts for this change? Again, pride of place must go to Austen-Leigh. Jane Austen was twenty-three—a brilliant girl, in her nephew's terms—when she finished the last of the three manuscripts that would later become the novels of the early phase. Her father was still alive and well, their family home in Steventon still unthreatened by the prospect of removal. By the time she began *Mansfield Park* at the age of thirty-five, however, her father had died; her family had moved house six times, among three different towns, with long intervals, after two of the removals, of shuttling from friend to friend; she had accepted a proposal of marriage just short of her twenty-seventh birthday—the age by which Charlotte Lucas has become desperate enough to accept the hand of Mr. Collins—then rejected it the next morning; she had sold the manuscript of *Northanger Abbey* (then called *Susan*), only to see it languish on the publisher's shelf; and at last, her family having settled in the Chawton cottage she would call home for the rest of her life, she had seen *Sense and Sensibility* accepted for publication and put into proof. The brilliant girl had become a mature woman.[4]

But something else happened during those twelve years, something that could not have failed—and as I will argue, did not fail—to have a profound impact on Jane Austen's art. Her long period of silent growth, together with the six subsequent years of continued development until her death, coincided with and can to a considerable extent be attributed to the most significant literary event of her lifetime: the flowering of the poetic movement that later became known as British Romanticism. It was not known as such until many years later, nor were the poets eventually grouped under that rubric classed together at the time.[5] But by the middle of the first decade of the nineteenth century—1807, at the latest—it had become clear to literate Britain that something very important was happening in English poetry: that Wordsworth and his fellow "Lake Poets" were leading a revolution in poetic form, diction, and subject matter, as well as in the very idea of what it meant to be a poet.[6] *Lyrical Ballads* appeared in September 1798, just after Austen had begun work on *Susan*.[7] By 1816, the year she finished *Persuasion*, nearly all of Wordsworth's significant work (excluding, of course, the *Prelude*) had seen print. Nor were Wordsworth and Coleridge the only important new voices. All but one of Scott's verse romances, as well as the first three of his novels, appeared during the period, all of them to tremendous acclaim. And while Blake would have been unknown to Austen and the careers of Shelley and Keats not yet sufficiently underway by 1816 to have attracted attention, in 1812 Byron burst onto the scene with *Childe Harold I–II* and, within two years, his four Turkish Tales.

Wordsworth, Coleridge, Scott, and Byron: Austen responded not to a movement, but to four powerful individual talents, just as she had earlier responded to some of the leading talents of the mid- to late 18th century—

Richardson, Johnson, Cowper, Burney. That Austen was profoundly shaped by the literature she read as a youth—that hers is an art that begins in imitation, parody, and creative adaptation—has been a matter of critical consensus and intensive scholarly investigation for as long as critics have been writing about her work.[8] It is striking, then, how little thought has been given to what she read as an adult and how it shaped the very different kinds of novels she wrote as an adult.[9]

Criticism liberated itself from the notion of Austen as exclusively a figure of the eighteenth century several decades ago, but it has yet adequately to consider in what form and in what ways she absorbed the ideas and perspectives of the new century.[10] Richardson, Johnson, Cowper, and Burney first incited her to fiction, gave her narrative and linguistic forms, models of consciousness, themes and attitudes to play with and react against. Wordsworth, Coleridge, Scott, and Byron pushed her to the new recognitions for which her longer experience of life had stored her. However magnificent the achievements of her early phase, Austen's encounter with the Romantics deepened her art, darkened it, made it more intuitive, ambiguous, and unsettled, but also more bold and mature.

That Austen has affinities with, and was even influenced by, the Romantic poets, is not as strange an idea as it once would have seemed. For a long time, Austen and the Romantics occupied two different critical worlds: prose versus poetry, eighteenth century versus nineteenth century, conservative versus radical, female versus male.[11] More recently, especially with the rise of feminist criticism, connections between Austen and Romanticism have been traced in a number of ways. But attempts to expand the British Romantic canon, as well as related attempts to define a specifically female Romanticism, however valuable in themselves, while they do usually relabel Austen as Romantic, do not bring her any closer to the poets in question.[12] The same may be said of attempts to define a Romantic form of the novel.[13] A number of studies have identified Romantic characteristics in Austen's work as a whole and/or general thematic similarities between the novelist and the canonical, or formerly canonical, poets, especially Wordsworth.[14] Others have pointed to specific novels, or more commonly, specific characters, scenes, or elements, as displaying typically Romantic attributes.[15] But while these lines of investigation have yielded valuable insights, they imply no more than a *Zeitgeist* kind of affinity. A few studies do begin with specific allusions to argue for a more direct appropriation of Romantic materials on Austen's part, but only a very few, and only with respect to *Persuasion*, the sole novel of hers in which such allusions are obvious.[16] No study yet exists that argues for a sustained, major influence, one that structures whole novels and pervades an entire phase of her career.

In making such an argument, I will not be seeking to answer the question of whether Austen is a Romantic, still less that of what "a Romantic" or Romanticism is.[17] Nor will I be scoring the novels of the major phase against some checklist of Romantic attributes.[18] I will not be seeking to discover Austen's ideas about the Imagination, or Nature, or freedom, or the self as creator of values. Nor, as I indicated above, will I be discussing her work in relation to the whole of British Romantic literature, so much of which was unknown to her. There will be no consideration of Blake, Shelley, or Keats; Mary Shelley, Peacock, Hazlitt, or Lamb. The Wordsworth Austen knew had written no *Prelude* or *Peter Bell*, the Coleridge had published no *Sibylline Leaves* or *Biographia Literaria*. Austen's Byron wrote romances, not comic epics, her Scott mainly verse romances and as yet only three novels. Instead, I will trace the specific impact the works available to her had on the novels she wrote after they became available. My second chapter will argue not only that there is a systematic set of differences that distinguish the novels of the major from that of the early phase, but that this system of new perceptions, attitudes, and concerns bears unmistakable witness to an encounter with the four poets in question, and in particular, with Wordsworth.

My chapters on *Mansfield Park*, *Emma*, and *Persuasion* will each discuss her exploration of a specific concern that she can be seen to have drawn from the poets. These concerns each relate to some question of feeling and relatedness; each novel can be seen as an investigation into a hidden mechanism of psychic and affective life: "substitution" in *Mansfield Park*, "ambiguous relationships" in *Emma*, "widowhood" in *Persuasion*. But if Austen began with what she drew from the poets, she proceeded in her own directions, by her own means, and within the armature of the literary form she had already brought to perfection, the novel of courtship and education, the female *Bildungsroman*. In retracing these explorations, then, I will begin where the influence of the poets is most openly gestured to, with specific allusions and echoes, but as each chapter progresses, the poet or poets in question will gradually fall out of the discussion as I follow Austen across the new ground she charted for herself. Such is the nature of influence: not a shackling of consciousness into imitative postures, but a startling of the imagination into the pursuit of new possibilities.[19]

Several preliminary questions remain, however. First, couldn't those aspects of Austen's later work that suggest the influence of the British Romantic poets be attributable to such "proto-Romantics" as Thomson and Cowper, poets with whom she had been intimately familiar from an early age? Alternatively, weren't certain ideas and aesthetic impulses simply in the air in the first decade and a half of the nineteenth century? Next, whatever these poets' fame, what evidence is there that Austen read Wordsworth, Coleridge, Scott, and Byron, and more important, what evidence is there for what she thought of them?[20] Finally, given that each of her first three novels underwent some revision during the last years of her life, how legitimate is it to consider them as products of Austen's youth in the first place, and thus to divide her career into two distinct phases?

The first two questions are quickly answered. The very fact that the attributes in question show up only in the later novels indicates that they are not the result of the influence of the authors she already knew as a youth. Whatever was done for her by Thompson and Cowper—and Richardson and Johnson and Burney—was done by the time she began the first of her three early manuscripts. As for certain ideas and aesthetic impulses being "in the air" in the first decade and a half of the nineteenth century—yes, they were, but what was the "air" of that period composed of, with respect to the issues most important to the work of those four poets, if not that work itself? Those ideas and impulses were in the air because they put them there.[21]

Which brings us to the third question: how familiar was Austen with the work of Wordsworth, Coleridge, Scott, and Byron, and what did she think of it? The standard view holds that she probably did not read the first pair, or if she did, thought no more of them than of the second—which is to say, not very much at all.[22] None of the four is among the authors her family mentions as her favorites. Her brother Henry, in the biographical notice affixed to the posthumously published *Northanger Abbey/Persuasion*, tells us that "[a]t a very early age she was enamored of Gilpin on the Picturesque; and she seldom changed her opinions either on books or men . . . Her favorite moral writers were Johnson in prose, and Cowper in verse."[23] He also makes it clear that her admiration of Richardson, particularly *Sir Charles Grandison*, was very strong. Austen-Leigh offers a similar enumeration: "[a]mongst her favorite writers, Johnson in prose, Crabbe in verse, and Cowper in both, stood high."[24] There is no explicit mention of Wordsworth in her novels or unfinished manuscripts until we find him in *Sanditon* among the favorite authors—along with Scott, Burns, and others—of the absurd Sir Edward Denham, that Don Quixote of Don Juans.[25] Coleridge is not mentioned at all in her novels or manuscripts, nor is either poet referred to in her letters. Scott and Byron, of course, are alluded to prominently in *Persuasion*;

Scott is mentioned—along with Cowper and Thomson—as among the favorite authors of Marianne Dashwood and is quoted admiringly by Fanny Price; and both poets are referred to in the letters, Scott several times, Byron once.

To begin with Scott and Byron, the traditional critical assumption is that, because they are the authors *Persuasion*'s Captain Benwick reads as a way of wallowing in his grief, and because the novel seems to ask us to see Captain Benwick as overemotional and even perhaps, at the deepest level, insincere, Austen must have regarded them with derision.[26] To this are added two pieces of evidence from the letters. On Scott: "Ought I to be very much pleased with Marmion?—as yet I am not."[27] On Byron, with supposedly damning irony: "I have read the Corsair, mended my petticoat, & have nothing else to do."[28]

There is good reason to question the standard reading of this evidence, however, in part because it is far from the only evidence that bears on the question. To begin with, we have Anne and Benwick's agreement, in their conversation about poetry in *Persuasion*, as to the "richness of the present age," a characterization that clearly refers primarily to Scott and Byron ("the first-rate poets") and that Austen gives us no reason to take with anything but complete seriousness (121). As for Scott in particular, the remark about *Marmion* is hardly the letters' only mention of him, or even of that work. Less than seven months later, we find Austen sending a copy of *Marmion* to her brother Charles, and over four years later, we find her quoting it from memory.[29] Apparently, despite what her brother Henry would later say about the tenacity of her opinions, she did learn to be "very much pleased" with it. That this was her reaction to Scott's verse in general may be deduced from her comment on the publication of his first work of fiction: "Walter Scott has no business to write novels, especially good ones.—It is not fair . . . [I] do not mean to like Waverley if I can help it—but fear I must."[30] Finally, in later letters we find her casually alluding to a circumstance in *The Antiquary*, his third novel, and eagerly anticipating his two works on Waterloo, *The Field of Waterloo* and *Paul's Letter to His Kinfolk*.[31]

As for Byron, that remark about *The Corsair* tells us, in my view, precisely nothing—except that Austen was interested enough in Byron's work to have read his latest effort within five weeks of its publication. The letters are full of that kind of irony, directed at things Austen admired and took seriously as well as things she did not. What is more, as the fuller context makes clear, the remark is not aimed at Byron at all, but at the fact that she finds herself writing to her sister—something she took very seriously indeed—yet again.

Having just posted a letter two days before, she begins the new one with, "Do not be angry with me for beginning another Letter to you. I have read the Corsair, mended my petticoat, & have nothing else to do." It is the "triviality" of writing to Cassandra, not of *The Corsair*, that is being sent up. Far more relevant to an assessment of Austen's opinion of the poet is the fact that she took the trouble to transcribe his poem "Napoleon's Farewell" from the periodical in which it appeared, one of only five known occasions on which she copied out someone else's verse. Nor did she transcribe it verbatim, but rather made some half-dozen alterations that signify a high degree of involvement with its sentiments.[32]

Far more important than this interesting but incidental evidence, that Austen put Scott and Byron in *Persuasion* and Scott in *Sense and Sensibility* to satiric use is the highest evidence not that she scorned their work, but that it deeply stirred her. To see Austen's satire as a mark of disdain is fundamentally to misunderstand it. Who else, after all, does she satirize? More than anyone, Cowper and Gilpin.[33] For Austen, satire was the sincerest form of flattery. Nothing could be more obvious from the juvenilia than that the fiction she ridicules with such merciless glee she also passionately, guiltily adored. For one thing, she could never have known such books well enough to lampoon them as brilliantly as she does if she had not been reading them by the bucketful—and no one keeps reading what they simply despise. Parody, at that point, was an indirect way of handling her own divided response, her feelings of guilty pleasure.

In the novels—*Sense and Sensibility*, *Northanger Abbey*, and *Persuasion*—she confronts that response directly. Cowper, Gilpin, Scott, Byron: what, after all, does she satirize about them? Not their work itself, but—and this is substantially true of Radcliffe and Burney in *Northanger Abbey*, as well—the way their work was read, or misread. And yet she was not trying to protect her favorite authors from bad readers; she was one of those bad readers, as the juvenilia tell us, and she knew it. She was trying to protect bad readers—which is to say, all readers—from being carried away by their emotions. It is the central insight of Marvin Mudrick's celebrated study that Austen feared what she most loved, and that what she most feared were exactly the kinds of extreme passions those authors inspired.[34] She recognized the claims of sense, of course—of reason, of prudence—but the claims of sensibility—of energy, of desire—she did not have to recognize; they thrust themselves upon her. She esteemed "Elinor," but she loved "Marianne." She esteemed Pope, of the poets she encountered in her youth, but she loved Cowper;[35] of the poets she encountered in her maturity, she esteemed

Crabbe, but it is to Scott and Byron that she paid the supreme compliment of creating a character who loves them not wisely, but too well.

As for Wordsworth and Coleridge, given their great prominence, it is virtually certain that by 1811 a reader such as Austen would have long known their work very well.[36] A reader whose reading was, as her brother tells us, "very extensive in history and belles lettres" and whose memory was "extremely tenacious";[37] a reader carefully attuned and exquisitely responsive to the latest developments in the fiction, poetry, and drama of her day; a reader who, as a writer, is always very careful to show us what her characters read, and that the most avid readers among them read what is most up-to-date[38]—that such a reader would have neglected to read just those two poets, two of the half-dozen most important new poets of her adulthood, is improbable to the point of being incredible.[39] As for what impact they had on her, the evidence, admittedly, can only be indirect. Coleridge does not seem to have been a major influence in his own right, though his contributions to *Lyrical Ballads*, as well as individual poems she may have encountered elsewhere, surely contributed to her reception of the great complex of Wordsworthian-Coleridgian ideas and themes I discuss in my next chapter.[40] But Wordsworth is a different matter. Although this has seldom or never been recognized, Austen makes allusions to his work in both *Mansfield Park* and *Emma*. In both cases, however, these allusions are also and more obviously allusions to other authors. In both cases, in other words, Austen, in making her Wordsworthian reference, plays a complex and sophisticated double game.

The source of the allusion in *Mansfield Park* is less controversial. A number of critics have seen the representations hanging in Fanny Price's East room as pointing, at least two of them, to Wordsworth: "three transparencies, made in a rage for transparencies, for the lower panes of one window, where Tintern Abbey held its station between a cave in Italy, and a moonlight lake in Cumberland."[41] The more obvious reference here is to Gilpin, whose immensely popular series of books on the picturesque beauties of the British landscape included one devoted to the region of the River Wye—the book that made Tintern Abbey famous in the first place—and another on the Lake District of Cumberland and Westmoreland. Indeed, the presence of the transparencies argues that Fanny, like her creator, was "at a very early age . . . enamored of Gilpin on the Picturesque." But while Fanny may look at them and think of Gilpin, Austen expects us to think of both him and Wordsworth.

I will discuss this double reference more extensively in my chapter on *Mansfield Park*, but suffice it to say for now that Austen is suggesting not simply that the kind of looking Fanny does in that scene is Wordsworthian, but that it is Wordsworthian as opposed to Gilpinesque. In other words, Austen is doing exactly what Wordsworth himself was doing by setting his poem "a few miles above Tintern Abbey": alluding to Gilpin as a way of marking his or her distance from him—and in Austen's case, her closeness also to Wordsworth. Is it credible that Austen would have expected her readers to recognize "Tintern Abbey" as a reference primarily to Wordsworth? Gilpin's volumes remained quite popular, but by the time *Mansfield Park* appeared in 1814, their initial publication lay some two or three decades in the past. Wordsworth, meanwhile, as we have seen, had become one of the most prominent figures in contemporary English poetry.[42]

By the time *Emma* appeared at the end of 1815—with the publication the previous year of *The Excursion* and, earlier in 1815, of the first collected *Poems*—he had become more prominent still.[43] Austen could have felt even more confident that her readers would recognize a reference to his work, and she capitalizes on this familiarity to play the same kind of game she did in *Mansfield Park*. This time the double allusion sets Wordsworth against Cowper, again precisely as Wordsworth himself does in the passage to which the allusion points. Knightley, "however he might wish to escape any of Emma's errors of the imagination," cannot help but observe "symptoms of intelligence . . . symptoms of admiration . . . a look, more than a single look" that give him suspicions of a private understanding between Frank and Jane. Still, he worries that he might be mistaken, might be acting "like Cowper and his fire at twilight, 'Myself creating what I saw.' "[44] But while Knightley is thinking of Cowper, Austen knew that her readers would be thinking of Wordsworth, of the use he makes of Cowper's famous line in "Tintern Abbey": " . . . eye, and ear,—both what they half create,/ And what perceive" (106–107).[45] For what Knightley is doing at that moment, after all, is precisely "half-perceiving, half-creating"—observing signs and imagining, correctly, what lies behind them.

This is not quite the kind of imaginative half-creation Wordsworth has in mind, but it does offer the same contrast to Cowper's (and Emma's) creation-from-whole-cloth—a responsible use of the imagination, grounded in careful observation, to discover hidden truths. And this is exactly the use of the imagination Austen demands of her readers throughout the novel, both through the many puzzles and riddles she has us play along with her characters and, more important, through the very structure of the novel itself, a grand mystery story or puzzle-text that continually forces us to read clues and guess at the hidden truths that lie behind them.

Again, Austen is taking a text that Wordsworth had already played a variation on—a text a generation old, but still very well known—and playing her own variation on both the author of her youth and that of her maturity. In so doing, she is also measuring the distance between the work of her youth and that of her maturity. If *Northanger Abbey*, with only Gilpin at its disposal, could only ridicule too "picturesque" a way of seeing, and if *Sense and Sensibility*, with only Cowper at its disposal, could only ridicule too "poetry-of-sensibility" a way of seeing, now Austen has Wordsworth to help her envision the positive converse of these negatives, uses of vision and imagination that deepen rather than distort the perceptible surface of things. That the allusions in both novels refer to the same poem strikes me as giving more weight to this reading rather than less. "Tintern Abbey" seems to have been a poem that laid hold of Austen's imagination very strongly indeed, as it did of the imaginations of so many readers after her.

Finally, the last of the preliminary questions I enumerated above: is it legitimate to consider Austen's first three novels as products of her youth? We know, after all, that Austen-Leigh's chronology is misleading in more than just the small matter of the completion date of Austen's first attempt at *Northanger Abbey*. That manuscript was worked on again in 1803 and possibly yet again in 1816, though in both cases the changes were probably quite minor, as I will discuss below.

Far more significant are the revisions she is thought to have made to the manuscripts of *Sense and Sensibility* and *Pride and Prejudice* in the years just prior to their publication in 1811 and 1813, respectively. If either of these revisions was extensive—and it has long been common wisdom that the revisions to *Pride and Prejudice*, at least, were very extensive—then we are far less justified in regarding the novel or novels in question as creations of her early twenties and therefore far less justified in seeing the differences between her first and last three novels as resulting from whatever may have happened after 1799, whether in Austen's outward experience or in her inner life as a reader. Indeed, at least one critic enumerates her major novels not as *Mansfield Park*, *Emma*, and *Persuasion*, but as *Pride and Prejudice*, *Mansfield Park*, and *Emma*.[46] This common wisdom, however—the standard account of the evolution of Austen's manuscripts—is, as I hope to show, seriously flawed: based on circular logic, doubtful premises, and unwarranted inferences. There is no hard evidence to refute the claim that *Pride and Prejudice* is—in all its essentials of conception, design, and execution—the work of an astonishingly gifted young woman, but of a young woman nevertheless.

Nearly all the information we have about the evolution of Austen's manuscripts comes from the testimonies of three members of her family, each writing at an increasingly greater distance of time.[47] By far the most extensive and reliable of these is the memorandum made by her sister Cassandra, presumably shortly after the novelist's death. Omitting the information she provides about the three later novels, the chronology of whose composition has never been in serious dispute, the memorandum reads as follows:[48]

> First Impressions begun in Oct 1796
> Finished in Augt 1797. Published
> afterwards, with alterations & contractions
> under the Title of Pride & Prejudice.
> Sense & Sensibility begun Nov. 1797
> I am sure that something of the
> same story & characters had been
> written earlier & called Elinor & Marianne[. . .]
> North-hanger Abbey was written
> about the years 98 & 99[49]

To begin with the most contentious issue, that of the transformation of *First Impressions* into *Pride and Prejudice*, Cassandra does not say when those "alterations & contractions" were made or how extensive they were. Austen-Leigh, however, writing fifty-two years after his aunt's death, adds that "The first year of her residence at Chawton [1809–1810] seems to have been devoted to revising and preparing for the press 'Sense and Sensibility,' and 'Pride and Prejudice.' "[50] We also have testimony from Austen's own hand on this point, though it is very brief and raises more questions than it answers. Fretting to Cassandra about the shortness of the finished novel, she writes, "I have lopt and cropt so successfully however that I imagine it must be rather shorter than S. & S. altogether."[51] There are two things to note about this much-pondered statement. First, it gives no indication when the lopping and cropping took place; as the letter was written the day after the novel's publication (on January 28, 1813), Austen couldn't have been referring to something that had happened very recently. It could have happened in 1812, as most critics now believe, or it could have happened two years earlier, during "the first year of her residence at Chawton." The significance of this uncertainty will become clear below. Far more important for the matter at hand, whenever this revision occurred, Austen's statement gives no support to the theory that it involved anything other than shortening and tightening, "lopping and cropping."

As for the evolution of *Elinor and Marianne* into *Sense and Sensibility*, additional testimony comes from *Jane Austen: Her Life and Letters* (1913), published ninety-six years after the novelist's death by William and Richard Arthur Austen-Leigh, the son and grandson of J. E. Austen-Leigh. Relying on the unpublished memoir of J. E. Austen-Leigh's sister Caroline (written in 1867 and consulted by her brother during the preparation of his own *Memoir* two years later), the authors of the *Life* claim that *Elinor and Marianne* had been an epistolary novel and was read out to the family before 1796.[52] This may or may not be true,[53] but in fact the question has no bearing on the present discussion, since it leaves undisturbed Cassandra's claim that *Sense and Sensibility* assumed its present title, and began to assume its next form, in November 1797. When it finished assuming its next form— that is, when the work begun in that month was completed—Cassandra does not say, though presumably it was sometime in 1798, before the start of work on *Susan*. It must surely be seen as significant, however, that Cassandra's memorandum mentions no later revision, so that the changes made to it during "the first year of her residence at Chawton," if any, were surely not very extensive.

As for *Susan/Northanger Abbey*, in 1816 Austen finally bought the copyright back from the publisher who had purchased it in 1803. She then altered the title to *Catherine* and composed a short advertisement that begins by noting that "[t]his little work was finished in the year 1803."[54] There is no saying exactly what "finished" means—whether the production of 1798–1799 was altered only in some small way or more extensively revised. Nor can we say what else may have happened to the manuscript in 1816–1817 other than the change of name. In March 1817 we find Austen writing that "Miss Catherine is put upon the Shelve for the present, and I do not know that she will ever come out."[55] The letter is dated five days before Austen is believed to have broken off work on *Sanditon*, the novel she had begun some seven weeks earlier.[56] Illness clearly forced the cessation of the new project; whether she had actually done any work on *Catherine* or only contemplated doing so we do not know.[57] The critical consensus, however—which in this case I see no reason to question—is that neither in 1803 nor in 1816–1817 was the earlier work significantly altered.[58]

And that is all we can say about the evolution of Austen's manuscripts based on these direct and indirect testimonies.[59] The very sparseness of these testimonies, however, has encouraged scholarship to say a great deal more, especially with regard to *Pride and Prejudice*. Why? I spoke above about circular logic. Many critics profess themselves unable to believe that so accomplished a work of art could have been written by so young a person (or perhaps, given what Keats and others achieved at comparable ages, so young a woman). *Pride and Prejudice* as we have it could not have been written by a twenty-one-year-old—so the reasoning goes—therefore the revisions at Chawton must have been extensive; the novel is investigated, the revisions at Chawton are found to have been extensive, and the conclusion is drawn that the novel was not written by a twenty-one-year-old. In fact, that is precisely the logic that motivated the investigation that originally established the idea of an extensive revision in 1812.

The theory was first proposed by R. W. Chapman in his still-standard edition of the novels. At the end of the appendix in which he puts the theory forward, Chapman writes that "*Pride and Prejudice* has always seemed to me a book of greater maturity than is credible if we suppose it to have been written, much as we know it, when its author was only one-and-twenty."[60] "Has always seemed to me": a conviction in search of a proof. But is it really not credible that *Pride and Prejudice* was written by a twenty-one-year-old? For one thing, its relative immaturity is precisely what Austen-Leigh has in mind in the epigraph that heads this chapter; it is also implicitly what I will be discussing throughout the next chapter. *Relative* immaturity—we would do well to keep in mind what Virginia Woolf says about the astonishing artistic maturity Austen already displayed at fifteen.[61]

More important, who are we to say what Jane Austen—what a mind like Jane Austen's—was or was not capable of at any given moment in her development? Personally, I don't find it credible that *Pride and Prejudice* was written by anyone, at any age. The human quality represented by the creation of a *Pride and Prejudice*—call it genius, or talent, or creativity; a gift from the gods or genetic good luck—is never easy to understand, or perhaps even accept, by those of us who do not possess it (and often even by those who do). A writer like Austen, and especially the early Austen, only makes the matter worse, for as with Shakespeare, the magnitude of the achievement seems utterly incommensurate with what is known of the life that produced it. We know what feats of preposterousness this has led to in Shakespeare's case. In Austen's it has led only to the doubtful premises and unwarranted inferences I spoke of before.

Chapman's work on *Pride and Prejudice* was based on that of Sir Frank MacKinnon, who sought to ascertain the internal chronology or "dramatic date" of *Mansfield Park* by comparing the few full dates given in the text with the calendars of the twenty years or so in which Austen is likely to have set it.[62] MacKinnon's method is based on the premise—a very doubtful one, in my view, for reasons I will explain below—that Austen consulted almanacs in constructing the chronologies of her novels in order to ensure that those chronologies would be internally consistent. MacKinnon concluded, to both his satisfaction and Chapman's, that *Mansfield Park* takes place in 1808–1809 (from July to May).[63] This has since become the accepted dating of the novel's internal chronology.[64]

There are two problems, however. The first, which MacKinnon himself recognized, is that while Easter is said in the novel to be "particularly late this year," Easter 1809 fell on April 2—a very early date indeed.[65] The other problem is that in the autumn of the period in question—that is, putatively, the autumn of 1808—we find Fanny Price reading George Crabbe's *Tales*. Crabbe's *Tales*, which were very well known, were not published until September 1812.[66] It seems to me that one can only conclude that the main part of the novel takes place in 1812–1813, at the earliest. In fact, as *Mansfield Park* was published in May 1814, and as the novel's action is continued somewhat beyond the May of the principal events, the novel *must* be regarded as occurring in 1812–1813. To suppose otherwise is to suppose that Austen believed that her readers would recognize "Thursday, December 22" as a date in 1808 more readily than they recognized Crabbe's *Tales*, and that an author supposedly so scrupulous about keeping her chronologies consistent would have had no qualms about committing so egregious an anachronism as inserting the name of a work into a novel that takes place four years before that work was published. (Nor is this the only anachronism she would have been guilty of if MacKinnon's theory is right.[67]) Indeed, the presence of Crabbe's *Tales* argues that Austen herself was unaware of the calendrical significance of "Thursday, December 22," or indeed of any full date; that she did not use almanacs in the composition of her novels; and that she was unconcerned with the internal consistency of her chronologies.

Chapman clearly felt otherwise. Using MacKinnon's methodology, he concluded that the full dates mentioned in *Pride and Prejudice* agree with the calendar of 1811–1812. This in turn led him to conclude that Austen had consulted the almanacs of those years in revising the novel and that she must therefore have revised the novel during those years. Chapman concluded, in a much-quoted judgment, that "we must infer that the book as we know it was substantially written in 1812; for it is certain that so intricate a chronological scheme cannot have been patched on to an existing work without extensive revision."[68] Chapman presumably means that Austen revised the novel during this period for different reasons and naturally used the contemporaneous calendars to keep her internal chronology consistent.

Like MacKinnon's conclusions with regard to *Mansfield Park*, however, Chapman's redating of *Pride and Prejudice* is not without its problems. For one thing, at least one of the novel's full dates does not fit. Chapman's explanation is that Austen confused the date of one event with that of a similar event that occurs fifteen days earlier.[69] This is plausible, though not entirely convincing: why would a novelist who took such pains to keep her chronologies consistent make such a mistake at all? More important, though, why would she take such pains to keep her chronologies consistent? This is a question Chapman brings upon himself, for at the end of the painstaking explication of his theory he writes, astonishingly, that "Miss Austen's punctilious observance of the calendars of 1811 and 1812 . . . was for her own satisfaction; she did not expect her readers to play the detective. We are still free, therefore, to suppose, if we choose, that she at all times conceived the events as belonging to the closing decade of the 18th century."[70] For one thing, this admission makes nonsense of MacKinnon's argument for the dramatic date of *Mansfield Park*, since that argument is premised on an identity of the calendrical and dramatic dates (as well as on the assumption that Austen did indeed "expect her readers to play the detective"). For another, Chapman's admission redoubles the question of why Austen would bother paying attention to her internal chronologies, because now it appears, bizarrely, that she did not even care whether those chronologies matched the years in which the novels' actions supposedly take place.

In fact, a cogent argument was made a long time ago—in reference to *Pride and Prejudice* in particular—that Austen did not care about the consistency of her internal chronologies. In an analysis that deserves to be much better known, P. R. S. Andrews, minutely sifting the evidence once again, finds that not one, but two full dates mentioned in the novel are incompatible with the calendar for 1811–1812, and that fully four major anomalies must be taken into account by any attempt to make sense of the novel's internal chronology.[71] Andrews's own conclusion is that some of the dates correspond to the calendar of 1802, and that Austen therefore undertook a revision of the novel around that time. He does not seek to reconcile these dates with others in the novel; dates taken from different calendars, during different revisions, were used, he says "[w]ithout any regard for overall consistency."[72] I am not persuaded by Andrews's theory of an 1802 revision any more than I am by Chapman's of one in 1812 (among other things, Andrews's also seems motivated by the kind of circular logic I discussed above).[73] Rather, I believe that the overall thrust of his analysis demonstrates that, as he says, Austen had no regard for overall consistency, and that any argument about the dates of revisions based on dates given in the novels— any of the novels—is without foundation.[74]

In short, there is no good evidence to conclude that the *Pride and Prejudice* we have is not substantially the same work as the *First Impressions* of 1796–1797. In fact, Austen's recent biographers agree with this judgment.[75] In terms of its plot structure, thematic concerns, image patterns, significant allusions, even its characteristic diction and syntax, *Pride and Prejudice* remained, like *Northanger Abbey* and *Sense and Sensibility*, what it had originally been: the work of a writer in her early twenties.[76] If that strains our credulity, the problem, as I have suggested, is with our credulity. But I do not believe it should strain our credulity, not if we accept, as nearly everyone does, that *Northanger Abbey*, at least, is the work of Austen's early twenties. This is not the place for a detailed explication, but that "little work" is far more sophisticated than it is usually given credit for being. Its satirical program, along with the fact that it is always enumerated as the first of Austen's novels, makes it all too easily seen as continuous with the juvenilia.[77] But it did not come right after the juvenilia, and its satire has very little in common with theirs.[78] It came after Austen had already written two full-length novels (and revised one of them), two works in which, whatever one thinks they looked like then, she was giving herself a thorough education in how to shape and manipulate her readers' responses, how to anticipate and defeat their expectations. And that is exactly the knowledge she puts to use in *Northanger Abbey*.

The juvenilia are mainly burlesques; author and reader laugh together at the kind of fiction being parodied. But in *Northanger Abbey*, it is the reader who is being put to the test. Austen puts us to the test, in part, by putting us—in an almost Escher-like tangling of representational levels—inside the novel, in the person of its heroine. The very first sentence, which encapsulates the game Austen is playing, induces an ontological vertigo from which we never recover: "No one who had ever seen Catherine Morland in her infancy, would have supposed her born to be an heroine" (13). The more you think about that sentence, the harder it gets to understand—the more its layers of irony unfold like the petals of a Venus flytrap. There is no other sentence in Austen's work comparable to it in the imperturbability of its surface and the cunning of its designs upon the reader. No other sentence but one, of course: the first sentence of *Pride and Prejudice*. I don't suppose there is anyone who doesn't think that, if any part of *Pride and Prejudice* was written in Austen's maturity, it is that sentence. But if Austen could have written the first sentence of *Northanger Abbey* when she was twenty-two (and the novel so depends on it that it could not have been tossed in later), then she could have written the first sentence of *Pride and Prejudice*—and every other sentence, too—when she was twenty-one. And not only is there no solid reason to believe that by about 1800 the first three novels were not "substantially the books we know,"[79] there is a very good reason to believe the reverse: the systematic set of differences between those novels and the novels of the major phase, to which I now turn.

CHAPTER TWO

Early Phase Versus Major Phase

The Changing Feelings of the Mind

But seven years I suppose are enough to change every pore of one's skin, & every feeling of one's mind.

—*Letters*[1]

W hat did change, in Jane Austen's art, in those seven years and more between *Susan* and *Mansfield Park*? The few attempts to differentiate the second "trilogy" from the first have been general and brief, yielding, in sum, only a disconnected series of distinctions: "a more intensified sense of the influence of place and environment on personality and action, a broader and more thoughtful social critique, and a much greater power of imagining . . . figures within the social and geographical spaces they inhabit";[2] a greater focus on questions of bodily health;[3] a new emphasis on fulfillment through socially useful labor;[4] a new insistence on the claims of desire;[5] a deeper involvement with nature;[6] a new "sense of hazard to the larger community";[7] and a new consciousness of the Napoleonic War.[8]

While these characterizations are, by and large, unobjectionable, they fail to add up to a coherent account of how Austen's art matured. Nor do they go very far in explaining either our common readerly intuitions about the higher merits of the later novels—their greater emotional depth, artistic complexity, and psychological profundity—or our sense of the thematic developments and attitudinal shifts that mark those novels, as we note in critical shorthand, as belonging to the nineteenth rather than the eighteenth century.

A more thorough analysis is required. As the one I present in the ensuing pages argues, the differences between the novels of the major and early phases are both systematic, exhibiting a mutual coherence, and comprehensive, touching matters of narrative structure, characterization, language, and theme—touching, indeed, Austen's fundamental beliefs about those issues central to her art, the nature of personal growth and of the mind.[9] And my analysis indicates one more thing about these changes: that they are, to put it a bit too simply, Wordsworthian.[10] The influences of Scott, Byron, and, of course, Coleridge (not always distinguishable from that of Wordsworth) can also be recognized, but as we make our way through this system of changes, we will find that attribute after attribute bears the unmistakable imprint of Wordsworthian ideas and concerns. And those that do not will be seen to have grown out of those that do, to represent a development, within a novelistic framework that necessarily introduces aesthetic considerations of its own, of those same ideas and concerns.

For in those seven years and more, much, indeed, had changed. English poetry had changed, with the appearance of the new poetry of Wordsworth and Coleridge: a poetry of change, of the growth of the mind through the development of feeling; a poetry of memory and loss, interiority and solitude, ambivalence and openness—a poetry of process. And as the late novels make clear, Austen's beliefs had also changed, about those very questions, the most important questions with which her art, and especially her late art, concerns itself. In their form, language, and themes, but more, in the very sense of exploration with which they proceed, the novels of Jane Austen's major phase reflect her absorption of the new poetry.[11]

Of course, nothing of what follows should be taken as a disparagement of the early novels. Were they the only of Austen's works that we had, her place in the front rank of English fiction would still be secure; as it is, *Pride and Prejudice* in particular remains central both to her popularity and to her critical reputation, and in many respects nothing in the major phase surpasses its achievement. What is in question here is rather the greater overall merits of the late novels, merits that, as I began this study by noting, critics have sensed from the very first and that can be connected, as I will argue, to Austen's reception of the Romantic poets.

To begin with what has already been fairly well noted: Austen's late novels display an entirely new receptivity to nature and attitude toward natural contemplation.[12] In both *Sense and Sensibility* and *Northanger Abbey*, characters' observation of nature serves only to exhibit and ridicule stereotyped modes of response. Henry and Eleanor Tilney survey the country around Bath in strict accordance with the principles of the picturesque, and Catherine, their all-too-apt pupil, proves "so hopeful a scholar, that when they gained the top of Beechen Cliff, she voluntarily rejected the whole city of Bath, as unworthy to make part of a landscape" (99).

The more passionate Marianne Dashwood supplements picturesque conventions with effusions derived from Thomson, Cowper, and Scott, but she fares less well with her auditors, one of whom, Edward Ferrars, clearly represents Austen's approved way of evaluating a rural scene at that point in her career. "[M]y idea of a fine country," he says, is one that "unites beauty with utility . . . I do not like crooked, twisted, blasted trees. I admire them much more if they are tall, straight, and flourishing . . . I have more pleasure in a snug farm-house than a watch-tower—and a troop of tidy, happy villagers please me better than the finest banditti in the world."[13] Edward's ideal, in fact, is more than a union of beauty and utility, it is beauty understood in terms of utility, of the health and prosperity of a country's human inhabitants. As for *Pride and Prejudice*, it deliberately swerves away from an engagement with nature. Elizabeth and her uncle and aunt plan to visit the Lake District, for "[w]hat are men to rocks and mountains?"[14] But because their trip is delayed they can venture no farther than Derbyshire, where their attention is indeed brought back, willy-nilly, to "men."

The heroines of *Mansfield Park* and *Persuasion*, by contrast, display an attentiveness and spontaneous emotional responsiveness to nature that is in no way criticized or ironized. Though Anne, on the walk to Winthrop, "repeat[s] to herself some few of the thousand poetical descriptions extant of autumn," her response has a relationship to poetry the very reverse of Marianne's.[15] The earlier heroine projects onto the landscape feelings derived from verse; Anne recollects lines of verse to express feelings the landscape spontaneously evokes. In her farewell to Uppercross, as has been noted, she does more.[16] There, as in so many of Wordsworth and Coleridge's best-known nature poems, observation and emotion, outer and inner worlds, interact dialectically.[17] A mood of melancholy turns her attention to the dreary outer scene (that she looks out through misty panes reinforces the sense of a semipermeable membrane between self and world), which in turn prompts memories of her whole sojourn at the place—memories of pain as well as of reconciliation, but both modified under the influence of the scene, the ones softened, the others made melancholy. As in Wordsworth and Coleridge, feeling and observation are mutually reinforcing, mutually deepening. In the words of one critic, landscape in *Persuasion* becomes "a structure of feeling which can express, and also modify, the minds of those who view it."[18]

Fanny Price's interludes of natural contemplation, while not exhibiting the dialectical complexity of Anne's, embody other important Wordsworthian-Coleridgian ideas. Gazing out at a brilliantly starlit night, "solemn and soothing, and lovely," she is roused to feelings of tranquility and rapture and moved to profess the conviction that "there certainly would be less" "wickedness [and] sorrow in the world" "if the sublimity of Nature were more attended to, and people were carried more out of themselves by contemplating such a scene" (94–95). We might smile at this, especially as Fanny's tone approximates the sentimental ardors of Marianne Dashwood, but neither here nor in connection with any of her other effusions (on memory, for example) does Austen give any hint of satiric intent. And we should remember that the morally healing power of immersion in nature is precisely Coleridge's theme in "The Dungeon," Wordsworth's in "The Convict," and Wordsworth's again in the passage in "Tintern Abbey" that speaks of the influence of "beauteous forms": "On that best portion of a good man's life, / His little, nameless, unremembered, acts / Of kindness and of love" (23, 33–35).

Sometime later, sitting in the Mansfield Parsonage shrubbery, enjoying the "sweets of so protracted an autumn," Fanny remarks on an example of the kind of human adaptation of nature that would have cheered Edward Ferrars—the fact that the spot had only three years before been "nothing but a rough hedgerow"—but her purpose is less to praise the utility or even the beauty of the transformation than to remark on the contrast between past and present: "and perhaps in another three years we may be forgetting—almost forgetting what it was before. How wonderful, how very wonderful the operations of time, and the changes of the human mind" (173–174). Alterations in nature, as Wordsworth explores most fully in "The Brothers," become the yardstick for measuring alterations in the self.[19] Indeed, as Austen has Fanny suggest—and this is an idea that lies at the heart of Wordsworth's poetic encounter with the natural world—the life of the mind and of vegetation are not only parallel phenomena, they are, equally, natural ones, alike subject to "the operations of time"—persistence and decay, remembering and forgetting.

They are interlinked phenomena as well. Thus while *Emma* contains no scenes of natural contemplation,[20] it embodies even more fully than the other late novels the more general principle of which the human interaction with nature—whether in *Mansfield Park* or *Persuasion*, Wordsworth or Coleridge, or Scott, for that matter—is ultimately only a particular instance: the shaping of the self by place.[21] The second scene discussed above in connection with each of the other late novels—Anne's leave-taking from

Uppercross and Fanny's reflections in the shrubbery—exhibits this same principle. Anne's time at Uppercross has given new forms to her feelings and understandings, ones that—as that scene of mingled recollection and contemplation makes clear—are inseparably interwoven with the specific sensual textures of the place. Fanny's rootedness at Mansfield is even more heavily emphasized, especially since she first comes there having been shaped very differently by a different place and her ultimate inseparability from Mansfield is revealed to her precisely by a return to that same place. As Edmund tells her apropos of Henry Crawford, whose courtship threatens to take her away to yet a third place, "before he can get your heart for his own use, he has to unfasten it from all the holds upon things animate and inanimate, which so many years growth have confirmed" (288).

The shrubbery scene makes the point, as points about Fanny are often made, by contrasting her with Mary Crawford. Responding to Fanny's effusions, Mary declares that " 'If any body had told me a year ago that this place would be my home . . . I certainly should not have believed them!—I have now been here nearly five months!' " (175). Five whole months—hardly enough time for Fanny's tears to have dried. Mary—like her brother, a creature of mobility and instability—feels no such attachments as Fanny's; home, for her, is wherever she happens to be living at the moment. And yet, ironically, it is further evidence of the novel's investment in the idea of place as the shaper of self that that very instability, along with everything else about the Crawfords, is a product of their upbringing in London.

And *Emma*? Emma's rootedness to place is far less obvious than Fanny's or Anne's, because it receives no emphasis whatsoever. It does not have to: it is so fundamental that it helps constitute the very form of her novel itself. Alone among Austen's works, the scene of *Emma* never shifts from the place in which it is set. Alone among her heroines, Emma never ventures away from that place, never even thinks of doing so. Highbury and its environs are as essential to her constitution as a character as Dublin is to Leopold Bloom's; she is simply inconceivable without them, and everything she is she is because of them. Indeed, the story of the novel is, in one respect, the story of how Emma comes to recognize that very rootedness, her inseparability from and responsibility toward the community that includes Miss Bates, Robert Martin, and everyone else.

Elizabeth Bennet, by contrast, has no particular relationship to Meryton and its environs, owes nothing of herself to their influence, and is able to live very well without them. Much the same could be said of her novel; *Pride and Prejudice* could take place anywhere, or even nowhere—one of the reasons it has proven so adaptable to the stage. *Northanger Abbey* depends on certain social particularities of Bath and certain architectural ones of Northanger, but its characters have no essential relation to either locale, still less to Catherine's home village.

Of the early novels, *Sense and Sensibility* is the one most concerned with place, as it is most concerned with nature, but as with respect to the latter theme, that circumstance in fact allows it to serve in drawing a sharper contrast between the two groups of novels. Willoughby's moral failings, like the Crawfords', are associated with London, but they are, precisely, only associated with it. They are revealed there, but the city has played no role in creating them. As for the novel's depiction of the attachment to place, that attachment is purely a matter of sentiment and sentimentality. The Dashwood women are certainly sad to leave Norland, and Marianne apostrophizes it upon their departure in a storm of exclamation points, but it is essential neither to their constitution nor, as it turns out, to their happiness. Before long, both they and the novel have all but forgotten it.

As the foregoing discussion has already begun to make clear, the idea of place as the shaper of self is intimately connected, in Austen's late novels as in the four poets, with the idea of home. "If any body had told me a year ago that this place would be my home . . . "; home, for Mary Crawford, is anywhere. For the mature Austen, as for the poets, it is one place only—the place that has made you who you are.[22] Again, this is an idea essentially absent from the early novels. While each is intensely concerned with finding its heroine or heroines a suitable husband, in no case does that quest also involve finding them a suitable home, still less solacing them for the loss of a home they already have. Catherine Morland's home all but doesn't exist, while Elizabeth Bennet's is, if anything, something to get as far away from as possible. The Dashwoods' loss of Norland has just been discussed, and Barton Cottage, while a boon for them as a decent house, develops scarcely any resonance as a home. If anything, its proximity to Barton Park soon makes it almost as inhospitable to Elinor and Marianne as Longbourn is to Elizabeth.

The idea of home has similarly little relevance to the places in which the early heroines eventually settle. Henry's parsonage is as briefly touched upon as Catherine's childhood home. In settling Elinor and Marianne "almost within sight of each other" (323), *Sense and Sensibility* comes closest of the early novels to preserving for its heroines the home of their youth. Still, whatever Elinor's love for Marianne, relations between the sisters have never been easy, and the novel's final, disturbing note makes the mere absence of tension seem the highest blessing their relationship, and thus their common "home" (we never do get a glimpse of their actual houses), can hope for.[23] The best candidate among the early novels for a house that is also a home may be thought to be Pemberley, the beauties and comforts of which are dwelt on at great length. But Pemberley functions in the novel as an estate, a socioeconomic unit whose condition bears witness to its master's character. He has formed Pemberley, in other words; Pemberley has not formed him. At issue in its presentation is the way it has been managed, not the affective richness of the life that has grown up within it. For Elizabeth, it will be a place to be "mistress of," not, per se, to dwell in (201).

What is new in the late novels—and may be new in the European novel altogether, though it is at least as old as Homer—is the idea of home as a psychic necessity, together with the correlative idea of the loss of home as an irreparable psychic wound. That home is vital to the emotional health of each of the late heroines—as it is for Wordsworth and so many of his characters (Poor Susan, Leonard in "The Brothers"), for Scott's Lieutenant Brown in *Guy Mannering*, for Childe Harold—needs little additional emphasis. We have already seen how this is true for both Fanny and Emma, and for the former it is abundantly confirmed by her acute misery, first at leaving Portsmouth for Mansfield, then at leaving Mansfield to revisit Portsmouth. In Anne's case the demonstration is almost wholly negative. As I will discuss more fully in my chapter on the novel, *Persuasion* is, to a great extent, a novel about homelessness and the effort to create a home away from home—for Anne, for the naval officers both at sea and upon their return to shore, even, in their own very limited way, for Anne's father and elder sister.

While Anne finally finds that home-that-is-not-a-home, Fanny and Emma never even have to leave their homes.[24] In Emma's case, home is only slightly less important than husband, as her husband quickly finds out. But Fanny almost seems to cling to Edmund just because he can guarantee her continuation at Mansfield. (The interlude at Thornton Lacey is, tellingly, virtually elided.) Or rather, her loves for him and for Mansfield are inextricable, emotions of a single growth, and it is not at all clear which is the more important. At the novel's close, we find her gazing not into her husband's eyes, but out at the estate; it is really that "union" that the novel finally celebrates. So important has the idea of home become, in this late novel at least, that it overshadows the romance plot altogether.

There is good reason why the ideas of place as the shaper of self and of home as the place where the self has been shaped are absent from the early novels. In the early novels, the self is not "shaped" at all. Elizabeth, Marianne, and Catherine all change during the course of their novels, but as I will discuss more fully below, their alterations each involve an abrupt change of consciousness rather than a continuous modification of personality. More to the point at hand, who they each are at their novel's outset is simply a given. Missing from the early novels, in other words, is another great Wordsworthian theme, that of childhood.[25] That Elizabeth even had a childhood we can only guess, for there is no evidence she had any life whatsoever prior to the opening of her novel; she simply pops into existence on its first page.[26] The opening chapter of *Sense and Sensibility* outlines the Dashwood family's past, including the sisters' childhoods, but those childhoods receive no elaboration and bear no relation to the characters sketched at the chapter's end. That Elinor, at nineteen, possessed "strength of understanding," "coolness of judgment," and "an excellent heart" and that Marianne, at sixteen, "was sensible and clever; but eager in every thing" remain unexplained and—in line with what the younger Austen apparently believed, for it is true of the Bennet sisters, as well—seem to be matters of innate disposition (6). Of the early heroines' childhoods, only Catherine's is sketched. We watch her pass rapidly from ten to fourteen to fifteen to seventeen, but her development is devoid alike of particularity and emotional significance, instead mingling and playing with two generalized developmental paradigms: the physical and attitudinal changes of puberty and the reading program of a "female Quixote."

At first glance, only *Mansfield Park* seems to differ from the early novels with respect to the significance of its heroine's childhood. Fanny's is dwelt on, not at the length that George Eliot, in her most Wordsworthian novel, would later devote to Maggie Tulliver's, but enough to show how the patterns of behavior and feeling established then shape her actions and responses throughout the rest of the novel. Her transplantation to Mansfield at age ten, placing her in the company of four older cousins vastly her superiors in knowledge, confidence, and social standing, makes her into the timid and self-doubting creature who creeps through the next three volumes, concealing her desires, doubting her choices, and suppressing her resentments. But Fanny is not the only one in the novel decisively shaped by the treatment she receives as a child; both her cousins and the Crawfords clearly are as well, each of the six in ways that reflect differences not only in place and parents, but also in gender and birth order.[27]

Of the childhoods of Emma and Anne nothing directly is shown, but the summary information Austen gives on the first two or three pages of each of their novels is enough to show how their early treatments, too, have produced the young women who appear at the start of their narratives proper. In Anne's case, this significant past includes not only her accession to Lady Russell's pressure not to marry, but extends back well into her adolescence and indeed helped give rise to that fateful choice at age nineteen. If Anne's life from nineteen to twenty-seven has been haunted by that choice, the previous six years had been haunted by her mother's death. Austen's presentation is uniquely understated here, but what she asks us to infer is clear: at a crucial point in her life, right around the onset of puberty, Anne, until then her mother's favorite, became the family member most disregarded and disdained by her emotionally frigid father and equally withholding elder sister.[28] That is, when she was at home at all, for the first consequence of that untimely death was Anne's removal to a Bath boarding school for three gloomy years. Not only did her mother's loss teach Anne an excessive reliance on Lady Russell's advice, then, it also established her voicelessness and powerlessness within her family, her melancholic disposition, her distrust of her own judgment, and her tendency to put her own needs and desires last.

Emma Woodhouse, handsome, clever, and rich, could hardly be more different from the meek and marginalized Fanny and Anne, but her upbringing was no less unfortunate than theirs, precisely for giving her so unshaken a confidence in her own powers and prerogatives. Again, as with the other late heroines, the early loss of a mother is decisive. The death of Mrs. Woodhouse in Emma's infancy left her younger daughter to the guidance of a weak father, a too-compliant governess, and a sister whom all acknowledge as her inferior.[29] Where Fanny and Anne must learn to speak, to desire, and to will, Emma must learn to do less of all three. The early lives of Austen's late heroines are not Wordsworth's happy childhoods in nature, but unfortunate childhoods in society. All three young women struggle throughout their novels with the legacies of a misshapen upbringing.

Two further developments follow from this new emphasis on childhood, one interesting but minor, the other of the very first significance. Children become more prominent in the late novels, if not quite as much as in Wordsworth and Coleridge,[30] and they acquire a specific new function relative to the heroine. The only children to appear in the first three novels, other than the Gardiners' in *Pride and Prejudice*, who figure very briefly, are Lady Middleton's brats in *Sense and Sensibility*, who seem to exist for the sole purpose of showing how revolting children can be. In each of the late novels, by contrast, the heroine has a significant care-giving relationship with a group of children within her own family—Emma's nieces and nephews, Anne's nephews, and Fanny's younger sisters in Portsmouth. Not only are these children shown in a more positive (though far from idealized) light— their feelings taken seriously, as in Wordsworth—the fact that the heroine cares for them, and cares for them well, counts as important evidence to the goodness of her character.

Far more significantly—another way in which her childhood or adolescence shadows her young adulthood—each heroine's life continues to be dominated by her relationship with a difficult, domineering father or surrogate father. (This is not a kind of relationship that much interested the poets, though Wordsworth's "Anecdote for Fathers" is an interestingly subtle portrait of paternal tyranny, but it shows Austen working out the logic of ideas she drew from them along the lines of her own concerns and within the framework of her own literary form.) In the early novels, relations between the heroine and her parents may be easy or strained, but they are never particularly important. Their emotional texture is thin, even in the strongest case, that of Marianne and her mother, and parents play little or no role in their daughters' courtship. Elizabeth may be embarrassed by her mother, but she is hardly influenced by her. These young women do more or less as they please, at least as far as their own families are concerned. Parental figures connected to the heroes do function more prominently in the early plots, but only as comedic blocking figures. Notwithstanding the subtle delineation of General Tilney's tyranny over his children, these relationships, too, acquire little or no depth. Indeed, the early novels overwhelmingly concern relationships among the heroine's coevals, be they siblings, friends, or potential lovers.

In the late novels, by contrast, parental and especially paternal relationships loom very large indeed. Fanny's relationship with her uncle and Emma's with her father are second only to those with their future husbands as their most important, emotionally fraught, and complexly negotiated. It is no surprise that at the end of their novels, they marry or settle in a way that very much pleases papa. For Anne, again, it is a matter of negatives. Deprived of her relationship, one way or another, with both parents, she clings to substitutes. Lady Russell is the obvious example, but the emotional pull Admiral Cross exerts within the narrative—on the reader as much as on Anne—points to his most significant symbolic function. He is the kind, loving, accepting father Anne has always lacked, and it is no accident that he replaces her real father as the caretaker of Kellynch, her lost home, as her protector (when she is taken into his carriage as well as when he escorts her through the streets of Bath) and—though this is far more pronounced in the first version of the novel's ending—as the person who symbolically "gives her away" to her husband.

It has been noted that the late novels' blocking figures all come from within the heroine's family, but more to the point, they are all parental and, for the most part, paternal figures: Sir Thomas, Mr. Woodhouse, Sir Walter, Lady Russell.[31] The early novels are, like Burney's *Evelina*, stories of "a young lady's entrance into the world." In the late novels, the young lady is already in the world (Anne), never gets there (Fanny), or has no larger "world" to enter (Emma). In this phase of her career, Austen discovers an even more compelling narrative: the family romance itself.

This new attention to the shaping of the self in early life is only the beginning of the largest and most important difference between the two phases of Austen's career. The late novels represent a complete transformation in Austen's understanding of time: not simply in the depths of time they involve, but in their rendering of physical and social processes, of memory, of loss, indeed, of change itself. As time in all its ramifications may be said to be Wordsworth's greatest and most persistent theme, so is it the great theme of Austen's mature work.

We can begin by noting that the early novels not only occupy less time than do most of the late ones—this is trivial—but that in the former the very nature of time is different. Two passages from *Pride and Prejudice* may be taken as emblematic. The Netherfield ball has been announced, but five days remain before the big event, days that prove sadly inclement: the "younger Miss Bennets," cut off from Meryton, are especially distressed, "and nothing less than a dance on Tuesday, could have made such a Friday, Saturday, Sunday and Monday, endurable to Kitty and Lydia" (75). Sometime later, with the Netherfield party gone, Charlotte married, and Jane in London, Elizabeth has little to do but write letters, and so, "[w]ith no greater events than these . . . and otherwise diversified by little beyond the walks to Meryton . . . did January and February pass away" (127). "Friday, Saturday, Sunday and Monday," "January and February": two stretches of time in which, narratively speaking, nothing happens: nothing changes, nothing develops, time itself has no effect on feelings, thoughts, or relationships.[32]

But there is nothing anomalous about these utterly blank intervals; rather, as I suggested, they are entirely characteristic of the younger Austen's handling of time. Events in the early novels occupy time like beads on a string; they function as discrete entities the intervals between which have no significance and could thus be made arbitrarily greater or smaller without materially affecting the narrative. Nothing changes in Elizabeth's story between Christmas and her arrival in Hunsford in March, and again nothing changes between her departure from Hunsford the following month and her visit to Pemberley in July. Had she and Darcy met in Hunsford in January and Pemberley in April, their story would have been the same. Austen clearly had aesthetic reasons for having both *Pride and Prejudice* and *Sense and Sensibility* occupy the space of twelve months, and there were circumstantial reasons, such as the winter season in London, for setting certain scenes at certain times of year, but nothing internal to the narratives, no matter of emotional development or personal change, would have prevented either novel from occupying two years or six months.

As for the deeper past in the early novels—for in each it eventually turns out that a crucial event took place during the prehistory of the narrative—it exists in a purely schematic relationship to the present, as if the time between it and the start of the narrative proper were as blank as the intervals we just looked at. At a certain point in each work, forward movement is suspended for the recounting of some lurid tale that, like the opening of a secret door in a Gothic mansion, throws a stark light on the dark recesses of the villain's character and the hero's hidden wounds: Darcy's story of Wickham and Georgiana, Colonel Brandon's of Willoughby and the two Elizas. (In *Northanger Abbey*, the one novel in which the secret story, that of Mrs. Tilney's death, actually *is* told in a Gothic mansion, the satiric point is that neither is it lurid nor does it reveal dark secrets about General Tilney or his son.) But in each case, no organic relationship, no sense of continuity, connects past event and present moment. Each tale is framed and offered for inspection like a painting hanging on a wall. Indeed, in *Pride and Prejudice*, paintings hanging on walls become another way of gaining access to an isolated moment from the deep past—Darcy and Wickham's appearance as they were eight years prior to the narrative present. The device suggests something I will deal with more extensively when considering the question of memory: that in the early novels, memory functions, as we might say today, like a camera, a recorder of isolated mental images that remain unchanged by intervening lapses of time. Again, time in the early novels progresses in discrete quanta, not along a continuum of constant change.

Any sense of the physical effects of time is similarly absent from the early phase. Wordsworthian examples include, most famously, Simon Lee's swollen ankles and other signs of age and hard times, but also any number of others, including those that mark the old Cumberland beggar and Ruth. The early novels, to be sure, contain characters of all different ages, but other than Colonel Brandon with his rheumatism—an ailment that proves, precisely, no impediment to his marrying a woman a generation his junior—none is shown to have been physically affected by the passage of time. The counterexamples in *Persuasion* are too numerous to mention, for what with illness, injury, and simple aging, they include most of the characters in the book. In *Mansfield Park*, they include both Sir Thomas, who returns thin and worn from his two-years-plus in Antigua, and Fanny herself, who has blossomed during the same interval into an attractive young woman. In *Emma*, such effects are more subtle; we find no physical changes taking place during the span of the narrative, but we do find what we see nowhere else in Austen, the senescence of the elderly. Mr. Woodhouse is ostentatiously feeble. Mrs. Bates, as we are frequently reminded, is both hard of hearing and weak of vision. And Mrs. Churchill—continually ill, though no one will believe her, these past twenty-five years—bears witness to the ultimate effect of time on the human constitution and, doing what virtually no one else in the course of a Jane Austen novel does, dies.[33]

The late novels similarly display a new attention to social change. While such change is not absent from the early novels, it remains in the background. General Tilney's modernization of Northanger, John Dashwood's of Norland, the tension between Lady Catherine's old-fashioned understanding of the distance between aristocracy and gentry and Elizabeth's newer one—all these point to large-scale changes in English society that surround and contextualize the narratives. So too, at a smaller level, several of the novels' figures are themselves in the process of changing social position, but in each case the change lies outside the main action of the novel in question. The Dashwood women suffer a sharp decline in fortune as their story starts, but only as it starts, as a precondition of the narrative proper. So too, Elinor and Marianne enjoy an elevation of wealth and status when they get married—that is, as their novel ends. Their social positions, however, like those of everyone else in the early novels, remain static during the main course of their narratives. In the early phase, change both large and small happens around the edges; it is not an intrinsic property of the stories themselves.

In the late novels, change becomes pervasive at both the national and personal scales. Among the poets, Wordsworth registers social change particularly in his more extended portraits of the dispossessed rural poor—"The Female Vagrant," "Michael." But its leading exponent, of course, is Scott.

Most of the great historical novels would come after Austen's death, but Scott anticipated their rendering of large-scale change in verse romances that likewise reflect on the passing away of old sociocultural orders and the rise of new ones, as the very title of the first of them, *The Lay of the Last Minstrel*, suggests—a point I will take up more fully in my chapter on *Persuasion*.

In *Mansfield Park*, the drama of small-scale change is embodied by the fortunes of Sir Thomas: imperiled enough before the start of the main action to necessitate his trip to Antigua to take personal charge of his estates; improving handsomely upon his return with the marriage of his eldest daughter to a wealthy young man and prospective marriages of his younger son and adopted niece to two more wealthy young folk; contracting suddenly at the end with the collapse of all three matches. As for larger-scale changes, the issue of the improvement of estates, peripheral to *Sense and Sensibility* and *Northanger Abbey*, becomes central. In *Persuasion*, social change involves both the rise and fall of personal fortunes—Wentworth's and William Walter Elliot's rising, Sir Walter's falling—and, as I will discuss at length in the relevant chapter, the larger changes rippling through English society as it makes the transition from war to peace and, concurrently, from the leadership of the aristocracy to that of the professional middle-class.

In the virtually self-enclosed world of *Emma*, large- and small-scale social change are hard to distinguish; what counts in the other novels as small feels momentous here. Austen's presentational techniques are at their subtlest in tracing these movements; by a myriad of small strokes, she charts the rise of Highbury's second-rank families to greater prominence: the Coles, beginning to give dinner parties; the Perrys, thinking of setting up a carriage; and of course, the Eltons, intruding everywhere and talking up their wealthy connections at every opportunity.[34] Add to them Mr. Weston, recent purchaser of an estate; Mrs. Weston, just risen from governess to mistress of that estate; Harriet Smith, learning new ideas about what she can aspire to; Robert Martin, a "gentleman farmer" "on his way," in Lionel Trilling's phrase, "to being a gentleman pure and simple";[35] and Miss Bates, sinking ever deeper into genteel poverty; and there scarcely seems a single person standing still in this supposedly timeless idyll. In *Emma*, then, as in all the late novels, change—continuous change—becomes the very groundwork of the narrative and of its characters' existences.[36]

Of all that gives these novels their increased complexity and density as compared to Austen's earlier works, this fact of continuous change is surely one of the most important. To use a mathematical analogy, a kind of narrative arithmetic sufficed for the sort of analysis that Austen undertook during the first part of her career, that of fixed characters within a fixed setting. For the novels of her maturity, in which both self and world exhibit continuous alteration, she had to devise a narrative calculus.

The corollary of the late novels' insistence on the inescapable fact of physical and social change is the prominence they give to characters who resist change both within and without, figures willfully stuck in time. (This is not a type prominent among the poets, though Byron's Giaour is an example.) Mr. Woodhouse—"a valetudinarian all his life"; "a much older man in ways than in years" (8)—seems never to have been young. Sir Walter Elliot, a freeze-dried version of what he was thirty years before, seems never to grow older. It is no accident that they both so vehemently reject the alterations going on around them; just as they stand still, so do they want their world to stand still. Sir Walter does his best to ignore the changes sweeping through English society in these "unfeudal" times, changes the most deplorable effect of which, in his view, is precisely the opportunity they give to persons of low birth to elevate their social status (152). Mr. Woodhouse resists all change whatsoever, but what he especially seeks to wish away are the changes consequent upon marriage. Having apparently never felt the longings of youth himself—for newness as little as for sex—he literally cannot seem to understand how anyone else could feel them.

The case of Sir Thomas, a more complex figure than these other two patresfamilias, is less obvious. Time has marked his body, his household, and his estates, and he does not seek to remain oblivious to these alterations. But his orientation is fundamentally conservative, and his way of dealing with these changes is to seek to reverse them: to restore his estates, recover his health, and, emblematically, remove every vestige of the theatricals that have so disrupted his household.[37] But Sir Thomas's desire to continue living in the past shows itself most importantly in his high-handed, authoritarian way of conducting himself as a father.[38] Written and set during the Regency, a time when the British national household was headed by a disreputable prince filling the place of a father who had lost his mind, *Mansfield Park* documents an evolution in family life that has weakened paternal authority and strengthened the willfulness of children in resisting it.

Admiral Crawford, Mr. Price: fathers here are not what they used to be, and even if they don't know it, their children do. Sir Thomas solemnly admonishes his eldest son for his extravagant ways, and Tom laughs in his sleeve. He cautions his eldest daughter not to enter into marriage with a man she cannot respect, and Maria practically cracks her gum in his face. Even Fanny, who buys into her uncle's retrograde notion of the obedience due one who stands in place of a father, resists his commandment to marry Henry in favor of her own hidden desires. And so, because his authority will not bend, it finally shatters, his daughters breaking into open revolt. Resisting change, all three of these proud men cut themselves off from the people around them. To place oneself beyond the realm of change, in the late novels, is to place oneself beyond the realm of human connection.

Three proud men, three stern fathers. Given what we have seen about the hold these figures have over their daughters' imaginations, it is no wonder that each of the late novels gives us a young woman with something of this same resistance to change. Each case is different. *Persuasion*'s is the least interesting, since the daughter in question is not the heroine, but her elder sister. Elizabeth Elliot's freeze-dried quality exactly resembles her father's. Emma is not nearly as bad as her own father, but as we have begun to see, much of what is wrong with the way she conducts herself—her snobbery, her obstruction of Harriet's marriage to Robert Martin, her refusal to take her proper place within her community—stems from her resistance to the very social changes outlined above. And while she herself does change gradually throughout the novel, as I will discuss below, she does not see that she does, and indeed thinks that no alteration will ever be necessary on her part: "I am not only, not going to be married, at present, but have very little intention of ever marrying at all . . . I cannot really change for the better" (73). While the literal meaning of that last phrase refers only to a change of marital circumstances, its larger, unconscious implications point to the attitude embodied in Emma's every infuriating display of imperturbable self-possession—her belief that she has nothing to learn and no more growing up to do. Like Elizabeth Elliot, though in a very different respect, Emma is stuck at a certain stage of emotional development.

But what of Fanny? In her social values, as I have said, she emulates her uncle's conservatism, and in her visceral repugnance to any change in her personal circumstances, she approaches Mr. Woodhouse. If anyone would seem to constitute a counterargument to the idea that the late novels insist on the necessity of change, it is she. Doesn't she resist it in just the way Sir Thomas, Mr. Woodhouse, Emma, Sir Walter, and Elizabeth Elliot do? No, she does not. The resistance to change we find in those five figures is, as we have seen, a willful rejection of it: a refusal to acknowledge or yield to it. But Fanny's hatred of nearly every change that comes her way—her removal to Mansfield or, most poignantly, her recognition in Portsmouth that her parents no longer love her—is matched only by her resilience in accommodating herself to it.

The mature Austen does not insist that her characters like the changes happening to and around them, she only insists that they adjust to them. She never suggests that change is necessarily desirable, only that it is necessary. Each of the late novels, in fact, spends a great deal of energy exhibiting, examining, and evaluating the changes it documents. In each case, Austen chooses the middle way between the most radical agents of social change and its most conservative refusers: between Sir Thomas and the Crawfords, Mr. Woodhouse and Mrs. Elton, Sir Walter and William Walter Elliot. And in each case, that middle way is embodied, finally if not initially, by the hero and heroine.

The idea of change leads in turn to perhaps the most profound and important Wordsworthian idea of all, one that is also of the first significance for Byron and Scott: loss. As criticism has shown on a massive scale, the fact of loss and the attempt to come to terms with it is everywhere in Wordsworth, be it the loss of youth and youthful powers or the loss of beloved individuals. The lamentation for the loss of childhood places, friendships, and loves is the principal subject of Byron's early lyrics, while the Turkish Tales are, one and all, stories of bereavement. Scott's romances—as the conspicuous framing devices of the first and best of them, *The Lay of the Last Minstrel* and *Marmion*, make clear—mourn the loss of the very cultural and narrative traditions they memorialize.

But absent a true consciousness of change, Austen's early novels are likewise innocent of loss. In each, the heroine must give up someone she once cared deeply about, but in every case, as she is made at great length to learn, the person in question turns out not to have been worth having in the first place. Even the pain of error is made perfectly good, and so happiness finally comes at no real cost whatsoever—surely one important reason the early novels, for all their splendors, feel so much less profound than do the later ones. For the later ones are saturated with loss. In fact, in two cases, the question of loss will be my main focus in the later chapters of this study. Fanny must give up nearly everything she loves, starting with her home in Portsmouth, and do without nearly everything she wants, being forced, in each case, to find substitute objects of affection or desire. Anne, like almost everyone else in *Persuasion*, is "widowed" of the person she most loves, and even if she retrieves him at novel's end, the lost time remains lost, so many years of happiness replaced by so many of loneliness and self-reproach. And while the very structure of *Emma* works to conceal its heroine's losses from us—precisely because she cannot see them herself—we should not doubt that they are heavy and continuous. Until her final release, Emma's imprisoning egotism deprives her of nothing less than a full emotional life, true intimacy with those around her. That loss is embodied in Jane Fairfax, and by refusing to allow Emma a belated friendship with that young woman as the reward of her reformation, Austen tells us that things once lost cannot be recovered. In the late novels, time is real: too late is too late.

In discussing Austen's understanding of time in the later novels, my focus thus far has been on externals: physical appearance, social position, the loss of beloved objects. But the most important, pervasive, and subtle manifestations of this great new theme lie in the inner realm: in matters of feeling, reflection, recollection, relatedness, and personal transformation. It is also in these matters that we will find the grounds on which the new complexity and density of the late novels most significantly develop. I will turn to this large set of questions in a moment. First, though, I would like to touch on several other, strikingly Wordsworthian characteristics of the mature novels, ones that seem at first remote from these issues but will soon lead us back to them.

Few characteristics of Wordsworth's poetry in *Lyrical Ballads* and *Poems in Two Volumes* are more immediately striking than the attention it pays to the poor, the marginal, and the dispossessed. Many examples may be cited, including "Simon Lee," "The Old Cumberland Beggar," "Michael," "Resolution and Independence," and so forth. While such figures are entirely absent from Austen's earlier novels, they appear in all of the later ones, often with a great deal of emphasis. Fanny's family in Portsmouth may not be quite poor, but it is far down the economic scale from anyone in the early works. Miss Bates *is* poor, as is Mrs. Smith, and far poorer are the cottagers visited by Emma and Harriet.[39] Servants and dependents are newly visible, as well—nurserymaids, valets, laborers, tenant farmers, bailiffs—as are shopkeepers and the members of the less lucrative professions. In the late works, Austen opens her imagination to a whole world of economic realities that lies below the lives of the country gentry.[40]

As several of these examples suggest, this expansion of focus involves, in particular, a new attention to what Emma thinks of as "the difference of woman's destiny" (316). So too, most of Wordsworth's pictures of the poor and dispossessed are pictures of women, including "The Female Vagrant," "Goody Blake and Harry Gill," "The Thorn," "Her Eyes are Wild," "Alice Fell," and many others. Fanny, Jane Fairfax, Harriet, Miss Bates, Mrs. Smith, even Clara Brereton, *Sanditon*'s presumptive heroine ("[s]o low in every worldly view, as . . . to have been preparing for a situation little better than a nursery maid")[41]—all women in circumstances and with prospects far below even those of the Dashwood sisters, with their thousand-a-piece. It is to the pressures of such lives, not to the marriage plots of the relatively well set-up, that the late fiction gives the bulk of its attention.

These women share another, related characteristic: marginality within their family or community. Elizabeth Bennet, Jane, Elinor, Marianne, Catherine and her friends—all young and lovely, all cynosures of their circle, all avidly courted. But the late fiction gives most of its attention to young women whom no one regards: Fanny and Anne, of course, and—because *Emma* is told through the eyes of its heroine, who is herself fascinated by two more such women—Harriet and Jane. Yet because no one regards them, they (with the exception of Harriet) regard everything. As Fanny says, "I was quiet, but I was not blind" (300). Aside from Elinor's always-keen interest in Marianne, silent observation plays no significant role in the early heroines' lives. Scarcely more does silent contemplation, for the younger Austen tends to stage deliberative episodes as dialogues—Elizabeth with Jane or Charlotte, Elinor with Marianne, Catherine with Henry. The lives of these heroines are almost entirely absorbed by social activity; scarcely ever do we see them alone, their moment of transformation being in each case the one important exception. But the late heroines, including Emma, are frequently alone, and when alone are invariably immersed in introspection. Austen has discovered, in other words, the great Wordsworthian theme of solitude, essential to the flowering of a dynamic and ever-evolving inner life, a life of recollection and reflection. It is to that life that we now return.

The element of the inner life most obviously involved with time is that of memory. Memory plays only one role in the early novels, and though it is a crucial one, arising in connection with each novel's central scene, that of its heroine's transformation, it also exhibits the narrowness of Austen's conception of memory at this time in her career.[42] *Pride and Prejudice* provides the clearest instance, for its heroine's transformation, her self-recognition, is the most stunningly swift. Darcy's letter forces Elizabeth to reconsider all her judgments about him and Wickham, a reconsideration that in turn forces her to remember her impressions of the latter. The result proves distressing: "She tried to recollect some instance of goodness . . . But no such recollection befriended her . . . " (169). She reads on, and her memory becomes more particularized: "She perfectly remembered every thing that had passed in conversation between Wickham and herself, in their first evening at Mr. Phillips's . . . She was *now* struck with the impropriety of such communications to a stranger" (170, emphasis in the original). Her old judgments weaken, and only a paragraph later comes the catastrophe, the two dozen words on which the whole novel pivots: "She grew absolutely ashamed of herself.—Of neither Darcy nor Wickham could she think, without feeling that she had been blind, partial, prejudiced, absurd" (171). There are two things to note here. First, as I suggested above, the contents of memory undergo no change or decay from the moment of the event to the moment of recollection. Five months later, and Elizabeth still "perfectly remembered everything that had passed in conversation." It must be so, else the second and more important circumstance could not be true: the function of memory here—the only function it performs in the novel—is that of moral self-correction. The heroine remembers what she did, thinks about it, is heartily ashamed of it, and resolves to do better.

This is one of those instances in which an idea implicit in Austen, or at least in the early Austen, is identical to one explicit in Samuel Johnson: "Memory is the purveyor of reason, the power which places those images before the mind upon which the judgment is to be exercised, and which treasures up the discriminations that are once passed, as the rules of future action, or grounds of subsequent conclusions."[43] And so it is in *Northanger Abbey*, when Henry's rebuke opens Catherine's eyes to the "extravagance of her late fancies" (173). And so it is in *Sense and Sensibility*, for Marianne undergoes her transformation, not because Willoughby jilts her, not because her grief over him makes her ill, but because her illness "has given me leisure and calmness for serious recollection": "I considered the past; I saw in my own behaviour . . . I saw that my own feelings. . . . Whenever I looked towards the past . . . ," and so forth (293–294). Recollection, judgment, mortification, a resolution to judge and act better, and Marianne is cured in more than just the medical sense.

But because memory is confined to this one special role, its workings understood in so schematic a way, its potential impact on the sense of time in the early novels is negated. Time here is essentially Bergsonian *temps*—linear, unidirectional clock-time—with none of the thickening and deepening provided by those back-and-forth movements of consciousness that cause time present and times past to coexist in a complex temporal space. Compared with this mechanical understanding of memory's operations and limited view of its functions, the multifarious roles it plays in the late novels represent an immeasurable advance. From being Johnsonian, Austen's understanding of memory becomes Wordsworthian.[44]

So essential are the workings of memory to *Mansfield Park* and *Persuasion*, and so important will their exploration be to my chapters on these novels, that to give a full account of them here is neither desirable nor necessary. I will only touch on the most important points. We already began to see the ways in which memory operates for Fanny Price when we examined her response to nature in the shrubbery scene.[45] As opposed to what we find in the early novels, but very much like we see in Wordsworth and Coleridge's first-person lyrics, memory arises for her spontaneously. It also gives her a sense of rootedness in time, a way of understanding not only the past, but also the present. As in the greatest poems of memory Wordsworth published during Austen's lifetime—"Tintern Abbey," "The Brothers," "The Two April Mornings"—the present acquires significance because of the way it both echoes and alters the past. Memory thus makes palpable the distance between present and past, helping give time the weight it so lacks in the early works. Late in the novel, we find Fanny sharing the Portsmouth parlor with her father: "And the remembrance of her first evening in that room, of her father and his newspaper came across her. No candle was *now* wanted. The sun was yet an hour and half above the horizon. She felt that she had, indeed, been three months there" (362, emphasis in the original).

This passage, like the shrubbery scene, also shows memory connecting the temporal rhythms of Fanny's life to those of the life of nature, the passage of seasons and years ("five summers, with the length / Of five long winters! and again I hear / These waters . . . "). Another scene of recollection in Portsmouth suggests a deeper way in which the past gives meaning to the present through the action of memory. In a remarkable testament to the power of time to both alter and fix the affections, Fanny, greeting Mrs. Price for the first time in eight years, embraces a mother whose features she finds she "loved the more, because they brought her aunt Bertram's before her" (313). It is not that she so loves her aunt's features, as such; it is the electric charge of recognition, transmitted between memory's two poles of "then" and "now," that galvanizes her heart. The present is loved because it evokes the past, and the past is loved because it lives again in the present. Without the other, each is barren.[46]

But the supreme scene of recollection in *Mansfield Park*, as I mentioned in the previous chapter and will discuss at length in the next, is the first description of the East room, where Fanny, under the presiding emblem of Tintern Abbey, casts her glance about her and "could scarcely see an object in that room which had not an interesting remembrance connected with it.—Everything was a friend, or bore her thoughts to a friend." But what these beloved mementos speak of, in the first instance, are "the pains of tyranny, of ridicule, and neglect." Yet "almost every recurrence of either had led to something consolatory . . . and the whole was now so blended together, so harmonized by distance, that every former affliction had its charm" (126). Nothing could be more like Wordsworth, and especially the Wordsworth of "Tintern Abbey": memory's power, not to repeat the past, but to transform it, and in particular, to redeem experiences of suffering and loss.

In essence, the kind of temporal and therefore emotional depth Fanny experiences at particular moments undergirds the whole of *Persuasion*, constituting the affective ground bass of this, Austen's lushest orchestration of feeling. The whole narrative is a "now" shadowed by a "then," so that the novel itself may be said to remember: to possess a memory that grounds its sense of self, gives meaning to the present and weight to time, and finally redeems the past by bringing it again to life, immensely transformed. Of course, most of the novel's remembering is focused through the consciousness of its heroine, for whom, as for James in Wordsworth's "Brothers," memory becomes an almost physiological process.[47] Where Fanny courts memory, often her only friend, Anne has long suppressed hers, and so, when Wentworth's reappearance calls it forth, it seems to push its way to the surface from the very depths of her body. The mere mention of his name evokes blushes and sighs, effusions of blood and breath, that send her hastening out for a walk in an attempt to regain control of herself. With his actual approach, "a thousand feelings rushed on Anne,"[48] and with his appearance, her very senses rebel, rendering her scarcely able to hear or see (we can practically feel the blood pounding in her ears) and leaving her scarcely able to eat, her mind and body—if the distinction can still be maintained at this point—"resuming the agitation" that almost eight years "had banished into distance and indistinctness" (84–85).

We can scarcely speak of the past as being recollected here, because it seems never to have gone away. Both Anne's habit of suppressing her memories of Wentworth and the force with which those memories reassert themselves once that suppression is overborne arise, of course, from the grief she feels at having lost him. In this novel, whose central theme is loss and grief, memory is always closely allied to both. For what is grief but memory made visceral, memories felt in the body, and felt the more sharply for being only memories, for belonging to that which can never come back in another form?

Memory is clearly less important in *Emma* than in the other late novels, primarily because Emma is so different a figure from the melancholy, introspective Fanny and Anne. Where their thoughts tend to turn back to the past, those of Emma, a creature of energy and will, are busy striding forth into the future. But *Emma* is not unmarked by its author's new understanding of memory's place within a full human personality. Indeed, the narrative proper, which begins on Emma's governess's wedding day, begins in a manner that strikingly, if only lightly, anticipates *Persuasion*: "It was Miss Taylor's loss," we read, "which first brought grief" (7). Alone that same evening, Emma has "only to sit and think of what she had lost"—in other words, to remember. "She recalled [Miss Taylor's] past kindness—the kindness, the affection of sixteen years . . . but the intercourse of the last seven years . . . was yet a dearer, tenderer recollection" (8). Of the mother who had died in her infancy, we have already been told that Emma had no more "than an indistinct remembrance of her caresses" (7). As it is for Fanny and Anne, memory here is affective, even physical (those caresses seem more felt than anything else); helps ground the self by creating a sense of its history, including the different eras of that history ("sixteen years," "seven years"); and helps form, strengthen, and reform the affections. Already Emma dwells more deeply in time than do the early heroines, and in so doing, possesses herself more fully.

In discussing the quality of time in the early novels, I noted that the intervals between events possess no narrative significance, that time itself is a neutral medium. To say this is also to imply something about the nature of characters and relationships in the early works, of the feelings people have about each other and the ways they negotiate them—how these occupy and are affected by time.

In the early phase, feelings remain precisely as they are, with neither change nor growth nor decay, until some specific event, some confrontation or recognition, shocks them into a new, equally static condition. Darcy snubs Elizabeth, and from then on, she hates him; she reads his letter, and from then on she esteems him and regrets her behavior toward him; she meets him at Pemberley—perceiving what the estate says about its owner and what his behavior says about his feelings for her—and from then on, she loves him. The same analysis may be made of any of the less central feelings in the early novels (Jane, for example, has never stopped carrying a torch for Bingley, as we eventually learn, nor he for her), as well as of the major ones in *Northanger Abbey* and *Sense and Sensibility*: Catherine's for Isabella Thorpe and Henry Tilney, Marianne's for Willoughby—this last moving through sharply demarcated stages of passionate love endlessly dwelling on itself, passionate grief doing likewise, and finally a letting go of love and grief that happens, as we saw above, in the space of just a few days. True, Marianne's heart does "in time" become "as much devoted to her husband, as it had once been to Willoughby" (322), but this gradual transformation happens after the end of the narrative proper. The younger Austen may recognize that feelings can sometimes change with time and time alone, but she does not know how to dramatize that perception and for the most part disregards it. A graph of virtually any feeling in the early novels would resemble a set of stairs: a series of horizontal lines—steady states—linked by vertical jumps up or down—sudden shifts, as the personality that has hardened into one configuration is shattered by some dramatic event and instantaneously reassembles itself into a new one.

There are several implications and corollaries of this principle of sudden emotional transformation. Because changes in emotional state depend so much on confrontation and shock, melodramatic elements are much more prominent: stock events like Lydia's elopement, Catherine's ejection from Northanger, or those lurid tales Darcy tells of Wickham or Brandon of Willoughby; stock characters like the false, fortune-hunting female (Caroline Bingley, Lucy Steele, Isabella Thorpe) and the domineering dowager on the man's side (Lady Catherine, Mrs. Ferrars, Willoughby's Aunt Smith; General Tilney is a male version). We may also note, in this connection, how much more schematic are the early plots than the later ones, and how much greater is the family resemblance among them than among the later group. The younger Austen, having written out a certain narrative paradigm three times, had brought it to perfection; the mature writer clearly had no desire to repeat it, or in fact to repeat anything. Indeed, in trotting out Mrs. Clay, whose ambitions trouble Anne for about ten seconds, and William Walter Elliot, whose charms stand not the slightest chance of winning her over and whose perfidy she cannot finally be bothered to expose, *Persuasion* thumbs its nose at that very paradigm, with its lurid tales and its fortune hunters and its Mr. Wrongs.

With this relative simplicity of both emotional structure and narrative structure comes a relative simplicity of characterization. Complexity of character, to a great extent, *is* complexity of emotion. In many cases, in fact, figures in the early novels are not so much characters as caricatures, albeit brilliant ones. The late novels have their caricatures, too, but far fewer of them, and in far less prominent positions. We can see this deepening of characterization most clearly through a comparison of analogous figures. Collins and Miss Bates are both fools, but the latter is also a full human being, with complex feelings capable of being wounded, significant relationships, and a social role within her community, and that she is no mere figure of fun becomes, indeed, an extremely important idea at a certain point in the novel. John Thorpe and Yates are both "puppies," but while the first is a one-line joke, the latter is plausible as a real, albeit limited, young man. As a villain, John Dashwood's motives are as simple as his behavior is transparent; William Walter Elliot, to say nothing of Mrs. Norris, plays a more complex game, and for more complex reasons.

Just as the late novels are sparing of caricatures, so too do they abound in characters who are morally ambiguous. The early novels have none such; we know exactly what we are to think of everyone in them. But as the critical literature demonstrates, equivocal figures in the later works include, in *Persuasion*, Lady Russell, Mrs. Smith, and Captain Benwick; in *Mansfield Park*, the five most important figures at the very least—Fanny, Edmund, Mary, Henry, and Sir Thomas; and in *Emma*, pretty much everyone except Knightley and Mrs. Elton, the novel's moral poles.

Just as emotions and motives are so much less complex in the early novels, so too are relationships. That this is so, that relationships between characters are similarly unambiguous and shift in a similarly step-wise fashion, is already largely implicit in what I have said, but it bears on narrative form in ways well worth exploring. The younger Austen—it is one of her glories—is extremely fond of what might be called the narrative set-piece. So many of her most memorable scenes belong to this type: Catherine and Henry's teasing conversation during their first dance, Elinor and Lucy's set-to in the Middletons' parlor, Elizabeth and Darcy's sparring matches while Jane is ill as well as during the ball at Netherfield. We can recognize a general likeness between these scenes, as well as the great importance of each to their respective novels, but how can we characterize this likeness more precisely?

Most obviously, these episodes are all markedly performative. Austen constructs them like little plays, carefully setting the scene and disposing the characters in their places. (This is especially notable in Elinor and Lucy's encounter, where the break between chapters 23 and 24 functions as a kind of drumroll.) The scene set, she then withdraws, rendering the rest of the encounter almost entirely in dialogue. And the characters know they are performing—not for us, but for each other. The tension is high, because the stakes are high, too. Little plays, these set-pieces are also verbal fencing matches, impromptu debates—games, as Catherine and Henry's encounter makes clearest, albeit with unspoken rules. One more analogy: in their plotted, patterned, performed quality, their precise architectonics and balancing of opposed units, the set-pieces of the early phase are the scenic equivalents of the Johnsonian sentence, the syntactic form most favored by the younger Austen. As such, they may be said to spread out not so much in time as in space; their quality is pictorial rather than narrative. They do not advance their respective plots so much as reveal existing attitudes and the tensions between them. Indeed, as a game fences itself off from "real life," drawing a temporal boundary around itself, so do these scenes seem to arrest the narratives to which they belong, sticking out from their surface like rocks in a stream.

This last observation returns us to the relevance of the set-piece to the temporal quality of relationships in the early novels. Yes, Elizabeth and Darcy's relationship changes, in a very important sense, as a result of the sudden changes in their feelings about each other. But in another, equally important sense, their relationship never changes. The reason these set-pieces are so important, and much of the reason they are so memorable, is that each defines, once and for all, a central relationship. That is why each occurs early in its respective novel: the set-piece was the younger Austen's way of "pictorially" representing a certain crucial dynamic that would remain unchanged and would carry through the rest of the novel. This principle is less fully true in the case of Elinor and Lucy—their relationship is less central—but in the other cases the picture we get in those scenes—light-hearted, satiric Henry and wide-eyed Catherine; wickedly ironic Elizabeth and imperturbably forensic Darcy, at glittering daggers drawn—is the one we retain even after the narrative is over. However much these relationships may change during the course of their novels, what matters more is what they intrinsically, eternally are.

Set-pieces, stasis, sudden shocks and shifts—feelings and relationships in the late novels could hardly be more different. If events in the early works occupy time the way beads occupy a string, events in the later ones occupy time the way salt occupies water, so that it scarcely makes sense even to distinguish between "events" and "time."[49] Everywhere we find psychological states in continual flux, as characters respond to changing circumstances, not with stubborn rigidity or helpless collapse, but by means of gradual adjustments of feeling. This principle is everywhere in *Mansfield Park*, from Fanny's slow, painful, carefully documented adjustment to her initial removal to the way she copes with the arrival of Mary, with her own emergence as an attractive and desired young woman, with the several shocks of her return to Portsmouth, and with just about every other change that comes her way. This ability effortlessly to bring her feelings to a new state is precisely what underlies her resilience in accommodating herself to change. Nor are all these adjustments willed; some take her by surprise, especially those having to do with the Crawfords. In Portsmouth, she finds herself ("Here was another strange revolution of mind!") glad to receive a letter from Mary (326); she even finds herself beginning to feel affection for

Henry—just as he, to his great surprise, had once found that a similarly undiscerned shift in feeling had brought him to the condition of loving her. The prospect of another letter, from Edmund, surprises Fanny by evoking terror rather than delight, occasioning what we might regard as the novel's thematic statement about change both inner and outer: "She began to feel that she had not yet gone through all the changes of opinion and sentiment, which the progress of time and variation of circumstances occasion in this world of changes" (309).

Emma and *Persuasion* take place in this same world. *Persuasion*, as we said, is about grief, a psychological process that by its very nature involves gradual adjustment, as we see most clearly, if perhaps too quickly, in the case of Captain Benwick. But such adjustments also lie at the very center of the narrative, in the slow dance Anne and Wentworth do toward each other. The process is not symmetric: because Anne has never stopped loving him, her feelings are really about his, and we learn of his through her constant attempts to divine them: "Her power with him was gone forever" (86), she first sees; then a little while later, "She understood him. He could not forgive her,—but he could not be unfeeling" (113); then later still, she finds him "turning to her and speaking with a glow, and yet a gentleness, which seemed almost restoring the past" (134), and so the gradual transformation and gradual discovery go until she reads the note in which he passionately professes his love.

Emma, by unsurprising contrast, seeks frequently to measure the state not of a young man's feelings for her, but of hers for him, Frank Churchill. After his first departure from Highbury: "Emma continued to entertain no doubt of her being in love. Her ideas only varied as to the how much. At first, she thought it was a good deal; and afterwards, but little" (217). Later, hearing the news of his imminent return, she is set to "weighing her own feelings, and trying to understand the degree of her agitation, which she rather thought was considerable" (250), but a chapter later "[a] very little quiet reflection was enough to satisfy [her] as to the nature of her agitation on hearing this news of Frank Churchill. She was soon convinced that it was not for herself she was feeling at all apprehensive or embarrassed; it was for him" (261). Here not only do we see feelings changing day by day and even hour by hour, we see them changing under their own self-scrutiny, a minuteness of analysis on Austen's part, and a frequency of it on her heroines', absolutely foreign to the early novels.

Fanny and Anne experience no sudden recognition-cum-transformation—not, like Elinor, because they have nothing to reform, but because, like

Wordsworth and Coleridge in their first-person lyrics, they practice a continual reappraisal of feeling and experience and are thus continually changing. Emma is not quite so heroic as these two creepmice, but her transformation is every bit as profound. Critics have long noted that, unlike those of the early heroines, hers involves not one but a series of recognitions, the moment when the truth of her love for Knightley darts through her constituting only the final one.[50] But to reduce Emma's transformation to her several moments of repentance and recognition is to flatten what is in fact a comprehensive maturation of personality by fitting it to the pattern of the mere changes of consciousness experienced by the heroines of the early works. When we read, for example, in the novel's penultimate chapter, that Emma now feels that "[i]t would be a great pleasure to know Robert Martin" (389), we recognize that her transformation has involved not just an illumination of the mind, but an opening of the heart, a supplanting of snobbery by generosity and humility, a fundamental change of character that has been gradually, continually coming over her throughout the entire novel.

Because continuously evolving inner lives make for continuously evolving relationships, the major phase replaces the set-piece with what might be called the "serial scene." If Darcy were the one who wanted to enter the ministry and Elizabeth the one who disapproved, the two would have one cracking go at it, one fireworks display, in which their antagonistic positions were fully set out, and that would be the end of it (until Elizabeth broke down, perhaps, and confessed how wrong she had been). Instead, Edmund and Mary worry the question over and over, at different lengths, in different contexts, from different angles, with different degrees of levity or vexation, and with differently adjusted feelings and hopes: in the Sotherton chapel (75), during the walk in the wilderness (77ff.), at Mansfield manor (91ff.), at the Parsonage (200ff.), at the ball (230), and so forth. Comparable serial scenes in *Emma* include Emma and Knightley's long wrangle about the propriety of her behavior to those around her as well as Frank's many-chaptered, subtly shifting game of double meanings and pretend-flirtation with her and Jane. *Persuasion*, as we just noted, is at its core a serial scene writ large, that of Anne and Wentworth's many tentative encounters with each other. Like feelings, relationships in the late novels are in a constant state of reexamination and recalibration, with characters constantly repositioning themselves relative to one another.

That is why both feelings and relationships are often so hard to define. In the early novels, we always know where people stand with each other. But what *is* Emma's relationship with Frank? And what is it with Knightley:

brother and sister? friends? lovers? Wordsworth raises the same question about his relationship with his former schoolteacher in the Matthew poems. In fact, the issue of such "ambiguous relationships" will be the subject of my chapter on the novel. Again, how many shades of uncertainty and mutual misunderstanding must we account for in characterizing Fanny's relationship with Edmund at any given moment, and how many different ones at the next? About Anne and Wentworth's we needn't undertake such an investigation—as we've seen, Anne does it for us.

It is no wonder that just as relationships in the late novels are so often ambiguous, feelings are so often, what they never are in the early works, ambivalent. And, as in the Romantic poets—for whom ambivalent feelings are their favorite feelings of all—they are incomparably stronger for being so.[51] That this is the case in *Persuasion* has been noted more than once, specifically in connection with Byron as well as Keats and Shelley.[52] Again and again, Anne's encounters with Wentworth plunge her into agonizingly mixed states of mind, "compounded of pleasure and pain" (113) or of "agitation, pain, pleasure, a something between delight and misery" (185), the parade example occurring at the Musgroves' lodgings in Bath, where, waiting for the chance to open her heart to Wentworth, she finds herself "deep in the happiness of such misery, or the misery of such happiness" (233). Fanny's ambivalences tend to cluster around Edmund's attraction to Mary, as jealousy fights against guilt and hope against hopelessness. As she listens to the account of his final conversation with Mary, one that has crushed his own hopes, she cannot help but feel both "pain" and "delight" (375) and be "almost sorry" to have made him speak at all (377). Emma expresses similar feelings not only with respect to Frank, but also after the proposal scene, as her love for Knightley conflicts with feelings of duty toward her father and guilt toward Harriet.

About feelings in general in the late novels as opposed to the early ones, we can say that they are not only far stronger for being conflicted and far deeper for being rooted in a denser matrix of personal history, but also far more various. The early novels work with the limited repertoire of emotions proper to the marriage plot: love, humiliation, dejection, hope, happiness. But the later novels, while still ostensibly presenting pictures of courtship, in fact de-emphasize the marriage plot to such an extent that it becomes merely the vehicle of narrative resolution, and generally a hasty resolution, at that. The later novels spend almost no time on what almost exclusively concerns the early ones: the conversations and events of the hero and heroine's courtship. In the first two, in fact, the hero and heroine do not even discover that they are lovers until the very end, and in the third, they do not rediscover it until then.[53] Instead, each of these novels opens itself to a broad range of social situations and psychological states, which is why each traverses such a broad range of feelings. To take only Fanny, and only the first volume of her work, we watch her experience loneliness, despondency, gratitude, shame, guilt, jealousy, self-pity, terror, and moral revulsion. The rest of her story adds other feelings, the stories of Emma and Anne, others still.

In all this, then—the slow shaping of the self in childhood and adolescence, the multifarious operations of memory, the continuous conquest of self-knowledge, the gradual evolution of feelings and minute adjustment of relationships—we see how central was Austen's discovery of time in giving rise to the incomparably greater psychological complexity of her later novels. And we also see how unmistakably that discovery bears the imprint, in its central, structuring logic as well as in so many of its particulars, of the Romantic poets, and especially of Wordsworth.

We can go still further in delineating the impact of Austen's new understanding of time on her ideas and her art. The conceptual landscape of the early novels is dominated by the abstract moral vocabulary Austen inherited from the eighteenth century: "pride" and "prejudice," "sense" and "sensibility." It is fallacious, of course, to see Elinor as personifying sense and Marianne sensibility (we are twice told of the latter's sense in the very first chapter), but it is not fallacious to see the novel as organizing itself around a struggle between those two faculties. Pride and prejudice, in their novel, are rather mutually reinforcing than antagonistic, but they remain dominant terms of analysis. Nor are these the only important abstractions. In *Sense and Sensibility*, both characters and narrator spend a great deal of time identifying the story's various single men as "amiable," "agreeable," or the reverse. *Pride and Prejudice* simply cannot be fully understood without a grasp of what Austen means by such terms as "gentlemanliness," "respectability," "elegance," "dignity," "grace," "cordiality," and "warmth" (not to mention "address," "countenance," "manner," "air," and "features"). A powerful categorizing intelligence is at work.

But by the late novels, Austen's mind has grown into a far different shape. To be sure, the earlier mode of analysis has not been discarded, but it has receded into the background. The very titles point to the change, the paired abstractions having been replaced by names that may be understood as signifying, not collections of fixed qualities, but fields of possibility. How will Mansfield Park change? And famously, "[w]hat will become of" Emma? A phrase worth pondering, that: not only "What will happen to Emma," but also, "What will develop from Emma?" and "What will Emma become?" (35).[54] Become, indeed: from an artist of being, of static characters and abstract qualities, Austen becomes that most "Romantic" of creators, an artist of becoming.[55]

We can see it in her language. The greater "subtlety and flexibility of Jane Austen's mature prose" has long been noted.[56] At its worst, the language of the early Austen can practically drive itself dizzy with its Johnsonian juggling of paired and tripled abstractions. After Willoughby concludes his impassioned confessional monologue, "Elinor made no answer. Her thoughts were silently fixed on the irreparable injury which too early an independence and its consequent habits of idleness, dissipation, and luxury, had made in the mind, the character, the happiness, of a man who, to every advantage of person and talents, united a disposition naturally open and honest, and a feeling, affectionate temper" (280).

The late language displays its freedom most fully in the rendering of speech. Nothing can compare to Miss Bates's free-associative monologues of broken fragments, but a comparable freedom from syntactic order is often essential to the reporting of Fanny's speech, as well. This is a heroine whose first words are "'no, no—not at all—no, thank you'" (14) and who responds to the news that it was Henry who had arranged for her brother's promotion with, "'Good Heaven! how very, very kind! Have you really—was it by *your* desire—I beg your pardon, but I am bewildered. Did Admiral Crawford apply?—how was it?—I am stupefied'" (247; emphasis in the original).[57] Comparable examples from Anne's speech are harder to find, since she does so little speaking at all, but they are not at all scarce in Austen's notation of what passes through her mind. A scene discussed above, Anne's first meeting with Wentworth, provides what has become the best-known example: "Her eye half met Captain Wentworth's; a bow, a curtsey passed; she heard his voice—he talked to Mary, said all that was right; said something to the Miss Musgroves, enough to mark an easy footing: the room seemed full—full of persons and voices—but a few minutes ended it" (84–85).

As these last two examples suggest, the greater syntactic freedom of the late novels overwhelmingly serves one particular purpose: the moment-by-moment registration of feeling.[58] And this attention to the flux of feeling points, as we will see, to a development of the very first importance, nothing less than a revolution in Austen's conception of both the mind and the moral life. For even as we see the late characters' feelings develop moment by moment, so, very often, do we see their thoughts simultaneously doing likewise, evolving in snatches of half-formed and provisional formulations as their feelings search for expression. Nothing could be more like the poetic practice of Wordsworth and Coleridge, and often also of Byron, than this.[59]

The early novels know no half-formed thoughts, no feelings groping to understand themselves. Indeed, as we just saw with Elinor, thought in the early Austen tends to crowd out feeling, the diction and syntax of categorization asserting itself even at moments of intense passion, as if the only valid responses were rational ones.[60] But observe Emma's soliloquy as she tries to determine the exact degree of her love for Frank: " 'I do not find myself making use of the word *sacrifice* . . . I do suspect that he is not really necessary to my happiness. So much the better. I certainly will not persuade myself to feel more than I do. I am quite enough in love. I should be sorry to be more . . . *He* is undoubtedly very much in love—everything denotes it—very much in love indeed!—and when he comes again, if his affection continue, I must be on my guard not to encourage it' " (217). This is thought evolving on the page as feeling seeks to discover itself—indeed, it is feeling itself evolving before our eyes through the effort of bringing itself to consciousness.

To cite examples from *Persuasion* would be arbitrary, since much of the novel takes this form. One of the most prominent instances in *Mansfield Park* enables us to make a closer comparison between the early and late works, for it occurs in Edmund's long, tormented letter to Fanny about his prospects with Mary, a letter analogous in important ways to that of Darcy to Elizabeth. In each case, a young man speaks his mind at a moment of intense feeling, and because he is writing, speaks it in a way that enables him to monitor his thoughts as they take shape on the page. After a short introduction, Darcy's letter begins thus: "Two offenses of a very different nature, and by no means of equal magnitude, you last night laid to my charge" (162). The passage offers a fair sample of the forensic language in which the whole letter is couched as well as of the forensic structure by which it is governed. Feelings may be at stake, but feelings are not permitted to enter into the letter itself; Darcy even makes a point of assuring Elizabeth that "my investigations and decisions are not usually influenced by my hopes and fears" (163).

Edmund's letter could not be more different. To cite a passage from the middle of it:

I cannot give her up, Fanny. She is the only woman in the world whom I could ever think of as a wife. If I did not believe that she had some regard for me, of course I should not say this, but I do believe it. I am convinced, that she is not without a decided preference. I have no jeal-

ousy of any individual. It is the influence of the fashionable world altogether that I am jealous of. It is the habits of wealth that I fear. Her
ideas are not higher than her own fortune may warrant, but they are
beyond what our incomes united could authorize. There is comfort,
however, even here. I could better bear to lose her, because not rich
enough, then because of my profession.   (348)

What we have here is not a structured argument, but a spontaneous outpouring of emotions: determination, desperation, hope, jealousy, fear, comfort. Indeed, very shortly after this, Edmund interrupts himself to say, "You
have my thoughts exactly as they arise, my dear Fanny; perhaps they are
some times contradictory, but it will not be a less faithful picture of my
mind. Having once begun, it is a pleasure to me to tell you all I feel." "Perhaps they are some times contradictory"—the mind is not, at bottom, a
rational instrument. "You have my thoughts" as "[I] tell you all I feel"—it is,
instead, constituted by emotion, with thought merely the form feeling
assumes so that it may see itself.

The resemblance to the Romantics could not, again, be greater, and the
change from Austen's early work could not be more complete.[61] In the early
phase, feeling is dictated by reason, even (or especially), as Darcy's letter
reminds us, in the most important instances. Elizabeth misjudges Darcy,
therefore she hates him. Once her mind changes, her heart changes too.
That is why this revolution in Austen's conception of the mental life is a revolution in her conception of the moral life. The ethical doctrine at the center of her early novels is the idea that feeling can and ought to be shaped,
controlled, and educated by thought, a doctrine to which the flawlessness of
their plots, the mercilessness of their irony, and the supreme self-assurance
of their narrators give the inevitability of a mathematical demonstration.
The errors of the early heroines are errors of reason; that is why each of the
early novels can pivot on a single moment of clarified understanding, a sudden recognition of wrong thinking that opens the way for right feeling. The
heroine changes by changing her mind: once, decisively, and forever.

But the late heroines, as we have seen, change continuously, and not by
examining their judgments, but by discovering their feelings. The only
sudden recognition the late novels give us is Emma's, and what darts
through her with the speed of an arrow has nothing to do with realizing
that she has been thinking wrongly and everything to do with realizing that
all along she has been feeling rightly, only she hasn't known it. Elizabeth,
Marianne, and Catherine must reform their minds; Emma must make her-

self "acquainted with her own heart" (335). And it is only then—right feeling opening the way for right thinking—that "[s]he saw it all with a clearness which had never blessed her before. How improperly had she been acting by Harriet! . . . What blindness, what madness, had led her on!" (335–336). In *Mansfield Park* and *Persuasion* the way is opened to the lovers' union in precisely the same fashion, only there it is the heroes who at last become acquainted with their hearts.

Does this mean that the mature Austen believes, "Romantically," that feeling, desire, is always right?[62] Clearly not, in the sense that feeling must still be guided by principle. But it is true that none of the late heroines has to sacrifice her feelings or alter her desires, at least with respect to the man she loves.[63] Other late characters clearly do have improper feelings and desires, but such matters no longer concern Austen much. The author of *Pride and Prejudice*, *Sense and Sensibility*, and *Northanger Abbey* gave her opinion very decidedly for so young a person, but the mature Austen is no longer an artist of what ought to be, but of what is. She has become an explorer of emotions, an observer of fields of relational possibility, a connoisseur of process. Twelve years after *Susan*, she has turned her attention to the changing feelings of the mind.

One final issue. With her new belief in change, Austen faced a crucial narratological problem. How to bring to closure narratives that embody the ever-evolving nature of all things human? The answer she found, as has been pointed out in various ways, was to not bring them to full closure, to resist closure.[64] This resistance takes three forms: the creation of interpretive confusion about how properly to judge characters and actions; the leaving open of narrative possibilities subsequent to the end of the action proper and/or the acknowledgment that possibilities have been left unexplored within it; and the construction of endings that create readerly dissatisfaction, the sense of the right outcome not having been achieved.[65]

The first of these figures only in *Mansfield Park* and *Emma* and has already been well explored in the critical literature. From the beginning, *Mansfield Park* has inspired a sharply polarized debate about whether its heroine embodies Austen's moral ideals or rather an infantile prudery that we are meant to criticize—a confusion related to the question of whom she and Edmund should marry and thus to those other two forms of resistance, as we will see in a moment. As for *Emma*, the interpretive confusion it generates may be represented by Trilling's observation that "[w]e never know where to have it," never know "what it is up to"—a fact we already glanced at in noting that the novel contains hardly a single character whose moral worth can be determined with certainty.[66]

The second form of resistance, the opening of alternative, unexplored narrative possibilities, is most obviously present in *Mansfield Park*, where Austen not only tells us, around the middle of the novel, that Henry's suit would have been successful had Fanny's heart not been elsewhere engaged, but also, at the novel's end, that it would have been anyway, especially once Edmund had married Mary. This news comes in the very last chapter, as Austen spins out the subsequent fates of her characters, and represents a stunning last-minute bifurcation of the plot: had Henry not eloped with Maria, everything would have turned out differently. And that does mean everything, since—to return to the issue of interpretive confusion—such an outcome would have required us to judge everything in the novel in a very different light. Of course, even the way things did turn out is left somewhat open, Austen famously "abstain[ing] from dates" (387) so that we may each imagine for ourselves the length of time required for the transfer of Edmund's affections from Mary to Fanny—a gesture of incompleteness explicitly related to the indeterminacies of emotional process. *Persuasion* achieves this kind of incompleteness by carrying its story up to the present, and in a sly narratological turn, leaving one of its possibilities to be worked out in the "future." Mrs. Clay and William Walter Elliot have run off together, "[a]nd it is now a doubtful point whether his cunning or hers may finally carry the day; whether . . . he may not be wheedled and caressed at last into making her the wife of Sir William" (252). We have already glanced at a different kind of unexplored possibility in *Persuasion*: that the novel leads us to expect that Anne will expose William Walter Elliot's scandalous behavior toward Mrs. Smith, only to drop that narrative line as quickly as it had developed it.

This kind of resistance to closure, like the others, is most subtle in *Emma*, the most highly wrought and architecturally perfect of Austen's late, indeed of all her novels. The first form it takes can be expressed by a question we looked at before, that of "what will become of [Emma]." As with none of her other heroines, Austen leaves us with the sense that even at the end of her novel, Emma still has a great deal of "becoming" to do—that *this* story is not the end of *her* story.[67] It is a sense reinforced by the fact that she has yet to settle in her permanent home when the novel ends. Neither, for that matter, have Frank and Jane, nor has it all been decided whether Emma or Mrs. Elton will play the leading role in the future life of their community. Quite likely, they will continue to struggle over it, just as we imagine Emma and

Knightley continuing to struggle over Emma's behavior. But the novel's most compelling unexplored possibility is Jane herself. Any number of critics have testified to what most readers surely feel, the continually evoked, never fulfilled longing to see Emma become better friends, dear friends, with this beautiful and mysterious and fascinating young woman—a longing surely related to *our* desire to become "dear friends" with her, intimate with her, to know something, finally, about her. She is the Austen reader's great unrequited love.

As for the final form of resistance to closure, the arousal of feelings of dissatisfaction as to the correct outcome not having been achieved, I need hardly dwell on it in the case of *Mansfield Park*.[68] There is surely scarcely a reader who would not have preferred to see Fanny marry Henry and Edmund Mary, at least the first time through the novel. Not only did Austen clearly connive at this reaction, she seems to have shared it, at least in part. The bifurcated ending we just looked at suggests as much, that Austen's own heart tugged her at least part of the way in the other direction, as does her very rare use of the word "I" in the earlier of the two passages I alluded to in that connection: "although there doubtless are such incomparable young ladies of eighteen . . . as are never to be persuaded into love against their judgment . . . I have no inclination to believe Fanny one of them" (193).[69] In *Persuasion*, dissatisfaction of a different sort inheres in the sense that even if Anne and Wentworth have found each other, justice has scarcely otherwise been done, and that the world in which they will have to live is soured and bleak.[70] I will return to this point in my chapter on the novel; suffice it to note for now that the future of *Persuasion* is one in which Sir Walter will remain unshaken in his icy pride and vanity until his death, at which point Kellynch will be inherited by William Walter Elliot—and possibly, Mrs. Clay.

In *Emma*, we can hear the dark notes of the ending only if our ear has been properly tuned by the rest of the narrative. For who, at first glance, could see any reason for discontent in "the perfect happiness of the union" (396)? The only problem is that all three of those key words—"perfect," "happiness," and "union"—have been so ironized by the novel's handling of them as to make it a matter of very grave doubt whether they are not rather to be avoided.[71] The "union" of that last sentence echoes the language of the first, where "Emma Woodhouse, handsome, clever, and rich, with a comfortable home and a happy disposition, seemed to unite some of the best blessings of existence" (7). This first union, as we have seen, is in fact the start of all her woe: the vanity of being handsome, the willfulness of being rich and therefore independent, and the blind certainty of being clever, each trait the worse for being "united" to the others.

"Happiness" and its derivatives are words that—aside from also being compromised right from the beginning by that talk of Emma's "happy disposition"—belong, above all, to Miss Bates and Mrs. Elton. "Happy," for the first, is the slogan of her diminished, dependent existence. "And yet she was a happy woman," we are told upon first meeting her (20), and again, that "[s]he is a standing lesson in how to be happy" (210). This may sound admirable, but what is it but a pitiable making-do that forces her to lower her expectations to the level of her circumstances, no matter how far her circumstances have sunk? For Mrs. Elton, "happiness" is the name of the misery and false gaiety she inflicts on herself and everyone around her, with her "apparatus of happiness" at Donwell Abbey (296) and her outing to Box Hill, where, after the arrangements have been made, "[n]othing was wanting but to be happy when they got there" (303). Of the kind of happiness capable of being produced by the joint efforts of these two, by Miss Bates's abasement and Mrs. Elton's schemes, we get a fine sample in this picture of Jane after she accepts the position as governess: "She is as low as possible," says her aunt. "To look at her, nobody would think how delighted and happy she is to have secured a situation" (312).

As for "perfect," no word in the book is as insistently or emphatically undermined.[72] Of the dozens of times it or its derivatives appear, almost none is without qualification or irony, the leading example being the conundrum devised by Mr. Weston, that moral imbecile, on the very heels of Emma's cruelty to Miss Bates: "What two letters of the alphabet are there, that express perfection? . . . M. and A.—Em—ma" (306). To which Knightley gravely replies: "*Perfection* should not have come quite so soon" [emphasis in the original]. No—for a novelist of process, perfection can never come late enough. "[P]ictures of perfection," Austen wrote at around this time, "make me sick & wicked."[73] Wicked indeed is the game Austen plays with us throughout the novel, flattering us with our ability to see past Emma's blindness about Elton only the better to rub our noses in our own blindness about Frank, conjuring seductive appearances that continually giving way to hidden, hinted-at realities of a less pleasant nature. The logic of the novel's language makes its final statement into just such another happy deception, one that leaves us with a story in which nothing gets settled, an apparently "perfect" work that terminates in nothing but loose ends, a novel that refuses to stop playing games with us.

In short, like poetry of Wordsworth and Coleridge, the novels of the major phase are committed to notions of the ambiguous and continually evolving nature of human consciousness and human relationships, as well as to the use of exploratory and opened-ended processes in their own artistic construction. Indeed, in the major phase, as I noted above, the center of Austen's attention has shifted away from the courtship plot altogether. The narrative machinery that brings the lovers together, then separates them and bars their way to each other, which in the early novels occupies so much space, is in *Mansfield Park* and *Emma* entirely absent and in *Persuasion* relatively incidental.[74] The marriage plot now functions merely as the framework for deeper explorations from which the final unions emerge almost as epiphenomena. As my final three chapters will seek to explain, each of the novels of the major phase focuses its attention on one particular emotional structure or mode of relatedness that seized Austen's imagination as essential to the story she wished to tell. Or rather, the story she wished to tell seems in each case to have been constructed, in part, so as to enable her to explore that particular structure or mode. Again and again we can feel her improvising with language and emotions alike, groping her way toward new recognitions and new powers. The precocious certainties of the early phase have given way to the maturer wisdom of doubt.

CHAPTER THREE

Mansfield Park

Substitution

———————————————————————————

"[I]f one scheme of happiness fails, human nature turns to another."

Austen's encounter with Wordsworth, Coleridge, Scott, and Byron revolutionized her art by revolutionizing her understanding of the self as it exists in time. But even as the novels of the major phase exhibit generic similarities that distinguish them from Austen's earlier work and align them with the work of the Romantic poets, each also constitutes an extended exploration of one particular psychic mechanism or mode of relatedness that is likewise the bequest of these poets.

In *Mansfield Park*, the mechanism in question is one I will call, taking the word from the novel itself, "substitution," a set of psychic processes whereby individuals adjust to deprivation or loss by accepting alternative objects of desire. Thus, as will become clear, like the explorations in *Emma* and *Persuasion*, that in *Mansfield Park* is deeply rooted in Austen's new understandings of mental and relational processes. In fact, the first form of substitution to consider is memory itself, for it is in the novel's most concentrated exploration of memory, and specifically of memory as substitution, that its key Wordsworthian allusion appears. I have already glanced twice at the scene, the one that takes place in Fanny Price's East room presided over by a transparency of Tintern Abbey. *Mansfield Park* is the novel in which Austen first discovers the new, largely Wordsworthian perspectives of her major phase, and that scene, a rewriting of Wordsworth's greatest lyric of memory and loss, is the announcement of that momentous discovery.

The parallels between poem and scene are abundant and readily discovered.[1] Just as the stretch of the Wye a few miles above Tintern Abbey is deeply intertwined with Wordsworth's personal history, so is the East room with Fanny's. Having been the Mansfield schoolroom at the time of her arrival, the room was abandoned by the Bertram girls and ceded to her use some six years later, two years prior to the start of the novel's main action. It was at that point—Fanny was then sixteen—that she began to communicate with herself, like a contemporary teenager hanging posters in her bedroom, by surrounding herself with objects that gave outward form to her awakening impulses and understandings: "[h]er plants, her books . . . her works of charity and ingenuity" (126).

But the things in the East room betoken more than present feelings. Unlike the Bertram sisters, free of sentiment and memory alike, Fanny desires to remain in communication with past feelings, as well, and so discards nothing that evokes them. Here she has accumulated a collection of powerfully evocative mementos: "work-boxes and netting-boxes," "transparencies," "family profiles," "a small sketch of a ship sent four years ago from the Mediterranean by William," and so forth (127). In short, "she could scarcely see an object in that room which had not an interesting remembrance connected with it" (126). Fanny has gradually transformed the East room into a palimpsest of personal history, a theater of memory that makes the past visible to present awareness and so grounds the self in time.

This is very similar, of course, to the way the Wye valley functions for Wordsworth. In each case, the space in question becomes a physical projection of its beholder's inner self and, as such, the place where that self is uniquely nourished and uniquely whole. Indeed, each space becomes animated with the affective and imaginative energies its beholder—or we might rather say, its possessor, its lover—brings to it. Of Fanny's mementos we are told that "[e]very thing was a friend, or bore her thoughts to a friend" (126). As does Wordsworth, Fanny half-perceives, half-creates the scene before her, animating and personifying the otherwise dead world of objects, making things into "friends," merging the human and nonhuman, inner and outer, into a single realm.

There are other parallels. The stages of personal history lived in relation to each place are the same: childhood, youth, and maturity—for Fanny, as we will see, is far closer to womanhood than she suspects—albeit the ages that mark each transition are far younger in her case, as accords with the significantly younger age at which women were expected to marry, and their experiential content for her, a sheltered young lady, and for Wordsworth, a worldly young man, are necessarily very different.[2] Nor are the two spaces, the one a domestic interior, the other a verdant natural scene, as physically different as they first appear. The site of Wordsworth's poem is, as has been noted, a fundamentally interior space, one of enclosures and "seclusion[s]" that make up an inner landscape (8), an "inland" or "in-land" space (4).[3] And the East room, with its houseplants, is also verdant, or makes a gesture toward the verdant—a silly idea, this would be, were these not the only houseplants in all of Austen, appearing just here, of all places.

Nor does memory function in the scene merely to recall the past, but rather to transform it. This is memory at its most Wordsworthian: "though there had been sometimes much of suffering to her . . . though she had known the pains of tyranny, of ridicule, and neglect, yet almost every recurrence of either had led to something consolatory . . . and the whole was now so blended together, so harmonized by distance, that every former affliction had its charm" (126). Memory functions here in just the way that distinguishes Wordsworth's conception of it from that of the eighteenth century: not flatly recording the past, but transforming it, refiguring it, reinterpreting it, and in particular, as I noted in the previous chapter, redeeming experiences of suffering and loss by recognizing them as part of the texture of the self and its history.[4]

Memory can do all this, both poem and scene suggest, because it is an aesthetic faculty, one that "blend[s]" and "harmonize[s]" formerly discordant feelings into present "whole[s]." Austen's "harmonized" echoes two moments in "Tintern Abbey": "with an eye made quiet by the power / Of harmony . . . / We see into the life of things" (ll. 47–49) and "Thy memory [shall] be as a dwelling-place / For all sweet sounds and harmonies" (ll. 139–142). Neither occurrence is perfectly lucid in Wordsworth, but he seems to mean very much what Austen does, though more clearly in the second instance, where the apparent redundancy of "sounds and harmonies" asks us to discover the difference between the two words. "Harmony," the phrase suggests, is what memory creates out of the primary data of "sounds." It is the integrated, charming, consolatory whole into which memory's esemplastic power fuses whatever is jarring or untamed in immediate experience, be it Austen's "suffering" and "pains" or Wordsworth's "wild ecstasies" (l. 138). It is surely no accident that right after Austen tells us about memory's harmonizing power she shows us a whole array of pictorial representations: the transparencies, the profiles, the sketch of the ship—emblems of the mind's representational capacity.

It is from this harmonizing power that arises memory's ability to act as what I am calling a substitute: something one seizes upon as ostensibly equivalent when one cannot have what one really wants. For Austen's whole picture of the East room as a place of memory is developed in reference to the circumstance under which Fanny typically retreats there: "She could go there after any thing unpleasant below, and find immediate consolation" (126). Consolation in what? "[S]ome pursuit, or some train of thought at hand.—Her plants, her books . . . her works of charity and ingenuity." These are solaces, not substitutes, but as the long passage winds itself out, it becomes clear that the most important, the most deeply felt form of compensation Fanny habitually turns to is that of memory itself, acting precisely as a substitute:

> [O]r if undisposed for employment, if nothing but musing would do, she could scarcely see an object in that room which had not an interesting remembrance connected with it.—Every thing was a friend, or bore her thoughts to a friend; and though there had been sometimes much of suffering to her—though her motives had been often misunderstood, her feelings disregarded, and her comprehension under valued; though she had known the pains of tyranny, of ridicule, and neglect, yet almost every recurrence of either had led to something consolatory; her Aunt Bertram had spoken for her, or Miss Lee had been encouraging, or what was yet more frequent or more dear—Edmund had been her champion and her friend;—he had supported her cause, or explained her meaning, he had told her not to cry, or had given her some proof of affection which made her tears delightful—and the whole was now so blended together, so harmonized by distance, that every former affliction had its charm.

I quote the passage at such length because its very syntax mimics the associative movement of Fanny's mind, the seemingly endless sentence that comprises the bulk of it groping its way along as she gazes and muses her way back into memory, uncovering first one grief after another, then one consolation after another, until grief and consolation are finally fused together in a single memory. And what has become, meanwhile, of that "unpleasant thing below" that had sent her to the East room in the first place? It has been entirely forgotten.

Something very complex indeed is going on here. Fanny is not recollecting previous acts of consolation to serve in place of the consolation she wishes she were receiving in the present instance. Rather, a single composite memory of both pain and consolation displaces the present instance altogether. Consolation—the counterbalancing of present pain by present comfort—is not finally what happens here at all. Instead, memory—a harmonious aesthetic whole created by consciousness—entirely substitutes as an object of desire for whatever Fanny has been deprived of in the world outside her consciousness, be it liberty, esteem, or love.

Wordsworth himself does something remarkably similar, for "Tintern Abbey" pivots on a declaration of just such a substitutional act: "for such loss, I would believe, / Abundant recompense" (ll. 87–88). Attainable objects of desire displace ones that are no longer attainable. And what are these new objects, these substitutes? Surely, first, the powers the poet goes on to enumerate: his ability to "look on nature" in a new way and to feel in it a transfiguring presence. But the poem's self-reflexive nature—the fact that, like *The Prelude*, it narrates the conditions of its own emergence, telling the story of how the poet became the person who writes it—suggests that Wordsworth's most important form of recompense is the poem itself: an aesthetic unity that is also an act of recollection, a product of consciousness that fuses pain and consolation into a single harmonious whole. Wordsworth has lost the youthful energies memorialized in "Tintern Abbey," but what he gets in return is "Tintern Abbey." The poem thus exemplifies a principle central to all of Wordsworth's poetry. As a number of critics have noted, the writing of every poem is, for Wordsworth, a substitutional act, an attempt to compensate for loss with the very thing that records that loss.[5] But the very language with which Wordsworth announces this principle in "Tintern Abbey" points to the kind of self-deception substitution necessarily involves. Just as Fanny must conjure away her present reality before her substitutional strategy in the East room can be effective, so Wordsworth strikingly qualifies his central declaration. "I would believe": in other words, I would like to believe, I choose to believe—a near-oxymoron that, as we will see again and again in our examination of Austen's exploration of the intricacies of this great Wordsworthian intuition, perfectly captures substitution's half-willed, half-instinctive operation.

But perhaps all this is beside the point. After all, isn't the image that supposedly signals the connection between Austen's scene and Wordsworth's poem merely an innocent reference to Gilpin and the picturesque: "three transparencies, made in a rage for transparencies, for the lower panes of one window, where Tintern Abbey held its station between a cave in Italy, and a moonlight lake in Cumberland" (127)? As I argued in my first chapter, Austen does intend us to think of Gilpin—just as Wordsworth does—but only as the first half of a double allusion that incorporates both authors.[6] And if Fanny herself regards these images as Gilpinesque, that only sharpens the irony; she may think she sees like Gilpin, but she really sees like Wordsworth, a kind of seeing that is indeed "a few miles above Tintern Abbey."[7]

Gilpinesque vision bears about the same relationship to its Wordsworthian counterpart as Johnsonian memory, as discussed in the previous chapter, does to its. It is purely objective, purely "retinal," with no admixture of memory or feeling, no deepening by the imagination, no dynamic quality. What is more, as we saw in the previous chapter when noting Catherine Morland's rejection of Bath "as unworthy to make part of a landscape" (NA 99), it does not seek to enjoy a natural scene so much as to judge it against a set of preconceived ideas about the beautiful. Gilpin demonstrates the absurdities to which such a tyranny of expectation over experience can lead in the case, as it happens, of Tintern Abbey itself: "It has been an elegant Gothic pile; but it does not make that appearance as a *distant* object, which we expected. Tho the parts are beautiful, the whole is ill-shaped . . . and a mallet judiciously used (but who durst use it?) might be of service" in correcting these defects.[8]

Beauty as such is ultimately irrelevant to Wordsworthian vision, or rather, takes on a new meaning in relation to it. It was indeed its "beauteous forms" that first enamored the poet of the Wye valley, but the far deeper joy the locale now gives him is rooted in the scene's place within his inner life (l. 22). Just so, of the East room the narrator tells us that Fanny "would not have changed its furniture for the handsomest in the house, though what had been originally plain, had suffered all the ill-usage of children" (126–127). It may be true of Austen that "[a]t a very early age she was enamored of Gilpin on the Picturesque," but neither she nor her heroine is a little girl anymore.[9]

Nor is the scene in the East room the only time we find memory performing a substitutive function in *Mansfield Park*. The other most important instance becomes recognizable only in retrospect, at the moment that function ceases to be necessary. It is also profoundly, startlingly counterintuitive. Her brother William has returned to Mansfield after an absence of seven years, but for all of Fanny's "agitating happiness" at his arrival, "it was some time even before her happiness could be said to make her happy, before the disappointment inseparable from the alteration of person had vanished, and she could see in him the same William as before" (194–195). The shock of this unmild surprise is more than gentle. So effective a substitute object of attachment has Fanny's mental image of her brother been during those seven years of his absence that she now distressingly finds herself preferring the substitute to its original. And the living William regains his place in her affections only because she is able to discern in him a resemblance to that mental image. Again, as in "Tintern Abbey" and the East room, we find that substitution involves the subordination of the external to the internal world.

The artifices of memory, however, are only one of *Mansfield Park*'s many modes of substitution. Austen introduces us to any number of others right at the start, through the person of Mrs. Norris, one of the work's great substituters. The novel's introductory sketch sets out the story of the sisters Ward as a history of desires fulfilled and frustrated. Her younger sister having made a brilliant match, Miss Ward, advantaged by Maria's new position and quite as handsome as she, expects to do almost as well. But six years pass, barren of eligible offers. Miss Ward must now be in her late twenties, that last-chance zone for Austenian women, and so finds herself "obliged to be attached" to the virtually fortuneless Rev. Norris (5). The choice of words here precisely exemplifies the idea of substitution: not "obliged to marry" or "obliged to accept" but "obliged to be attached"—to love, or at least desire, or least pretend to herself that she desires. It is not just that her will must submit; her affections must be coerced, cajoled, hoodwinked.

The sequel is not hard to understand. The narrator's reference to the Norrises' "career of conjugal felicity" is, of course, bitterly ironic; their marriage is, in fact, loveless, as evidenced both by Mrs. Norris's eventual reaction to her husband's death ("[she] consoled herself . . . by considering that she could do very well without him" [21]) and by their failure to produce offspring. The prolificness of a fictional marriage often signals its degree of happiness, and that is certainly the case here: Mrs. Norris, who marries for money, bears no children; Mrs. Price, who marries for love (or at least for sexual attraction), bears ten; Lady Bertram, who marries for a combination of the two, bears four. It is no wonder that Mrs. Norris is such a bitter woman. Is there nothing she loves? Two things, in fact: "her love of money was equal to her love of directing." Indeed, Austen explicitly tells us that money substitutes for the offspring she does not have, becoming "an object of that needful solicitude, which there were no children to supply." As Mrs. Price bears a child a year, so Mrs. Norris "make[s] a yearly addition to an income which [she and her husband] had never lived up to" (9).

Substitution rules Mrs. Norris's life, and substitution motivates her to bring Fanny to Mansfield. It is her idea, after all, not Sir Thomas's. Fanny will become the child she never had—not the child to love, but the child to direct, to tyrannize. But a deeper motive seems to be at work, as well. It was Fanny's mother, another Fanny, who married for love—who, just when Mrs. Norris was making her first, determining substitution, rubbed salt in her wounds by refusing to do the same. And it is Mrs. Norris who made sure that the breach between Fanny Ward and the rest of her family became as deep as possible, Mrs. Norris who hatches the scheme of bringing one of the Price children to Mansfield, and Mrs. Norris who decides that the child taken should be, not the oldest boy, William—the one whom Mrs. Price had put forward in her letter of supplication—but the oldest girl, the one whose name just happens to be the same as her mother's. Mrs. Norris does not have Fanny Ward around to vent her spleen on, so she arranges for a substitute Fanny to be obtained for victimization.

This act of substitution leads to the next, as Fanny Price herself is introduced to the psychic mechanism that will rule her existence at Mansfield. I mentioned more than once in the previous chapter that Fanny must undertake a gradual, grinding readjustment of feeling upon being transplanted from Portsmouth to Mansfield. She must force herself, that is, to substitute one home for another. The language could not be plainer: "Fanny . . . was fixed at Mansfield Park, and learning to transfer in its favor much of her attachment to her former home, grew up there not unhappily among her cousins" (18). "Not unhappily" (the phrase is an example of litotes, a figure of speech to which I will return) is a good sample of the degree of felicity that substitution tends to involve. Five years later we find Fanny declaring, "I love this house and every thing in it"—evidence both of substitution's inexorable workings and the self-deception it invariably necessitates, for "every thing" would have to include not only Maria and Julia, about whom we have been told that Fanny "was often mortified by their treatment of her," but even Mrs. Norris (23, 18).

And that declaration of love involves a further irony, for she makes it in response to yet another threatened removal and thus threatened need for substitution, her impending transfer to Mrs. Norris's house. The declaration comes while Edmund is trying to persuade her "constant little heart" that the change will conduce to her "ultimate happiness" (24, 25). That is, he is giving her a lesson in substitution. Or rather, yet another lesson, for Fanny had approached him with news of the plan because, she says, "you have often persuaded me into being reconciled to things that I disliked at first" (23). In fact, the whole conversation turns out to be moot, since Mrs. Norris has never had any intention of taking her in, and in retrospect, Austen's sole purpose in devising it seems to have been precisely to show just how central in Fanny's life is the principle—we might even say, the ethos—of substitution.

Before continuing my discussion of the forms and implications of substitution, I would like to explore its causes. What is it about the world of *Mansfield Park* that makes substitution so important a psychic process there? We already began to glimpse the answer in considering Mrs. Norris's initial substitutional act: scarcity economics—more desire floating around than objects to satisfy it—and in particular, the scarcity economics of the marriage market. The novel opens with a merciless dissection of the way that market functions.[10] Men bring wealth—the ability to provide pleasure—and women bring wealth as well as beauty, a way of providing pleasure more directly. (This may seem an excessively utilitarian way of thinking about beauty, but Austen has Fanny, speaking of Mary, make the connection explicit: "she is so extremely pretty, that I have great pleasure in looking at her" [54].) How much you get depends on how much you can give. Wealth and pleasure purchasing wealth and pleasure, with the exchange rates calculated to a nicety: "[Maria Ward's] uncle . . . himself, allowed her to be at least three thousand pounds short of any equitable claim" (5). For the reader of Austen's previous novels, the statement has a familiar ring; this is a world governed by the values of John Dashwood, who had judged Marianne's illness to have dropped her market-price down to "five or six hundred a year" (SS 192).

Mansfield Park puts a magnifying glass to what Austen's early novels may have acknowledged but did everything they could to avoid dealing with. I argued in my first chapter that Austen had largely put *Pride and Prejudice* into the form we know as early as 1797, but she still came to *Mansfield Park* fresh from having condensed it and seen it through the press. *Pride and Prejudice* is that work of hers most fully ruled by the pleasure principle, a novel in which a virtually portionless young lady rejects one of the richest men in the kingdom only to be finally rewarded with him nonetheless. "The work is rather too light & bright & sparkling," Austen famously wrote upon its publication, "it wants shade,"[11] and from the very opening of *Mansfield Park*, the novel could hardly be a more direct corrective, more obviously a work in which reality returns to claim its own. "Miss Maria Ward, of Huntingdon," the first sentence tells us, "had the good luck to captivate Sir Thomas Bertram of Mansfield Park." "Captivate," that wicked double entendre, points to the thematics of slavery that have been so well discussed of late in the critical literature, but it points first of all to the fact that marriage in this world is, at least initially, a mutual enslavement, a buying and selling of human beings on both sides.[12]

It is no wonder that the language of courtship here is so much the language of commerce: "Miss Bertram's engagement made [Henry] in equity the property of Julia" (38); "Miss Price had not been brought up to the trade of *coming out*" (220; emphasis in the original). Nor is it a wonder that some suspect the game is fixed. Marriage, Mary says, "is, of all transactions, the one in which people expect most from others, and are least honest themselves." Mrs. Grant's reply, the novel's most explicit statement of the principle of substitution, is breathtaking in its cynicism: "if one scheme of happiness fails"—that is, if you were cheated out of the marriage you thought you were getting—"human nature turns to another; if the first calculation is wrong, we make a second better; we find comfort somewhere" (40). "Somewhere," indeed—substitution in its simplest mode. But Mary, ever the clever young woman, has a better "scheme." Rather than teaching herself to desire something else should she be deprived of her first object, she makes sure that her initial "calculation" is the right one. We might call this more insidious form of substitution by the appropriately oxymoronic name of "prudential desire": "[Mary] had felt an early presentiment that she *should* like the eldest best. She knew it was her way" (41; emphasis in the original).

Nor are the young man and woman the only ones involved in the marriage market's transactions. Sir Thomas, practicing some prudential desire of his own on behalf of his elder daughter, "intend[s] to value [Mr. Rushworth] very highly" (156). And if young women must choose a husband, younger sons, for their livelihood, must choose a career. How fortunate, then, that Edmund had "no natural disinclination" to overcome (litotes, again) in deciding to be a clergyman, since his father has kept a very good living—two, actually, at first—for him to come into (91). Scarcity economics: there may not be "so many men of large fortune in the world, as there are pretty women to deserve them," but there also are not so many estates and well-paying positions as there are fine young men to deserve *them* (5). We are shocked when Mary wishes out loud for Tom's death, less so, for some reason, when William Price wishes for that of his first lieutenant.

What happened to that other living, by the way, the one that was also to have been Edmund's? His brother had consumed it. Tom, "feel[ing] himself born only for expense and enjoyment," had become extravagant, and so "the younger brother must help to pay for the pleasures of the elder" (16, 21). How much must he pay? "You have robbed Edmund," his father tells Tom, "for ten, twenty, thirty years, perhaps for life, of more than half the income which ought to be his" (21). In retrospect, he may have robbed him of Mary, as well. Scarcity economics: what one eats, the other cannot eat.

This ugly business points to two more important things about *Mansfield Park*: how preoccupied its characters are with pleasure, and how unequal they each are in the getting of it. In none other of Austen's novels does the word "pleasure" appear so frequently or so prominently—to cite only a couple of the more prominent instances, the young people stroll through Rushworth's "pleasure-grounds" and Mary teases Henry about the yearly cost of his *"menus plaisirs"* (75, 188)—and in none other does pleasure figure so largely among the characters' concerns. All of Austen's novels take place among what we would have to call the idle rich, but these are the idlest and the richest. The first volume is largely taken up with two elaborate schemes of pleasure on the part of the young people, the visit to Sotherton and the theatricals. True, *Emma* also features a number of such schemes in quick succession—the ball, the visit to Donwell Abbey, the excursion to Box Hill—but the contrast is instructive. There, in Austen's most communitarian novel, the primary purpose of such schemes is not so much the pleasure they provide as the excuse they afford to collect everyone together. In *Mansfield Park*, their primary purpose is most certainly the pleasure itself, and everyone spends a lot of time arguing about who is to have the most, or at least the kind they like best—who is to sit where during the drive to Sotherton, who is to get which role in the play, and so forth.

Those with the most money tend to do best. Henry, having been brought up "in a school of luxury and epicurism," is our man of pleasure *par excellence* (387). Even a good sermon is valued by him as "a capital gratification" (282). As for his sister, whose idea of improving an estate is to hire someone to "give me as much beauty as he could for my money" (the logic of the male position in the marriage market), she declares that "[n]othing ever fatigues me, but doing what I do not like" (49, 58). This is life in the jungle, dressed up with fine manners and wit. And the beasts must feed: Dr. Grant is little more than a running joke about appetite; as for Henry, Fanny, schooled in the ways of Mansfield, rejoices in Portsmouth that he won't be exposing himself to her mother's servant's cooking, but rather treating himself to "the best dinner that a capital inn afforded" (341–342). But the choicest example of the paramount importance of the pleasures of the table has to be what Lady Bertram says to her sons as they argue over the propriety of the theatricals: "Do not act anything improper my dear . . . Sir Thomas would not like it.—Fanny, ring the bell; I must have my dinner" (118).

Yet while men of property and independently wealthy women or those already well-married do relatively well, the less advantaged—Edmund, Maria, Julia, Mrs. Norris, Yates (a younger son)—do less well, and Fanny does least well of all. In a social world that revolves around the getting of pleasure, desire will always be particularly keen, its frustration particularly bitter. And in a social world so very particular about how much pleasure each person, depending on their class, rank, gender, and birth-order, is entitled to ("[Edmund] is certainly well off for a cadet of even a Baronet's family," Henry tells us [189]), those at the lower reaches of the pecking order will do well to develop the habit of wanting what they can get—that is, of engaging in substitution.

In Fanny's case, wanting what she can get largely comes to mean not wanting at all. In the world of Mansfield, those who have no power of choice are conveniently regarded as having no desires or preferences in the first place. "[I]t will be just the same to Miss Lee," Mrs. Norris helpfully notes of the Mansfield governess, "whether she has three girls to teach, or only two" (10). Since Fanny is little more than a glorified servant ("Fanny, ring the bell"), she becomes "totally unused to hav[ing] her pleasure consulted, or to hav[ing] anything take place at all in the way she could desire" (232). So ingrained are the "habits of submission" in her personality as to have become virtually physiological (296). When satisfaction does occasionally come her way—"he found her trembling with joy"—her body can barely contain it (193). Her mouth, that orifice of appetite and self-assertion, is a particular problem. We often find her unable to speak her gratitude even for small favors or, in this novel of eaters, to swallow—to take pleasure, to develop desire. Her characteristic word is "no," her use of it an emblem not of will but of self-denial: from her first words ("no, no—not at all—no, thank you" [14]), to her meek disavowal of her desire to ride the horse that had been placed at her disposal ("No, I don't know, not if you want the mare" [59]), to that central (and fraudulent) disavowal of desire, the word she pronounces—or rather, cannot quite get herself to pronounce—when Sir Thomas asks her if she is rejecting Henry because her affections are already engaged: "He saw her lips formed into a *no*, though the sound was inarticulate, but her face was like scarlet" (261). That rejection points to the one, merely negative, expression of desire Fanny has left her: refusal. Like a Richardsonian heroine, but very much unlike an Austenian one, all she can say is "no."

Fanny's position as an utter dependent and her virtual lack of desire come together in still another psychological dynamic—really another form of sub-stitution, but one peculiar to Fanny—that Austen patterns into her heroine's life at Mansfield. We might call this one "emotional economics," because it makes Fanny's feelings into a kind of currency that she must use to repay her debt to the Bertrams.[13] (Since she can never fully repay it, though, the system places her emotions in perpetual hock.) The principle is laid down before she even crosses the Mansfield threshold, and it is laid down, not surprisingly, by Mrs. Norris: "Mrs. Norris had been talking to her the whole way from Northampton of her wonderful good fortune, and of the extraordinary degree of gratitude and good behavior which it ought to produce . . . of its being a wicked thing for her not to be happy" (13). No matter what feelings Fanny might want to feel, love, gratitude, obedience, and cheerfulness are the ones she must substitute for them. What might otherwise be loathed must be loved; what might otherwise be rejected must be embraced. We understand now with greater precision how Fanny "learn[s] to transfer in [Mansfield's] favor much of her attachment to her former home," how she comes to "love this house and every thing in it," even Maria, Julia, and Mrs. Norris.

The Bertram children already understand, no doubt for good reason, that money and feelings are interchangeable currencies, that presents of cash or things represent love and ought to be reciprocated with gratitude. Maria and Julia immediately make Fanny "a generous present of some of their least valued toys," and Edmund overwhelms her by enclosing half a guinea in her first letter to William (14). Of course, all the many "work-boxes and netting-boxes" that accumulate in the East room are products of the same logic. And in that same scene of the half-guinea, the scene that cements her everlasting love for him, Edmund also gives Fanny some further instruction in emotional economics, offering "a great deal of good advice" about "being as merry as possible" (16). As in the scene in which he tries to persuade her that moving in with Mrs. Norris would really be quite a happy thing, Edmund here acts as the acceptable face of Mansfield's harshest imperatives—as a younger son, no inapt apostle of substitution. Austen does nothing to conceal the operations of emotional economics; the language of emotion, like that of marriage, becomes the language of commerce: "she regarded her cousin . . . as entitled to such gratitude from her, as no feelings could be strong enough to pay" (33). It should be no surprise that Fanny so often experiences more gratitude than her body can handle.

It is in its ability to mobilize Fanny's feelings of obedience that emotional economics provides its real payoff for her creditors. While we looked at the scene in the East room in terms of the habitual role the place plays in Fanny's emotional life, the description of that generic situation functions as a prelude to the narration of one specific episode. It is an episode in which, as I will discuss more fully below, substitution eventually fails to function, but not because the imperatives of emotional economics make themselves felt with anything less than full force. Fanny has just refused to participate in the theatricals, the first time she has ever asserted her will against the Bertrams'. "I shall think her a very obstinate, ungrateful girl," her Aunt Norris has declared, "if she does not do what her Aunt, and Cousins wish her—very ungrateful indeed, considering who and what she is" (123). Already by the time she reaches her sanctum, Fanny "had begun to feel undecided as to what she *ought to do*" (127; emphasis in the original). When she does get there, the various objects with which she has been wont to condole as with friends come instead to accuse her: "as she looked around her, the claims of her cousins to being obliged, were strengthened by the sight of present upon present that she had received from them" (127). It is almost enough to break her resolution, and it prefigures a scene of essentially the same structure but of even greater import.

The setting is again the East room, where Sir Thomas has sought Fanny out to deliver the glad news of Henry's proposal. But the exchange quickly degenerates into her uncle's attempt to dictate to Fanny what her feelings ought to be on the occasion, and his long speech of rebuke, which utterly crushes her spirit, culminates in that most terrible of words, "*ingratitude*" (263; emphasis in the original). This, Sir Thomas clearly feels, is Fanny's big chance to repay what she owes him, or at least, as much of it as she will ever be able to. If there is any time to teach herself to want what is being offered, it is now.

As for Sir Thomas, he is himself a creature of substitution, though not in an obvious way. If one thing stands beside pleasure as the supreme value in the world of *Mansfield Park*, it is comfort. The word and its derivatives appear as frequently as do "pleasure" and its, and in positions of as great a prominence. Fanny's return to Mansfield after the cataclysm of the elopement extorts from Edmund the exclamation, "My Fanny—my only sister—my only comfort now," and from Lady Bertram, the rather odd one, doubly emphasized by being placed at the end of a chapter, of "Dear Fanny! now I shall be comfortable" (367, 369). Being comfortable is indeed Mansfield's highest ideal—Mansfield as distinct from the Crawfords. What is so exciting for the Bertram children about the arrival of Henry and Mary, in fact, is precisely that they bring with them a more intense and, for all but Tom, a hitherto unsuspected type of gratification, pleasure as opposed to comfort. In plainer language, they know how to have fun, and as long as Sir Thomas is absent and the Crawford ethos rules Mansfield, fun is what everyone has, or at least tries to.

But when Sir Thomas returns, what does he immediately declare but his "value for domestic tranquillity, for a home which shuts out noisy pleasures" (156)? "A home which shuts out": the Mansfield ideal, a purely negative one of happiness as that which causes no "agitation" or "vexation" or "trouble," Mansfield's great evils (and precisely those attendant on the young people's schemes of pleasure during Sir Thomas's absence). To cite only one of many examples, the Bertrams are distressed to find, upon Fanny's arrival, that her "little rusticities and awkwardnesses" make "grievous inroads on the tranquillity of all," but soon Sir Thomas and Mrs. Norris are relieved to find that she "seemed likely to give them little trouble" (16). "Tranquillity": half-asleep at her station on the sofa, Lady Bertram epitomizes the life of comfort as Henry does the life of pleasure. As "little trouble" as possible: what Sir Thomas, to his eventual sorrow, most wants his children to be.

This purely passive, negative ideal of comfort, as opposed to the active, positive one of pleasure, pervades Mansfield's very language, for it stands behind the trope we have already stumbled upon twice, litotes. It is Mansfield's characteristic turn of phrase, signifying not the presence of the wanted but the absence of the unwanted.[14] Dozens of examples may be cited: "not unamused," "not unwilling," "not undesirable," "less unpleasant," "less unreasonable," and the word Sir Thomas twice uses to describe Henry's proposal, "unexceptionable." "Not un-": the very spirit of Mansfield, that so terribly "not un-" kind of a place. No wonder the kids are so bored. Comfort, as we just said, is a lot less fun than pleasure. In fact, it is the position one falls back on when one finds pleasure to be too threatening—too agitating, too volatile, above all, too expensive. Sir Thomas, middle-aged and instinctively conservative, as we saw in the previous chapter, fears the pleasure-seeking passions of youth, and as a man whose position in the world rests on the relatively insecure foundation of mercantile wealth, he also has strong practical reasons for being averse to expense and risk.[15] Pleasure is what he might hunger for had he the landed wealth of a Henry Crawford. Instead, he has unconsciously adjusted his desires in favor of a pallid substitute, comfort.

Does Austen think of it as pallid? As about many of the most important issues raised by her later work, she appears to be ambivalent. On the one hand, the novel makes comfort its explicit authorial ideal. "Let other pens dwell on guilt and misery," the final chapter begins. "I quit such odious subjects as soon as I can, impatient to restore every body, not greatly in fault themselves, to tolerable comfort" (380). So too, just a few pages earlier, the narrator had named "an escape from many certain evils" as the "best of blessings" (370). Substitution itself, the larger principle of which the ideal of comfort forms a part, seems similarly authorized as a good, specifically an ethical good—for it is one of the novel's highest lessons that only those can feel who know what it means to do without. Those who do nothing but pursue pleasure—Henry, Admiral Crawford, Dr. Grant—become monsters; those who refuse to accept the limitations their situation in life imposes on their pleasure—Maria, Julia, Yates—become miserable. Pleasure-seeking establishes a psychic economy in which "dullness" ever threatens and "amusement" becomes an addiction (96). It is empty and cruel and, in its constant stoking of desire, inherently self-defeating. During the period of the theatricals, "[s]o far from being all satisfied and all enjoying, [Fanny] found every body requiring something they had not, and giving occasion of discontent to the others" (136–137). The only hell the wicked require, it seems, is one another's company.

So yes, *Mansfield Park* makes a strong case that substitution, the acceptance and even embrace of diminished expectations, is better than its alternative, the pursuit of one's true objects of desire—but only in the world of *Mansfield Park*. It is the best thing under the circumstances, but what does that say about the circumstances? Implicit in Austen's stoic endorsement of an ethic of making-the-best-of-it is a deep despair at a world that demands such an ethic in the first place, a world of scarcity economics and jealously guarded economic prerogatives.[16]

In discussing the social conditions that make substitution so central a psychic process in *Mansfield Park*, I have been considering issues peculiar to Austen's fictional world. But in turning now to the novel's most complex and disturbing forms of that process, we will see, as we did with that first scene in the East room, just how deeply informed by the Wordsworthian thematics of loss and compensation is Austen's exploration of it. Far from being specific to "Tintern Abbey," substitutional logics and mechanisms would have greeted Austen throughout Wordsworth's poetry. Indeed, the closest link between Austenian and Wordsworthian substitution concerns the presence in *Mansfield Park* of what I will call "fetishes": objects invested with extraordinary emotional power, and even felt, totemically, as possessing a life or spirit of their own, through their association with an individual in some way absent or unattainable. The most obvious, though least powerful examples are those very "work-boxes and netting-boxes" and other objects in the East room. More potent fetishes are to be found in the trio of gifts Fanny wears to the ball—William's cross, Henry and Mary's necklace,

Edmund's chain; in the scrap of paper on which Edmund had been writing the note that would have accompanied that chain; and in the much-fought-over silver knife that makes an otherwise inexplicable appearance as a narrative focus in the Portsmouth section.

The investment of psychic energy in some place or thing, some image that the mind can fix on and imaginatively manipulate: what is this but the idea of the omphalos developed by Geoffrey Hartman in his seminal work on the poet?[17] It is true that Hartman's "omphalos feeling" necessarily attaches to a place, some structure or spot of ground, but in discussing *Lyrical Ballads* in particular, he widens this notion of psychic clinging to include other kinds of fixation: "This physical or imaginative cleaving . . . results from a separation . . . They cleave," he says of the protagonists of *Lyrical Ballads* and similar poems, "to one thing or idea in order to be saved from a still deeper sense of separation."[18] That deeper sense of separation, for Hartman, is from Nature as a whole, but clearly such poems can be read as dealing exclusively with the trauma of that first separation, the loss of some supremely beloved object, be it a child, a native place, or something else. The cleaved-to thing—Michael's unfinished sheep-fold, the sailor's mother's bird—betokens the lost beloved. Like a memory, it stands in for what it represents, but being, unlike a memory, a physical object, it makes itself available all the more readily as a substitute focus for the emotional energy that can no longer be lavished on the beloved.

Hence the fetish's elevation to ritual or even magical status. The sailor's mother, holding the bird beneath her cloak—that is, against her breast—bestows on it the maternal affection she can no longer give her son, shielding it from the "raw," "wet," "foggy," day as she was unable to shield him on the high seas (ll. 1–2). The picture is a pathetic one, undercutting the poet's first view of the woman as "majestic" and full of "strength" and "dignity," for it suggests an inability to accept her loss, to distinguish emotionally between son and bird, and thus a desire magically to assert control over that which has already slipped out of her control (ll. 5, 10). As for Michael, he swings between the need to deny the loss of his son by carrying on with his half of the covenant that Luke has already broken (an activity, the building of the sheep-fold, that, like the sailor's mother's guarding of the cage, involves the emblematic sheltering of innocent animal life) and the baffled half-acceptance of that loss suggested by his inability, on many days, so to carry on, his contrary need to commune in stillness with the wreck of his hopes. Two forms of ritual action, the building and the sitting, both tied to the psychic focus of the sheep-fold. In both poems, crucially, the grieving parent is denied the chance to see the physical remains of the lost son (Luke is not even dead), a circumstance that makes possible the denial we have just looked at and opens the way for the fetish object to serve as a substitute—in a sense, as a substitute for the body.

In choosing the term "fetish" I am of course importing Freudian overtones, willy-nilly, into my argument. Freud can help us here, but not in the most obvious way. His theory of the fetish as a perversion of the sexual instinct—that it is a replacement for the maternal phallus—is not particularly useful, but he also notes that "[a] certain degree of fetishism is . . . habitually present in normal love, especially in those stages of it in which the normal sexual aim seems unattainable or its fulfillment prevented."[19] This clearly describes Fanny's attachment to the cross, chain, and scrap of paper; in Freudian terms, substitution is often close to and sometimes identical to sublimation. But Freud's example of this normal kind of fetishism is interesting in itself. It comes from *Faust*, part I: "Get me a kerchief from her breast, / A garter that her knee has pressed."[20] *Faust* I is almost exactly contemporaneous with *Mansfield Park*. The point is not that Goethe may have influenced Austen—he almost certainly did not—but that both authors wrote at a time when ornaments and other luxury goods were coming to assume a role of unprecedented importance in the social and imaginative lives of the European middle and upper classes.[21] As someone very well acquainted with Bath, the first modern town designed exclusively as a place of consumption, Austen would have been highly aware of this new sensitivity to consumer goods—a sensitivity that is indeed registered throughout her letters and novels.[22] It is no coincidence that, other than Edmund's scrap of paper, all the fetishes in *Mansfield Park* are luxury items.

A better guide to these matters than Freud is David Simpson, who outlines the late-eighteenth-century debate over the taste for ornament in his book on fetishism and the imagination. Of special concern to this debate—which embraced social, moral, economic, and political questions and engaged such thinkers as Ferguson, Smith, Godwin, Rousseau, and Hegel—was the tendency of this taste for the tokens of wealth, status, and rank to set up such "trinkets and luxuries" as objects of veneration in their own right—that is, as fetishes, images which their worshipers have themselves created and empowered.[23] But Simpson's main interest here is to use this debate to contextualize Wordsworth's concern with the fetishistic dangers of the mind's own figurative power—its tendency so to believe in the reality of its creations as to allow them finally to supplant the objects they arise to represent. As Simpson puts it in an earlier study, "the mind's figurative faculty," for Wordsworth, "exists to make bearable the experience of loss" and thus to reintegrate the self into the world. But if it performs this task too completely—as it does in so many of his poems and pointedly avoids doing in others—it risks "the death-in-life of fetishism (fixation on one exclusive object, to which all mental energies are directed)."[24] We return here to Hartman, with a sharpened sense of the ubiquity in Wordsworth of the substitutional act.[25]

Of course, there are marked differences between the fetishes in *Mansfield Park* and those in Wordsworth. Most of the former betoken individuals unattainable rather than dead; like most of the novel's substitutions, they redress deprivation rather than loss in the purest sense. Nor are any of these fetishes clung to with the single-mindedness or intensity Hartman and Simpson describe. But all this only means that Austen pursued the start Wordsworth had given her imagination in her own direction, adapting what she found in his poems to the purposes of her own novelistic world. It is a world much more densely social than that of Wordsworth's lyrics, one that makes compromises and adjustments continually necessary. Wordsworth's figures, including that of the poet himself, live solitary or virtually solitary lives; their passions burn with a hard, gemlike flame. Austen's characters live in a tight web of social relations, obligations, and expectations. Fanny is an extremely passionate young woman—to my mind, the most passionate figure Austen ever created—but her passions are necessarily divided: among many impulses, many people, many objects.

The first of those objects are the ones in the East room, each of which, we may recall, either bears Fanny's thoughts to a friend or is itself a "friend." A strange personification, this second possibility, one made more pointed by the inclusion among these objects of a collection of family profiles, as if the Bertrams themselves were present as spirits inhabiting the things they have given her. Indeed, those two possibilities can be understood as shading into each other: those things are friends, we might say, which so forcefully bear Fanny's thoughts to friends that she has developed an independent emotional relationship with them. We can see how this situation would have arisen. Those "friends" in the East room are a lot more reliable than the ones downstairs. Since the latter so often offer her nothing but tyranny and ridicule and neglect, Fanny has taken to managing her relationships with them imaginatively, silently improvising happy endings to unpleasant scenes with the help of her little Maria-puppets and Julia-puppets and Edmund-puppets. What reality will not offer she can try to coax her fetishes into providing.

Retreating to her sanctum during the theatricals, she hopes "to see if by looking at Edmund's profile she could catch any of his counsel"—an attempt at imaginative manipulation pointedly undercut by the appearance of the young man himself just a paragraph later to inform her that he, too, plans to take part in the theatricals. In the meantime, as we have seen, her other fetishes have turned on her with a vengeance, the sight of her cousins' presents so reinforcing their givers' claims to obedience that it is as if she can literally hear those embodied Bertrams spirits rebuking her. Her imagination, it turns out, has indeed endowed these fetishes with a life and power of their own. Needless to say, there is something terribly sad about this befriending of things, suggesting the lonely girl in need of true friends. That this mediation of human relationships through relationships with objects—this substitution of things for people—has become one of the most deeply ingrained habits of Fanny's psychic repertoire we soon see, as she seeks to manage her feelings during the most emotionally fraught time of her life.

Though never named as such, Fanny's ball is an event she undoubtedly hoped would never have to happen, her "coming out" into society. The young woman who shrinks from notice, who has only very recently begun to adjust to "the idea of being worth looking at" (165), will for the first time be on display as an object of observation and desire. Other pressures are bearing on her as well. Henry's attentions have been too pronounced to escape notice. Edmund and Mary's courtship has been gaining momentum. William's arrival, as we have seen, has brought disappointment as well as delight. But her brother has also brought with him what is to be her symbolic defense against the threats of the ballroom in general and Henry in particular. As painfully uncertain as she is about how to dress for the event, the one thing she has decided is that she will wear the amber cross that William bought her in Sicily. It is to be a kind of magic amulet, symbolizing her desire to be shielded from the gaze of men, to remain inviolable, presexual, for it is both, in its association with William, an emblem of childhood and, in its association with Catholicism, an emblem of virginity.

It is precisely because Fanny is so attuned to the symbolic and emotional power of such tokens that she is suspicious—correctly, as it turns out—of Mary's offer of the necklace. Mary herself not only has so many "trinkets and luxuries" that none of them attracts much feeling, she is so cavalier about feeling itself, so mobile in her attachments, that feelings become as transferable as those trinkets themselves. "[W]ith the necklace," she tells Fanny, "I make over to you all the duty of remembering the original giver" (214). But Fanny, of all people, understands that gifts not only confer obligations but carry the ghostly, controlling presence of their giver. Possessing—for her, at least—all too easily slips over into being possessed.

As preparations for the ball, that nexus of desire and display, pick up pace, the fetishes start to come fast and thick. With the next one, Edmund's note, Fanny begins to win back some control over her situation, though, like that exerted by the sailor's mother, it is purely imaginative and imaginary. Because the note is the novel's one fetish that has no material value—the one, in other words, over which no one will contest possession or meaning—it is the one most docile to Fanny's manipulative intentions. The gods have dropped in her lap an object upon which she can unload all her suppressed romantic feelings for her cousin. The note is "a treasure beyond all her hopes"; even better than an object, it is a text, and thus affords apparently endless opportunity for imaginative overreading. "My very dear Fanny," it reads, "you must do me the favor to accept" (219)—and we can almost hear her completing the unfinished sentence with the word "me." So excessive is Fanny's response—"there was a felicity in the flow of the first four words, in the arrangement of 'My very dear Fanny,' which she could have looked at for ever"—that as with the analogous incident in *Emma*, Harriet's ceremonial burning of her "*Most precious*" court plaister and pencil-stub, Austen treats the moment with a touch of comedy (E 280–281).[26]

But there is nothing comic about her treatment of what soon follows; indeed, her symbolism becomes uniquely overt and uniquely sexual, as she collaborates with her heroine to create a fetish of supreme significatory power. While Henry's necklace will not go through the ring of the cross, Edmund's chain will, a circumstance that expresses both Fanny's desired and Austen's eventual answer to the question of which of the two men will earn the right to chain her up in marriage, to put his long, hard thing through the hole in the cross of her still childish (still virginal) body—or to make that hole, we might say, remembering Henry's project of "making a small hole" in Fanny's heart, with its overtones of dehymenization (191). I am not suggesting that Fanny recognizes this symbolic dimension of the circumstances Austen has created, but she does capitalize on those circumstances to create a symbolic system of her own, finally repossessing the tokens—and thus, imaginatively, the people—that had slipped out of her control: "having with delightful feelings joined the chain and the cross, those memorials of the two most beloved of her heart, those dearest tokens so formed for each other by every thing real and imaginary—and put them around her neck, and seen and felt how full of William and Edmund they were, she was able without an effort to resolve on wearing Miss Crawford's necklace too" (224).

Edmund and William together, "the two most beloved of her heart," Henry pointedly excluded.[27] Fanny is playing with puppets again, voodoo dolls, passing an emotional fiction on herself, making happen in her little play-world of objects what she cannot make happen in the real world. That "seen and felt" is also worth pausing over: thinking of Wordsworth's mad mother and other women unbalanced by unfulfillable longing, we might almost begin to fear for Fanny's sanity, as her very senses now participate in her willed subjectivization of the exterior world.

The novel's final fetish, the silver knife, is less emotionally loaded than those connected to the ball but participates in a uniquely complex system of substitutes, as the novel becomes increasingly self-conscious about the theme of substitution as it draws to a close. Portsmouth as a whole is indeed for Fanny a swirl of substitutions and memories and memories-as-substitutions, beginning even before she gets there, as "[t]he remembrances of all her earliest pleasures, and of what she had suffered in being torn from them, came over her with renewed strength, and it seemed as if to be at home again, would heal every pain that had since grown out of the separation" (306). Her experience of William's return to Mansfield, when the solacing substitutions of long-cherished memories had been destroyed in an instant by contact with the altered shape of the present, has done nothing to teach her to anticipate a less paradisal reunion. Nor does she recognize, surprisingly, that a return to her family implies another separation, that she will soon be struggling with the loss of Mansfield, the substitute home for which her original home must now serve as a substitute.

We saw in the previous chapter how the self-protections of memory go to work as soon as Fanny gets to Portsmouth, prompting her to love her mother's face the more because it reminds her of her Aunt Bertram's. How interesting it is that neither face ever reminds her of her Aunt Norris's, and if we needed any further evidence of the necessary selectivity of Fanny's memory, we have this reaction to the chaos in her father's house: "At Mansfield, no sounds of contention, no raised voices, no abrupt bursts, no tread of violence was ever heard; . . . every body had their due importance; every body's feelings were consulted" (325).[28] Her anticipatory memories of Portsmouth had undoubtedly been as accurate a picture of that happy family as is this recollection of Mansfield.

Meanwhile, another recollected similarity of feature has already surprised her, that of Betsey, her mother's youngest daughter, to Mary Price, Fanny's favorite sister before her removal to Mansfield. Mary, "very pretty" and "remarkably amiable," had died a few years after Fanny's departure, "and when the news of her death had at last reached Mansfield, [Fanny] had for a short time been quite afflicted" (320). Now, in a kind of delayed substitution, "[t]he sight of Betsey brought the image of little Mary back again." But as Fanny contemplates the resemblance, Betsey, unaware of what is going through her sister's mind, is "holding out something to catch her eyes." It is the silver knife, given by that same Mary, on her deathbed, to Susan, the eldest of the sisters still in Portsmouth, and cherished by her ever since. Another substitution, this one undoubtedly all the more urgent in that Susan, like her sisters, "never had been much" to Mrs. Price, and thus has had yet another deprivation for which to compensate herself (323).

So a substitute for Mary is holding a substitute for Mary—the narrative almost seems to be free-associating here—and we next learn that the silver knife had functioned as a fetish for Mary herself, the cherished token of old Mrs. Admiral Maxwell, the godmother who had given it to her a few weeks before *her* death. We might think here of that other Mary, and not only because a secret wish for her death might well be a part of what lies behind Fanny's sudden recollection of Mary Price. Mary Crawford, with her pile of necklaces so high that no single one matters much, helps us understand why, in a family with so little to spend on "trinkets and luxuries," one piece of silver must perform multiple duty, passing from hand to hand as the subject of successive investments of desire and feeling and meaning. In other words, we see here again the inverse relationship between privilege and the need for substitution. It is no coincidence that Fanny—who might well understand how important the knife must be for Susan—puts a stop to the contention over ownership by buying a new knife for Betsey—the first time, we are told, she has ever bought anything for any one. Wealth steps in to terminate the substitutional chain. And if we have any doubt that Austen is holding out the theme of substitution here in such a way as to catch *our* eyes, we might recognize that the entire episode—knife, Betsey, Mary Price, Mrs. Admiral Maxwell—is irrelevant to the plot, something otherwise almost unexampled in her work.

Finally, not only do memories and objects substitute for missing individuals, so, most importantly and most disturbingly, do other individuals. This is dark doctrine: we are commodities for one another, Austen tells us.[29] We love whom we have because we cannot have whom we love. This final form of substitution, too, she would have found in Wordsworth. The title characters of "The Mad Mother" ("Her Eyes are Wild") and "The Emigrant Mother"—the first of whom clings to her baby boy as a replacement for the husband who has abandoned her ("'Thy father cares not for my breast . . . But thou wilt live with me in love' " [ll. 61–67]), the second of whom replaces her lost child with the child of another—are obvious examples. But Wordsworth's most moving portraits of this form of substitution involve its refusal. As Hartman notes (his terminology coinciding here with mine), "[t]wo Matthew poems suggest there are things the heart cannot replace. Substitution (in contemporary terms, sublimation) is questioned."[30] Frances Ferguson draws a similar conclusion about "The Brothers," noting that Leonard's loss of the object of his affections leads to a loss of the affections altogether, as he essentially writes his own epitaph and turns his back on the human world.[31] But Austen's characters do not turn their back on the human world; either they are not as strong as Wordsworth's, or her view of human nature is less flattering, or the world of *Mansfield Park*, in which possession is the highest value, makes greater demands for accommodation and adjustment than does Wordsworth's.

This final substitutional pattern begins insidiously, almost unobtrusively, after Sir Thomas's departure for Antigua, with Lady Bertram "astonished to find how very well they did" without him, "how well Edmund could supply his place in carving, talking to the steward, writing to the attorney, settling with the servants, and equally saving her from all possible fatigue or exertion" (30). But then, Lady Bertram is an extreme case. Passionless; anesthetized; morally speaking, virtually dead—she is the novel's most devastating portrait of the effects of the marriage-market economy on the individual's capacity for feeling, its tendency not just to make people see each other in terms of utility, but to fool them into thinking that what they are feeling is love.

A more complex set of instances, one that involves Fanny herself, begins to take shape during the rehearsal of *Lover's Vows*. The period of the theatricals, as we noted before, proves to be a time of discontent and envy for nearly everyone, as an atmosphere of erotic frustration descends on the group. Maria and Julia struggle over Henry, Rushworth sulks, Fanny pines, Mary frets over Edmund's career plans, Edmund frets over her fretting. The various would-be lovers use the rehearsals, of course, as a way of expressing feelings they cannot openly avow—the deeper meaning of the chosen play's title. This is a kind of substitution, too—an odd kind, a displacement of desire that involves shifts in both the desired object and the desiring subject. But even this is as yet, for Mary and Edmund, too frank, so each looks to Fanny to provide an alternative to the alternative. "You must rehearse it with me," Mary tells her "that I may fancy *you* him," and Edmund too, possessed by the same idea, shows up in the East room himself a few minutes later (140; emphasis in the original).[32]

This strange triangular episode is not yet the substitution of one person for another, but it prepares the way for it, for Mary's plea to Fanny—"You must rehearse it with me, that I may fancy *you* him"—foretells the future of the two women's relationship. Enamored of the same man, they begin to use each other as his surrogate, a form of substitution that becomes the basis of the rather ambiguous friendship they develop.[33] It begins the day that Fanny, forced by a rainstorm to take refuge in the Parsonage, ends up listening while Mary plays the harp. Soon Mary insists on playing her "Edmund's prime favorite," and as she does so, Fanny "fancied him sitting in that room again and again . . . listening with constant delight to the favorite air" (173). Each woman is clearly using the other to dream herself into proximity to the man she loves—a man each has good reason to think she will never really be able to have—Mary again fancying one cousin to be the other, Fanny undertaking a more complex emotional operation, compounded of self-torment, voyeurism, and a strange sort of vicarious pleasure, but one that apparently gratifies her even against her will.

Despite rushing home immediately after the air is over, and despite feeling neither love for Mary nor pleasure in her company, from that day she begins compulsively to pursue a closer intimacy with her: "Fanny went to her every two or three days; it seemed a kind of fascination; she could not be easy without going" (173). Mary, for the time being, is the closest Fanny can get to Edmund. Her obsession with her cousin's beloved—virtually erotic, in some critical accounts—is a displaced version of her erotic obsession with her cousin himself. Once again—as with the initial scene in the East room, as with Fanny's manipulation of her fetishes, as with much else in this darkly complex book—Austen's exploration of substitution sends her groping along dim byways of feeling, apparently as uncertain about where she will come out as her characters are themselves.

One of the dimmest of those byways, and the one the exploration of which has lately proven most disturbing to Austen's readers, concerns what is finally the most difficult and momentous process of substitution Fanny undergoes, the replacement in her affections of William by Edmund. Much has been written about the novel's incestuous ending, including how Fanny's quasi-incest with Edmund becomes her best available alternative to incestuous (if nonphysical) union with William.[34] But while both the marriage and the impulse it substitutes for have been rightly criticized as narcissistic, they are driven by a thoroughly Wordsworthian logic.[35] This is a novel in which authentic personhood is rooted in memory, and the narrator's conspicuously Wordsworthian paean to fraternal love occasioned by William and Fanny's reunion praises that love in precisely those terms. The love between brothers and sisters, we are told, will in one important respect always trump conjugal love, being grounded in "the same first associations and habits" (195). What prompts that paean, in fact, is an act of joint recollection strikingly reminiscent of the "Tintern Abbey" scene in its Wordsworthian redemption of painful experiences through the harmonizing power of memory. Now that William and Fanny are at last reunited, "all the evil and good of their earliest years could be gone over again, and every former united pain and pleasure retraced with the fondest recollection" (195). Next to this, her love for Edmund can never be more than second best.

But Fanny's predicament is more complicated still, for by the time of William's return it is clear that, whatever she might think, even her regressive fantasy of "the little cottage" in which she and William are "to pass all their middle and latter life together" would not satisfy her (311). Having spent seven years displacing her fraternal feelings for William onto Edmund, and at least a couple of years developing sexual feelings for the latter, she now finds herself caught between the two men. Her divided childhood has left her with divided desires, and her adolescence has complicated those desires still further.

The only thing that could really satisfy her would be a fusion of brother and beloved cousin—in the light of which fact it is worth looking again at the passage in which she combines William and Edmund's two gifts. The passage reads, "having with delightful feelings joined the chain and the cross . . . and put them around her neck, and seen and felt how full of William and Edmund they were," not " . . . and seen and felt how full of William was the one and of Edmund was the other" (224). The syntax captures the necessary blurring of feeling.[36] We can now see that the joining of the cross and chain signified for Fanny more than the exclusion of Henry in favor of "the two most beloved of her heart"; it signified the imaginary—we might even say, the mystical—union of that pair, the creation of an ideal object of desire we would have to call William-Edmund. Fanny's acceptance of Edmund is thus finally a strange kind of second-order substitution—Edmund halfsubstituting for William during the years after her arrival in Mansfield, Edmund substituting again—once the realm of private fantasy gives way, as it must, to daylight possibility—for the hybrid creature thus created.

But Fanny's acceptance of Edmund is also and more obviously a refusal of substitution, that of Edmund himself by Henry. Only twice do we see Fanny making such a refusal, but those two instances are the great mileposts on her path to adulthood. The first, again, is the occasion of Fanny's retreat to the East room. The nature of that occasion constitutes yet another parallel between that scene and "Tintern Abbey," for if "Tintern Abbey" is a poem of crisis, this is a scene of crisis every bit as momentous, if very different in kind.[37] It concerns Fanny's relationship with the Bertrams, the benefactors to whom she feels herself so indebted as to be beyond repayment and to whom her customary relationship is that of a well-treated servant. But now she is refusing to set aside her own desire to avoid exposure in favor of their imperious demands that she serve their pleasure. "I shall think her a very obstinate, ungrateful girl," Mrs. Norris has said, "considering who and what she is" (123). But who and what she is are exactly the questions this moment thrusts upon her. The "friends" with which she has surrounded herself, as we have seen, now come to accuse her, just as the sight of his beloved valley reminds Wordsworth all the more of what he has lost since first beholding it. For both, the very constancy of the scene allows for the measurement of alterations in the self. But while Wordsworth recognizes that he is "changed, no doubt, from what I was when first / I came among these hills" (ll. 66–67), her own alteration Fanny does not see. But we see it: she is crossing into adulthood. She is no longer who and what she was. Out of the conflict between dependence and desire, a new self is being dragged painfully into life.

The difficulty of the process continues through its major phase, the struggle with Sir Thomas—and with Edmund and Lady Bertram and everyone else—over Henry's courtship. As always, Fanny's first impulse is to regress. As Sir Thomas approaches the East room for the confrontation I glanced at above, "[t]he terror of his former occasional visits to that room seemed all renewed, and [Fanny] felt as if he were going to examine her again in French and English" (257–258). (Interestingly, it is precisely when he sends her back to the scene of her earliest childhood that she at last begins to feel like an adult.) The last thing she ever wants to do is stand up for what she wants to do. But though she has learned that it is better for someone like her not to have desires at all, there is one desire she will not give up, for she has vested it with all her hopes for the future, and even though circumstances are about to tear it from her anyway, she refuses to assent to her fate. At the last moment, her creator rescues her—but what then becomes of the ethic of substitution? Is it just because Fanny has substituted so many times that she is finally allowed one relief from substitution? Or is her triumph Austen's one gesture of defiance against a world that makes substitution necessary in the first place?

If so, it is a solitary gesture, for the novel's final events enforce the sub-stitutional imperative more massively than anything that has come before. But before turning to these events it is worth considering one last scene in the East room, one final layer added to the semantic archaeology of this, a space of uniquely complex significance in Austen's work. It is also a scene of recollection, one that illuminates Austen's handling not only of memory, but also of personal change and the way it complicates questions of moral worth. As such, as we will see, it bears crucially on the novel's final substitutions. The East room has already been the site not only of the "Tintern Abbey" scene and of Fanny's confrontation with Sir Thomas, but also of Mary and Edmund's rehearsal and of Edmund's note-writing. The final episode in that by-now very resonant place brings Mary up to rebuke Fanny for having refused Henry's offer. But before she can launch in, she is brought up short by a spontaneous outpouring of recollection. Yes, Mary—one of those unfixed, heartless, amnesiac Crawfords. "[A]m I here again? The East room. Only once was I in this room before! . . . Only once before. Do you remem-ber it? I came to rehearse . . . A delightful rehearsal. I shall never forget it . . . Oh! why will such things ever pass away?" (296). The rhythms are those of genuine feeling, and the effusion ends with Mary falling silent "in a reverie of sweet remembrances."

Memory, sorrow, attachment: she sounds like Fanny Price. What has hap-pened in the ten chapters since the trick with the necklace? What has hap-pened is that she has begun to change. The love of Edmund, the friendship of Fanny, the examples of both, and no doubt also her failure to bend Edmund to her will (only those can feel who know what it means to do without)—all this and perhaps more have opened her to new emotions, new values, less giddy desires. As she confides to Fanny just after this, regarding her plans to leave Mansfield, "Mrs. Fraser has been my intimate friend for years. But I have not the least inclination to go near her. I can think only of the friends I'm leaving; my excellent sister, yourself, and the Bertrams in general. You have all so much more *heart* among you, than one finds in the world at large" (297–298; emphasis in the original). Mary has discovered what it means to have a heart, and her brother, who had sought only to make a hole in Fanny's, has discovered it too. At his leave-taking, Fanny notes, he "really seemed to feel.—Quite unlike his usual self, he scarcely said any thing. He was evidently oppressed" (302). The Crawfords initially deserve all the censure criticism has traditionally heaped on them, but they also exhibit a moral growth from those very unpromising beginnings that makes the conversion of a Marianne or Elizabeth look merely notional by comparison.[38] This is the start of the path to the alternative outcome I discussed in the previous chapter, one that Austen gazes down several times but ultimately declines to follow. As such, it is related, though not obviously, to the novel's final substitutions.

The most conspicuous, but by no means the only one of these final substitutions is Edmund's acceptance of Fanny in place of Mary—reminiscent of Marianne's "acceptance" of Colonel Brandon at the end of *Sense and Sensibility*, but different in the precise degree to which substitution differs from coercion. For Marianne does not so much accept Colonel Brandon as have him forced on her, and while she eventually seems to adjust to the disappointment, that is a very different matter from the psychic mechanism at work here.[39] Substitution, as I have said, is a voluntary process, which is precisely what makes it so effective and so chilling. Edmund actually persuades himself to believe that he is happier with what he gets than with what he wanted in the first place, that "a very different kind of woman might . . . do just as well—or a great deal better" (387). Austen's reference on this occasion to "the cure of unconquerable passions, and the transfer of unchanging attachments" is every bit as cynical as her initial glance at Miss Ward's obligation to be attached to Rev. Norris. Indeed, she is even consciously mendacious in suggesting that Edmund need only "learn to prefer soft light eyes to sparkling dark ones"—as much a trivialization of the difference between the two women, and of Edmund's attachment to Mary, as it would have been to describe an analogous shift from Edmund to Henry on Fanny's part as merely a matter of learning to prefer short men to tall. But of course, the entire novel has been about "the cure of unconquerable passions, and the transfer of unchanging attachments."

True, Austen goes on to do all she can to persuade us as to the naturalness and rightness of the substitution, but her deep ambivalence about the outcome she has chosen continues right through the novel's final paragraphs. For the shift of Edmund's affections is far from the novel's final substitution, and those that follow it, in their very swiftness and thoroughness and even casualness, ironize any protestations Austen makes as to his acceptance of Fanny being anything more than a matter of taking what you can get. Fanny herself returns from Portsmouth with her own replacement, in the person of her younger sister. In less than a paragraph, Susan supplants in Lady Bertram's heart the niece who has been her dutiful companion and servant for eight years, functioning "[f]irst as a comfort to Fanny, then as an auxiliary, and last as her substitute" (389; this is the passage from which I have taken my key term). About Sir Thomas, we read this: "In [Susan's] usefulness, in Fanny's excellence, in William's continued good conduct, and rising fame, and in the general well-doing and success of the other members of the family, all assisting to advance each other, and doing credit to his countenance and aid, Sir Thomas saw repeated, and forever repeated reason to rejoice in what he had done for them all." The narrator mordantly mimics Sir Thomas's own mental and emotional operation. Maria, Julia, and Tom are forgotten; Susan, Fanny, and William are installed in their place. Sir Thomas has bought himself a new set of children. It is not for nothing that they are named "Price."

But even this is not the novel's final substitution, because as powerful as Sir Thomas is, as able to determine the destinies of his children and stepchildren, he is not the ultimate possessor of Mansfield Park. That figure reappears at the start of the final chapter: "Let other pens dwell on guilt and misery. I quit such odious subjects as soon as I can, impatient to restore every body, not greatly in fault themselves, to tolerable comfort, and to have done with all the rest" (380). But whose happiness does Austen really control? Finally, ours. All along she has manipulated us into desiring the marriages of Edmund to Mary and Fanny to Henry, making us believe, with her talk of the Crawfords' reformation, in the inevitability of that happy occurrence. And then she teaches us exactly what it feels like to be deprived of what one most wants, and what one has to do in order to deal with it. One has to teach oneself to desire, in retrospect, a different outcome, and the critical record is replete with examples of readers making ingenious efforts to do just that. I take Lionel Trilling's celebrated essay as representative: "although on a first reading of *Mansfield Park* Mary Crawford's speeches are all delightful, they diminish in charm as we read the novel a second time."[40] Pleasure, that is, on second thought, is not really so pleasurable.

This is a reader publicly reeducating his desires, and seeking to do the same to our own. And if we are to live happily in the world of the novel, we had better take his direction. That is the deeper meaning behind the game Austen plays with us as to the time it takes for Edmund to shift his desires from Mary to Fanny. "I purposely abstain from dates on this occasion," she writes, "that every one may be at liberty to fix their own, aware that the cure of unconquerable passions, and the transfer of unchanging attachments, must vary much as to time in different people." Those unconquerable passions and unchanging attachments are ours, for and to the outcome that has been stolen away. The end of the story of *Mansfield Park* does indeed vary in time from reader to reader, because the substitution that completes it is the one that Austen at last requires of us.

CHAPTER FOUR

Emma

Ambiguous Relationships

"[Y]ou know we are not really so much brother and sister as to make it at all improper."

"Brother and sister! no, indeed."

Although *Emma* alludes to "Tintern Abbey," as I noted in chapter 1, in connection with one of its central themes, that of the imagination, it is neither that allusion nor that theme that I will be discussing here. For while Wordsworthian ideas about the imagination as a cognitive faculty clearly inform the novel, *Emma*'s greatest debt to the British Romantic poets lies elsewhere. From Wordsworth in particular, but also from Coleridge and Byron, Austen drew ideas here about new possibilities for intimate relationships—their complexity and depth, their freedom from conventional social hierarchies and categories, their transformative potential. Indeed, the novel initiates its exploration of such ambiguous relationships in its very first lines.

For the opening of *Emma* is strangely proportioned. A single sentence characterizes the heroine, a second her relationship with her father, then fully four more her relationship with her governess. That last passage is itself strange, and worth quoting in full:

[Emma's] mother had died too long ago for her to have more than an indistinct remembrance of her caresses, and her place had been supplied by an excellent woman as governess, who had fallen little short of a mother in affection.

Sixteen years had Miss Taylor been in Mr. Woodhouse's family, less as a governess than a friend, very fond of both daughters, but particularly of Emma. Between *them* it was more the intimacy of sisters. Even before Miss Taylor had ceased to hold the nominal office of governess, the mildness of her temper had hardly allowed her to impose any restraint; and the shadow of authority being now long passed away, they had been living together as friend and friend very mutually attached, and Emma doing just what she liked; highly esteeming Miss Taylor's judgment, but directed chiefly by her own.   (7; emphasis in the original)

"Governess," "mother," "friend," "sister"—what, after all that, *was* Miss Taylor's relationship to Emma? The more labels the narrator deploys, the farther she seems to get from finding the right one. Not only do these terms keep displacing and thus mutually qualifying one another, each is itself qualified as it makes its appearance, its adequacy undermined even before it can be enunciated: "little short of a mother," "less as a governess," "more the intimacy of sisters." "Friend" does seem to win out by the end of the passage— a circumstance to which I will return—but before we put too much stock in that alternative, we should note that the "friend" of "friend and friend," the phrase that marks the final stage of Emma and Miss Taylor's relationship, clearly means something different from the "friend" of "less as a governess than a friend," one of the competing definitions of the earlier stages. These different stages, however, do give us a way of making sense of this profusion of relational terms. We can conjecture that Miss Taylor, hired as a governess, was first something like a mother to the orphaned five-year-old, then, as Emma matured, became a kind of friend, then finally, after further maturation on Emma's part, achieved something of the intimacy of a sister.

But however accurate this conjectural narrative might be, the text gives us no reason to believe that these relational modes displaced one another; rather, it suggests a layering process, one in which maternal and amicable and sororal feelings and ways of interacting accumulated over time in an ever-denser affective palimpsest. No wonder that opening description is so long: it must be, to capture a relationship of such complexity—of such ambiguity. And no wonder that each of the relational terms it employs must be so hedged by qualification. For it is precisely Austen's purpose here, at the very start of the novel, to expose the inadequacy of such labels to characterize the kinds of relationships she will be concerned to explore, relationships that, in their fruitful, liberating ambiguity, continually push beyond conventional categories, conventional boundaries, conventional roles.

Emma's relationship with Miss Taylor is the only one whose ambiguity is made explicit, but all her major ties, with one exception I will discuss below, are similarly complex, even if, with the others, Austen leaves us to try to supply the labels ourselves. To her widowed and childish father she is at once daughter, wife, and mother, in addition to being what the novel's second sentence calls her, the "mistress of his house."[1] Knightley is not only her neighbor, but what the narrator calls "a very old and intimate friend of the family": a term, "friend of the family," the familiarity of which conceals its own complexity, for it seems to imply both a close connection between the Donwell and Hartfield households—we see how easily he drops in for a visit—and also the existence of friendships, of different sorts, between him and each member of the Hartfield family, not excluding the erstwhile Miss Taylor (10). Knightley has also been Emma's brother-in-law for the previous seven years—more ambiguity-within-ambiguity, for as this chapter's epigraph reminds us, Austen's society made no verbal distinction between such a relationship and that of a brother pure and simple, even while recognizing important differences between them. Of course, he has also been for far longer a kind of elder-brother- or father-figure to Emma, and he will eventually become, without dropping any of these other roles, her lover and husband.[2] The ambiguous relationship Emma develops with Frank we will consider later, but we may take this opportunity to note, with respect to Miss Taylor, that in addition to the four relationships approximated in the novel's opening, she has also been for Emma a kind of wife.[3]

Such relationships, however, are in no way peculiar to the heroine. What Frank is to Mrs. Weston, who "stand[s] in a mother's place" to him, "but without a mother's affection," and even what he is to his father, to whom he is practically a stranger, are not to be specified by a simple label—certainly not "son"—as his interactions with each testify (124). Indeed, we can scarcely find a significant relationship within the novel that could be so specified. Even Mrs. Goddard, the schoolmistress, is referred to as "motherly" (20). And the novel also shows us important relationships that may be thought of less as ambiguous, with regard to conventional relational terminology, than as indeterminate. Knightley and Mrs. Weston, John Knightley and Jane (who have an extended conversation toward the end of volume II that exhibits a surprising degree of intimacy)—it is not so much that these relationships attract too many labels, as that they do not attract any. Like the other ties we have been surveying, they reveal the same inadequacy of conventional relational terms that Austen takes pains to expose at the novel's outset, and thus prompt the same questions: What kinds of relationships become possible once those conventional roles and categories have been transcended? What kinds of feelings lie—or rather, grow—at the interstices of received emotions? What happens when people are brought together and left to find their own way toward each other, free of traditional expectations?

We have never seen anything like this before in Austen's work.[4] The world of the early novels is one of clearly defined roles—daughter, father, neighbor, suitor. (Elizabeth Bennet's relationship with her father may be light-hearted, but it is unmistakably a father-daughter relationship nonetheless.) This lack of ambiguity is not oppressive, but rather allows characters to understand how they are situated relative to one another and to respond accordingly. Indeed, it is part of what makes for the simplicity and clarity of emotions in Austen's early work. In the authoritarian world of *Mansfield Park*, however, the lack of relational ambiguity *is* oppressive. Their rigidly prescribed roles as Sir Thomas's sons and daughters (different roles for each sex, and for the older son as distinct from the younger) are exactly what three of his children rebel against. As for Fanny, her position does entail some initial ambiguity, but that very uncertainty about her role and her relationships makes for a debilitating anxiety, and in any case the Bertrams soon obligingly imprison her in her long-term position as "the lowest and last" (184).

Of course, the issue of substitution, as explored in the previous chapter, complicates the picture relative to her relationship with Edmund. But there is an important distinction to be made. Fanny, having partly substituted Edmund for William, feels emotions for him that hover ambiguously among those of a cousin, a sister, and a lover, but precisely because she knows that one in her position must conceal those last two forms of feeling, her relationship with Edmund itself, her actual behavior toward him, is, for the great bulk of the novel, well defined, stable, and conventional. That is exactly why Edmund is completely unaware, once he finally develops amorous feelings of his own toward her, that those feelings have long been reciprocated. For some nine years, he is the kind, patronizing older cousin, she the adoring, obedient younger one. We might think of them as closer to brother and sister, but they do not; in Mansfield, everyone knows their place. Only toward the end of the novel does Edmund call Fanny "sister" (367), and only at the very end, after the close of the dramatized part of the narrative, do the cousin-siblings also become lovers and spouses.

Still, Austen's exploration of substitution and its culmination in this most disturbingly ambiguous of relationships clearly gave her ideas. The suggestion with which *Mansfield Park* ends becomes the one with which *Emma*, a novel so different in most every other respect, begins. But the discoveries of the earlier novel were not the only thing that gave Austen ideas about ambiguous relationships. Once again, she would have found them already explored and elaborated in Wordsworth.

Ambiguous relationships can be found throughout British Romantic literature, and are by no means confined to that most celebrated of species, those that "incestuously" blend fraternal and erotic impulses.[5] Among the poems she had available to her, Austen would have found such relationships in "The Mad Mother," with the mingling of maternal and erotic passions I noted in the previous chapter ("Thy father cares not for my breast . . . But thou wilt live with me in love" [ll. 61–67]); in "Lines written at a small distance . . . ," which alternately refers to its addressee as "My sister! . . . my Friend . . . my Sister!" (ll. 9, 19, 37); and, echoing this last but with redoubled emotional force, in—once again—"Tintern Abbey," with its passionate call to "thou my dearest Friend, / My dear, dear Friend," a figure who only after some delay is also revealed to be "My dear, dear Sister!" (ll. 115–116, 121). But to see the passions expressed in these last two poems as incestuous or quasi-incestuous distorts Wordsworth by reading him through the lens of Romanticism as a whole—or perhaps more to the point, of Freud. Rather, Wordsworth means us to understand that such heights of passion can be reached outside the realm of the erotic, that one can feel fraternal or amicable feelings with an erotic intensity. And he also wants us to understand that a large part of what conduces to such intensities is precisely a blending of different kinds of feelings, a dynamic ambiguity of relationship.

Such notions are indispensable to Wordsworth's most extensive exploration of ambiguous relationships, at least among the works published during Austen's lifetime, the Matthew poems. Teacher, friend, brother, father—in a series of lyrics that beautifully unfolds the relationship between the two men, Wordsworth gradually develops the idea that Matthew was all of these at once to him—or even, as the narrator of *Emma* might say, more than a teacher, a special friend, almost a brother, little short of a father. The placement of the poems is itself significant, for they constitute, with the Lucy poems, one of the two foci of the second volume of the two-volume *Lyrical Ballads*. The volume thus centers on two triptychs that lament the loss of an intensely beloved figure, one loved in a straightforwardly sexual fashion, the other in a highly complex but nonsexual one.

At the same time, the 1800 expansion rearranges the order of the first, 1798, volume to highlight "Expostulation and Reply" and "The Tables Turned" by placing them at the head of the entire compilation. Those, too, must be seen as Matthew poems, Wordsworth's intention being to have us recall that "good friend Matthew"—about whom all we know at first is that he *is* a good friend—when we arrive at the Matthew poems proper those many lyrics later ("Expostulation and Reply," l. 15). It comes as a shock to discover in "Lines written on a tablet . . . " ("Matthew") that "Matthew"—so familiarly named, as an equal and intimate—is in fact the poet's former schoolmaster, even more of a shock to learn in "The Fountain" that of this "pair of friends," one is "young," the other "seventy-two" (ll. 3–4)—and that it is the latter who is the man of "glee," "frolics," and "fun and madness" (l. 20; "Lines," ll. 17, 22). As in *Emma*, as we will see, more than one kind of conventional boundary is being crossed here, more than one conventional verbal usage discarded.

"The Two April Mornings," the most complex of these poems, is also the most complex link in their exposition of the two men's relationship. Matthew, recalling an April morning just like the one he is now sharing with the poet, recalls a highly charged double-encounter he experienced then—an encounter with the grave of his daughter and, at the next moment, with her living image tripping by. But though the experience happened on that distant day, he seems to understand and fully digest it—"The will of God be done!" (l. 4)—only now, because only now does he have someone intimate enough to share it with, and thus to share it with himself with. The two mornings are "brother[s]," and so, this poem of doubles urges us to see, are the two men (l. 28). Finally, in "The Fountain," the third of the Matthew poems proper, the poet proposes a final link: "Matthew, for thy children dead," he declares, "I'll be a son to thee!" (ll. 61–62). Matthew refuses, but his refusal signals not a rejection of ambiguous relationships—the very refusal is accompanied by a spontaneous affirmation of intimacy ("At this he grasped my hand, and said, / 'Alas! that cannot be' " [ll. 63–64])—but an understanding of them that far exceeds that of the "young" and, as he paints himself here, emotionally callow poet (l. 3).

Austen would not have known "Address to the Scholars of the Village School of —," one of the Matthew poems not published until long after her death, but she would not have needed to read it to understand that Matthew was, for the poet and his fellow schoolchildren, "Our common Friend and Father" (l. 4). The paternal dimension of the relationship hovers over all three of the poems published in *Lyrical Ballads*; the poet's faux pas in "The Fountain" lies in trying to make it too literal, too explicit. For doing so would destroy the very ambiguity that keeps all those relational options in play, allowing the two men to move from one to another—from teacherly reproof to friendly discourse to fraternal empathy to paternal counsel—as circumstances and feeling prompt them to do, but more importantly, allowing them finally to create an intermediate zone of relatedness that blends all these modes together into a connection that is richer, deeper, and freer than any conventional one, at any moment, could be.

We see this same enriching, productive flexibility in the ambiguous relationships in *Emma*, and especially in the most important of them, the one that ultimately emerges as the novel's ideal relationship, that between Emma and Knightley. Thinking of Matthew and his young friend, we may note that theirs is also an intergenerational tie. And thinking of the interactions between Sir Thomas Bertram and his eldest son and daughter that we glanced at in the second chapter of this study, we may note that Emma and Knightley's characteristic encounter involves the delivery of some kind of counsel or reproof on his part. But what a difference between the way such advice is given and received here and those analogous interactions in *Mansfield Park*, where father and children are locked into stereotyped patterns of behavior and emotion.

Two scenes in *Emma*'s first half develop these intricacies particularly well—the first in chapter 1, on the evening after the Weston wedding, the second in chapter 21, when Knightley drops in to congratulate Emma on having treated Jane so handsomely the previous evening at Hartfield—and as such are representative of the strengths and subtleties characteristic of all of the novel's ambiguous relationships. It is therefore worth examining at least one of these scenes in detail. The first part of the later one reads as follows:

Mr. Knightley . . . was expressing the next morning . . . his approbation of the whole; not so openly as he might have done had her father been out of the room, but speaking plain enough to be very intelligible to Emma. He had been used to think her unjust to Jane, and now had great pleasure in marking an improvement.

"A very pleasant evening . . . particularly pleasant. You and Miss Fairfax gave us some very good music. I do not know a more luxurious state, sir, than sitting at one's ease to be entertained a whole evening by two such young women; sometimes with music and sometimes with conversation. I am sure Miss Fairfax must have found the evening pleasant, Emma. You left nothing undone . . . "

"I am happy you approved," said Emma, smiling; "but I hope I am not often deficient in what is due to guests at Hartfield."

"No, my dear," said her father instantly; "*that* I am sure you are not. There is nobody half so attentive and civil as you are. If any thing, you are too attentive. The muffin last night—if it had been handed round once, I think it would have been enough."

"No," said Mr. Knightley, nearly at the same time; "you are not often deficient; not often deficient either in manner or comprehension. I think you understand me, therefore."

An arch look expressed—"I understand you well enough;" but she said only, "Miss Fairfax is reserved."

"I always told you she was—a little; but you will soon overcome all that part of her reserve which ought to be overcome, all that has its foundation in diffidence. What arises from discretion must be honoured."

"You think her diffident. I do not see it."

"My dear Emma," said he, moving from his chair into one close by her, "you are not going to tell me, I hope, that you had not a pleasant evening." (142; emphasis in the original)

The complicating presence of Emma's father makes the interactions here especially intricate. "[N]ot so openly as he might have done had her father been out of the room"—both Emma and Knightley recognize that there is something potentially disturbing to Mr. Woodhouse about the full nature of their relationship, something that goes beyond his need to maintain his belief in Emma's perfection. Emma's father finds anything new, anything he cannot immediately recognize and comprehend, deeply threatening. He may unwittingly participate in an ambiguous relationship with his daughter, but he would never consciously assent to one, never be anything but extremely uncomfortable at the sight of people stepping out of their conventional relational roles. Here and elsewhere, Knightley accordingly employs a particularly obvious, stagy kind of condescension in speaking to him about Emma—"I do not know a more luxurious state, sir, than sitting at one's ease to be entertained a whole evening by two such young women"—a one-elder-to-another tone that pacifies the old man by performing the attitude he expects Knightley to adopt toward his daughter.

But having thrown him this bone, Knightley can turn to Emma and address her directly in far different accents: "I am sure Miss Fairfax must have found the evening pleasant, Emma . . . " The tone is familiar, all traces of condescension having dropped out of it, and Emma is addressed as "Emma," not as "Miss Woodhouse," a rare and important mark of intimacy. Still, Emma invariably finds Knightley's supervision, whether expressed in approval or rebuke, damaging to her self-love, so here, as usual, she responds to it as no child ever could, with a playful and even mocking parry-and-thrust: "I am happy you approved . . . but I hope I am not often deficient in what is due to guests at Hartfield." Her father instantly leaps to her defense, but no one is paying attention to him anymore—Knightley essentially talks over him—as something much more important goes forward outside his range of perception. "No . . . you are not often deficient; not often deficient either in manner or comprehension. I think you understand me, therefore." Brought up short by Emma's response, Knightley's tone hardens here, becoming clipped and almost stern, much less that of an equal. But Emma again defends herself, this time even more playfully, while following Knightley in veiling the full purport of their exchange from her father: "An arch look expressed—'I understand you well enough;' but she said only, 'Miss Fairfax is reserved.' " A further exchange, in which Knightley maintains essentially the same tone, then finally: " 'My dear Emma,' said he, moving from his chair into one close by her, 'you are not going to tell me, I hope . . . ' " "My dear Emma": his language, like his body, suddenly moves in close. Four distinct registers of discourse on Knightley's part in as many utterances, ranging from pompously formal all the way to warmly intimate, four different implicit relationships or modes of relatedness.

There are other things to note here as well. First, how the complexity of their relationship has tuned Emma and Knightley's sensibilities to be able to perceive the subtlest communicative inflections—small tonal shifts, facial expressions, body language—sometimes (like Matthew's simultaneous rejection of the poet's desire to stand in as a son and his warm grasping of the young man's hand) operating on more than one level at once. Second, because of this mutual attunement, how intricate a scene Austen is able to construct here, one that essentially keeps three conversations going at the same time: the one Mr. Woodhouse thinks he is having, the one Emma and Knightley are having out loud, and the one they are having silently. *Emma* is Austen's supreme achievement in precise and nuanced communication—both among characters and between author and reader—and we get a little better sense here of why. Third, because Emma and Knightley's relationship leaves so much room for negotiation—for disagreement, for face-saving, for new kinds of appeal—how much more effective a way it is for Emma to receive guidance than would be any sort of paternal dictate. Sir Thomas wants to correct his children; Knightley wants Emma to grow. If *Mansfield Park* so often seems to be about right and wrong, its heroine the character who is ultimately vindicated, *Emma* is about growth, its heroine the character with the greatest potential for development and change.

Fourth, how important to Emma and Knightley's relationship is Emma's playfulness—how it allows them to make the transitions between levels of discourse and lubricate the frictions between their ideas of what their relationship ought to be.[6] (Indeed, her very first words to him are uttered "playfully" [11].) The notion may be extended: in *Emma*, playfulness or play—room for improvisation, space for the exercise of freedom—is exactly what Austen introduces into the normally strict and well-defined system of social roles. Playing is exactly what she does with those roles, seeing how far they can stretch, how fully they can blend, what they can be made into. Both Emma's play and Austen's are directed toward a serious purpose; like Wordsworth's Matthew, they are capable of uniting the most giddy and most sober responses to experience.

And finally, as do the Matthew poems, the scene demonstrates that a fully realized ambiguous relationship involves not so much an alteration between stable relational modes as the achievement of a permanently ambiguous one in which all tones and attitudes are continuously available. I attempted to enumerate before the different relationships in which Knightley stands to Emma, but we would be very hard pressed to name, at any moment in the scene just examined, exactly which of those roles he is occupying, whether that of neighbor or friend of the family or father figure or any other. The lines between those roles or modes, then, do not so much get crossed and recrossed as effaced. Knightley is not finally all of those things to Emma at once, any more than Miss Taylor was at once a mother, a sister, and a governess. He is, as she was, something else altogether.

What he is is what he and Emma and the novel all eventually agree to call him: a "friend." And it is friendship, as typified by Emma and Knightley's relationship, that ultimately steps forth as the novel's new relational ideal, the ambiguous relationship *par excellence*. Now we have already encountered the term "friend" as one of the narrator's alternative, and thus inadequate, ways of naming Miss Taylor's relationship to Emma. "Friend" in that sense—a fixed and well-defined, and therefore stereotyped and imprisoning, form of connection—would be no more appropriate than any other label in characterizing this new kind of relationship.

But something happens to the term during the course of the narrative: it gets worked and reworked, discussed and debated, used by so many different people to mean so many different things, that by the end, friendship emerges as a new idea.[7] Or rather, a whole constellation of ideas. Friendship becomes the novel's supremely important relationship because it becomes its supremely flexible one, "friend" the one term able to denote the fruitful imprecision and rich complexity of ambiguous relationships. Just as that long opening description of Emma's relationship with Miss Taylor comes to rest on the term "friend"—and already there we see its relative flexibility, even as a conventional term—so too does the novel's entire exploration of ambiguous relationships. Friendship becomes the name for relationships for which there is no name.

But it also becomes far more than that. Because nearly every important relationship in the novel is ambiguous, nearly every one gets rewritten as a friendship. Friendship not only becomes the novel's most important kind of relationship—finally, it becomes virtually its only one. And in thus extending and apotheosizing the idea of friendship, Austen does nothing less than anticipate—and help create—the meaning and role that friendship has come to assume in the modern world. To quote Robert Brain, the leading scholar of friendship:

> In contemporary Western society the boundaries of friendship, kinship, and loving are disintegrating . . . Roles which were more exclusive in other societies have broken down. A wife is her husband's "best friend" and fathers and sons call themselves by Christian names—like friends . . . [T]here seems to be little difference between the love felt between kin and that between friends; sentiments found in the family are based almost completely on ties of love felt between unrelated friends . . . One chooses this or that uncle, this or that cousin, even this or that brother and sister to be friendly with.[8]

And even, as Brain suggests, this or that parent, as well as this or that coworker, neighbor, teacher, student. Friendship has become the relationship in terms of which all others are understood, against which they are all measured, into which they have all dissolved. It has become, in other words, the characteristically modern form of relationship. As Brain says, "We are friends with everyone" now.[9] And while it is clear that Austen has not fully arrived at this state of affairs—however ambiguous Emma's relationship with her father, the novel in no way regards it as a friendship—it is equally clear that she sets us down the road that has led to it, a state of affairs in which, for example, the notion of being friends with one's father is commonplace and unremarkable.

Why has friendship risen to such preeminence in modern imagination and practice? For one thing, its new status is clearly part of the larger reorientations of modernity toward individualism and egalitarianism, away from vertical ties and toward horizontal ones, and away from strong, stable social structures toward looser, more ephemeral ones.[10] But that is only part of the explanation. Another has to do with the concept's very flexibility, the flexibility that, as we said, is the key to its ability to function as the universal relationship, to mean so many different things in so many different situations—for while we may be friends with everyone now, we are not friends with everyone in the same way.

To regard that flexibility as inherent in the concept itself, however, is to beg the question of how it developed—to speak from our late point in the very historical process we are trying to trace. Friendship appears to us to have a complex semantic nature because it has a complex semantic history. Many different ideas have fed into it, and in particular, many different ideas were feeding into it in Austen's day; its complex history was never more complex than at the time she was writing.[11] The concept of friendship, the word "friend," was the site then of vigorous semantic contestation and rapid semantic change, as new social and existential ideas—ideas about the nature of the individual and his or her relationships with others—came into being and struggled with each other and with existing ideas. Nor was Austen the only writer to be inspired by this ferment, to seize on the possibilities it opened up to explore and elaborate meanings of her own. So too, as we will see, did the British Romantic poets, especially Wordsworth and Byron. Indeed, their innovations were crucial in inspiring hers. In short, *Emma*'s exploration of friendship takes place within a highly complex historical context. It is to that history that I now turn.

To begin with, one important sense of the words "friend" and "friends" was just on the verge of dying out in Austen's day, and may in fact have taken its last large breath in one of her earlier novels. For while I am claiming that in *Emma*, under the influence of Wordsworth and Byron, Austen engages the idea of friendship more deeply and complexly than ever before, an intense investment in the idea, as has long been recognized, pervades her entire body of work.[12] In *Sense and Sensibility*, in particular, "friend" is frequently and pointedly used in a way now obsolete but once integral to what Lawrence Stone calls the Open Lineage Family, the kind of extended kinship group that, he argues, dominated the upper reaches of English society through the early seventeenth century.[13] While Stone's chronology has been criticized as too rigid, and even he acknowledges that various family types coexisted at different times during the three centuries covered by his study, those types remain valuable as categories of analysis.[14] Indeed, while *Sense and Sensibility* itself bears witness to the persistent strength of the Open

Lineage Family through at least the late eighteenth century, it also shows how Stone's different family types were struggling (or still struggling) for allegiance among the upper classes.

The Open Lineage Family, according to Stone, consisted not only of parents and children but also of what were known as " 'friends'—that group of influential advisers who usually included most of the senior members of the kin."[15] The influence of such "friends"—who, as Stone's language makes clear, were not limited to blood relations, but included a family's "advisers," patrons, and important associates—was particularly important when it came to the question of marriage: "It was 'friends' who were the key advisers in the critical decision of marriage, not only among the nobility and gentry, but down to the lower middle classes."[16] How long did this meaning persist? Until Austen's very age: "[a]s late as the 1820s," according to Stone, though, as noted, he underestimates the continuing force that the usage, along with its attendant ideas about familial relations and personal identity, had at that late date.[17]

What is for Stone, by the turn of the nineteenth century, the semantic vestige of an old order is for Austen the sign of a dragon that still needs to be slain. The usage figures so prominently in *Sense and Sensibility* precisely because it is in that novel that Austen wages her most passionate battle against the hard-dying values and prerogatives of the Open Lineage Family, and in particular against the assumed right of its senior members to override a young person's desires in determining the marriage choice.

Sense and Sensibility may satirize sensibility's excesses, but it is squarely on the side of what Stone calls "affective individualism"—the new valorization of individual affection in the governance of personal relations—and against the old allegiance to family interest.[18] The old and new values face off in the struggle between, on the one hand, the Dashwood women, Colonel Brandon, and Edward Ferrars, and on the other, John Dashwood and the rest of the Ferrars family. And the linguistic ground on which that struggle is fought is exactly that of the word in question. While characters on the "good" side of the divide use "friend" both in Stone's old sense—it is an inescapable part of their world—and in what he calls the modern one—"one who supports you and comforts you while others do not, someone with whom to compare minds and cherish private virtues"[19]—John Dashwood, the novel's leading spokesperson for the old values, only ever uses it in its older denotation. Friendship in any other, warmer sense is alien to him. Here he is urging Elinor to secure Colonel Brandon (" 'a kind of [match] that'—lowering his voice to an important whisper—'will be exceedingly welcome to *all parties*' "): " 'Perhaps . . . the smallness of your fortune may make him hang back;

his friends may all advise him against it. But some of those little attentions and encouragements which ladies can so easily give, will fix him, in spite of himself' " (189; emphasis in the original). Again, later in the same conversation, he congratulates Elinor on "having such a friend as Mrs. Jennings. 'She seems a most valuable woman indeed.—Her house, her stile of living . . . ' " (191).

Mrs. Dashwood's way of thinking could not be more different, and she announces as much in a declaration that deliberately seizes control of our key word. Taking leave of Norland—having been more or less evicted by John Dashwood and his wife, in part out of their anxiety at Edward's growing attachment to Elinor—she makes her invitations to Barton Cottage:

> "It is but a cottage . . . but I hope to see many of my friends in it. A room or two can easily be added; and if my friends find no difficulty in traveling so far to see me, I'm sure I'll find none in accommodating them." She concluded with a very kind invitation to Mr. and Mrs. John Dashwood . . . and to Edward she gave one with still greater affection.   (SS 21)

The repetition of "my friends" is especially pointed, given the circumstances; the word's meaning, in effect, splits before our eyes. Two different kinds of invitations, for two different kinds of friends: friends as kin, whatever one feels about them, and friends as those for whom one feels affection, whether they be kin or not. The signal gesture with which the novel affirms the second of these meanings is Colonel Brandon's presentation of the living to Edward free of charge, an act of kindness that John Dashwood finds simply incomprehensible. The novel, recognizing the moment at which it stands in the history of language and personal life, enacts the victory of affective individualism over the imperatives of lineage, of friend-as-intimate over friend-as-benefactor.[20]

Although Stone undertakes no separate discussion of friendship as such—indeed, histories of friendship are quite sparse[21]—he touches on it again in his discussion of "companionate marriage," the ideal of marriage in which husband and wife stand together as "companions and equals."[22] While Stone is wrong to believe that companionate marriage arose only in the eighteenth century (Alan Macfarlane traces it back as far as the Middle Ages[23]), he is not wrong to suggest that it was acquiring a new ideological importance, a new literary and political emphasis, during that period. Mary Wollstonecraft, for example, invested the ideal with new political significance when she argued in *A Vindication of the Rights of Women* that marriage should be based on the lasting ties of friendship rather than the transient bonds of erotic attraction.[24]

Again, this is a dimension of friendship on which Austen's imagination had gone to work long before *Emma*. For if she did not invent the idea of marriage as friendship, she revolutionized it. Stone remarks that the "literary apotheosis" of companionate marriage in the eighteenth century "has to be found in Oliver Goldsmith's *Vicar of Wakefield*."[25] But to compare Parson Primrose's relationship with his wife to that of any of Austen's heroines with the man she will marry is to see what an immeasurable advance the latter represents in intimacy, mutual respect, and depth of communication. Goldsmith's couple live on easy and familiar terms and run their family as equals, but they are also constantly at cross-purposes, have little regard for each other's abilities and opinions, and don't so much talk with as jab at each other. Of the kind of intricate mutual knowledge and responsiveness we have already seen between Emma and Knightley, or even that which we find between Elizabeth and Darcy, there is not the shadow of a suggestion.

And there is a further difference between Stone's "conjugal friendship" and the kind of relationships we find in Austen. Austen's lovers become friends *before* they get married. According to Lillian Faderman, women in eighteenth-century England "were encouraged to live in an essentially homosocial environment, to distrust men, and to form close relationships only with other women outside of marriage."[26] As a result, "[w]hen genuine communication occurred between a man and woman . . . people had difficulty believing that the pair were not contemplating marriage." Faderman goes on to cite evidence from Austen herself, namely the assumption aroused by Elinor's friendship with Colonel Brandon that the two are courting, for "what had a man and woman to say to each other, after all?" The main point, however, is not just that Austen so vastly improved on the ideal of companionate marriage as that she had something to improve on. Both the newly important notion of marriage as friendship and Austen's own previous expansion and deepening of that notion constitute additional strands in the history that she had available to her when she came to write *Emma*.

Stone follows his discussion of companionate marriage with a brief account of foreign reaction that makes it clear how peculiarly English that ideal was: "The Duc de La Rochefoucauld noted with surprise in 1784 that: 'Husband and wife are always together and share the same society. [. . .] It would be more ridiculous to do otherwise in England than to go everywhere with your wife in Paris.'"[27] As Margery Sabin notes in her discussion of the differences between Rousseau's handling of the terminology of love in *The Confessions* and Wordsworth's handling of it in *The Prelude*, French thinking of the time tended to draw very careful and sharp distinctions between the different kinds of love, while English thinking allowed them to blend together.[28]

At the very time the English were giving new importance to their long-standing idea of spouses as friends, Rousseau was insisting that his unique feeling for Mme. de Warens, while not what people commonly call love, either, was certainly not friendship: "I have known friendship, at least, if ever a man has, and I have never had this feeling for any of my friends."[29] And though Rousseau describes this unique feeling in language that sounds, on its face, like Wordsworthian-Austenian ambiguity, it is really its opposite: "She was to me more than a sister, more than a mother, more than a friend, more even than a mistress."[30] Their relationship does not hover ambiguously between categories, it transcends them all. Where Wordsworth and Austen say "all of the above," Rousseau says "none of the above." In his novels, meanwhile, according to Allan Bloom, Rousseau trivializes friendship, at least between men, as a mere parasite of sexual love: asserting in *Emile* that it arises only in the wake of "puberty and sexual awareness"—for "[o]ne must have a friend with whom to discuss one's mistress"—and embodying that assertion in *La Nouvelle Héloïse*.[31]

Rousseau's strict separation of friendship from sexual love is scarcely surprising, coming as it does within a cultural tradition that, as Sabin shows, set the two so firmly at odds,[32] and his denigration of the former is no more surprising in a culture so exclusively focused on sexual relations—if not in actual fact, then certainly, as we are about to see, in the perception of Austen's England. The relevance to *Emma* of these distinctions between the French and English ideas of friendship, sex, and marriage is connected, of course, to Knightley's polemical distinction between "amiable" and "*aimable*," a passage to which I will return below (124).

There are further complexities to consider. According to *A History of Private Life*, "Friendship is difficult to analyze because it can be viewed in two extreme and contradictory ways. On the one hand it is often confused with everyday social relations, while on the other hand it is seen as something exalted, which, like love, has only an individual history."[33] Of course, we have already seen that it can be viewed in other ways as well, but the passage points us both to a meaning of "friend" that sets it roughly equivalent to "neighbor"—a usage prominent in *Emma*—and to the classical tradition of friendship as articulated by Aristotle, Cicero, Montaigne, and others and reworked by the seventeenth and eighteenth centuries and then still further by the Romantic poets.[34] The classical ideal sees friendship as a rare and exquisite relationship rooted in virtue and dedicated to the pursuit of goodness and truth. It can thus arise only between men—only they, in the classical conception, can possess the requisite loftiness of soul—only between equals, and only between adults, men of wisdom whose worth has been tested by the world, or at the very least, between an adult and an unusually virtuous and gifted youth.[35]

Aristotle, with characteristic thoroughness, defines three species of friendship, the useful, the pleasant, and the good, the second characteristic especially of youth and only the last corresponding to the foregoing description.[36] As for friendship between husbands and wives, Aristotle allows for it but classes it among the more limited kinds of friendship that subsist between unequals. Cicero waxes warmer in his characterization of the friendship of good men, speaking of a true friend as "a second self . . . For man not only loves himself, but seeks another whose spirit he may so blend with his own as almost to make one being of two."[37] Here we see a characteristic feature of the classical discourse of friendship, its tendency to parallel the rhetoric of erotic love, with the implication that true friendship constitutes a higher alternative to the sexual love of women, both the love and its object being of a higher nature. Bloom, thinking especially of the friendship of Socrates and Alcibiades—one from which, as represented in Plato's *Symposium*, Socrates insists on excluding sexual contact—speaks of an eros of souls rather than bodies.[38]

But surely the most fervent and extreme of the great classical expressions of male friendship is Montaigne's evocation of his bond with Etienne de La Boétie, "so entire and so perfect that certainly you'll hardly read of the like."[39] Montaigne contrasts such friendship to filial, fraternal, and erotic love, to marriage, and to homosexual love, and like Cicero, he regards it as available only to the mature man.[40] This, then, is the "exalted" union of which *A History of Private Life* speaks, something, to its exponents, far finer and rarer even than erotic love: "So many coincidences are needed to build up such a friendship that it is a lot if fortune can do it once in three centuries."[41]

But despite Aristotle and company's exclusion of women from this tradition, its revival during the Renaissance, as typified by Montaigne, soon spread to women and women writers, especially those of the upper classes.[42] Faderman traces the description and celebration of intense female friendships, both fictional and actual, across the literature of seventeenth- and eighteenth-century England and France. Like such "romantic friendships" between men, as they became known,[43] these involved mature and highly refined adults, were every bit as exclusive and all-consuming as erotic attachments, and employed the rhetoric of sexual love, though with no suggestion that they were, in fact, genital.

By the second half of the eighteenth century, Faderman notes, romantic friendship had become a popular theme in English fiction,[44] a fact that suggests both a diffusion of the ideal and its corresponding dilution. That it often degenerated into an overused and overblown cliché we learn from Austen herself.[45] Among the conventions of the novel of sensibility she so gleefully attacks in both the juvenilia and *Northanger Abbey* is that of the passionate and undying attachment that instantly springs up between young heroines of appropriately heightened sensibilities. The satire is most broad, as we might expect, in "Love and Freindship": "We flew into each other's arms, and after having exchanged vows of mutual friendship for the rest of our lives, instantly unfolded to each other the most inward secrets of our hearts."[46] The romantic-sentimental tradition is thus another element within friendship's rich history that Austen had engaged during the first half of her career, adding her own earlier imaginings and valuations to the store of material she had available to her in *Emma*.

Nor did the evolution of this tradition cease with the novel of sensibility, for it was taken up in yet new forms by the British Romantic poets. Most of the expressions that Romantic friendship found in the works and lives of these authors would have been unknown to Austen, but she would have encountered one of the period's most impassioned engagements with the theme in Byron's *Hours of Idleness* as well as in quite a number of the early lyrics not included in that collection. It is scarcely too much to say that the young poet was obsessed with the experience of friendship, and in setting down that experience in verse he added a uniquely Romantic dimension to the classical or classical-romantic ideal.[47] That he had absorbed that ideal by a young age some of his earliest surviving poems make clear. "To E—," written at age fourteen, celebrates a friendship rooted in "Virtue" (3). "To D—," composed a few months later, employs an extreme and frankly erotic rhetoric ("On *thy dear* breast I'll lay my head— / Without *thee! where* would be *my Heaven?*" [ll. 11–12; emphasis in the original]). "Childish Recollections," a somewhat later production, proclaims the superiority of friendship to heterosexual love ("The smiles of Beauty, though those smiles were dear / Could hardly charm me, when that friend was near / . . . / and Friendship's feelings triumphed over Love" [ll. 201–202, 206]).[48]

But Byron stands the classical tradition on its head by making friendship the exclusive province of youth.[49] Again, from "Childish Recollections":

Hours of my youth! when, nurtur'd in my breast,
To Love a stranger, Friendship made me blessed,—
Friendship, the dear peculiar bond of youth,
When every artless bosom throbs with truth;
Untaught by worldly wisdom how to feign,
And check each impulse with prudential rein;
When, all we feel, our honest souls disclose,
In love to friends, in open hate to foes.

(ll. 55–62)

Byron's conception of friendship, as the passage makes clear, is of a piece with the general Romantic revaluation of experience. Youth is elevated over adulthood, innocence over maturity, candor over prudence, spontaneity over self-restraint. "Youth" is rhymed with "truth": as in Wordsworth, youth *is* truth, the time of genuine feeling and perception before the corruptions of the social world take hold.[50] And "the dear peculiar bond of youth," associated with all its purity and frankness and artless innocence, is friendship. If youth is the Romantic Eden, Byron effectively says, then its Eve, or Eves, is one's beloved childhood companions.[51]

"Childish Recollections" is largely an extended encomium to those companions, one that ends with a paraphrase of the French proverb that seems to have seized hold of Byron's imagination around this time, late in 1806, "*l'Amitié est l'Amour sans ailes*" ("Friendship is Love without wings"): "Friendship bow'd before the shrine of Truth, / and Love, without his pinion, smil'd on Youth" (ll. 411–412).[52] Again, though Byron celebrates sexual love as frequently and as fervently in his early lyrics as he does male friendship, friendship is the higher relation: purer, more innocent, more constant.[53] But already in the poems of the first half of 1807, those that make their first appearance in *Hours of Idleness*, he is discovering that friendship does indeed have wings, does fly away—"For Friendship can vary her gentle dominion / . . . / like Love, too, she moves on a swift-waving pinion"—for the simple reason that youth does, as well: "Youth has flown on rosy pinion, / and Manhood claims his stern Dominion" ("To George, Earl Delawarr," ll. 5–7; "To Edward Noel Long, Esq.," ll. 23–24). If youth is Byron's Eden, the poems of 1807–1809 are a long lament over Paradise lost. Those addressed to individual friends ("To George, Earl Delawarr," "To the Earl of Clare," "To a Youthful Friend") are no longer erotic or celebratory, but elegiac, even—for some of his old companions have embraced the corruptions of court and society— bitterly accusatory. It is on this disillusioned note—the revealed transience of the friendship of men as well as of the love of women—that Byron turns his back on England.[54]

But if Byron and Wordsworth both idealize youth, their response to its loss is very different.[55] For Byron, what is gone is gone, but Wordsworth's entire poetic project—"Tintern Abbey," the Intimations Ode—centers on the attempt to carry the energies and feelings of youth into adulthood. While his most important vessel for doing so is poetry itself, another essential one, as the poems we have already looked at in this chapter make clear, is friendship. Wordsworth turns to his sister in the last verse paragraph of "Tintern Abbey" and, evoking her as "my dearest Friend, / My dear, dear Friend," embraces her as the living image and repository of the youth the loss of which he has spent the first two-thirds of the poem lamenting (ll. 115–116). The kind of vicarious access to his "past existence" that she offers him is clearly predicated on the nature and intensity of their connection (ll. 149). Her role in his emotional life—as "dearest Friend"—and in his psychic life—as the living record of his past—are not to be distinguished. The bond of youth, friendship, keeps him in touch with the energies of youth.

It is no different in the Matthew poems. Notwithstanding their darker notes of melancholy and loss, they portray a man who, though old, has cheated time by retaining the spirit of youth, that inextinguishable spirit imaged in the title of "The Fountain." Matthew has stayed so young at heart because he has lived his life among schoolchildren, and ignoring differences of age, befriended them as equals. But youth is not the gift only of the young. Matthew's friendship with the poet has allowed both men to stay in touch with youthful energies: Matthew, because the poet is the far younger man, but the poet himself, because Matthew has remained so much younger at heart. Note the seeming paradox: the poet remains young through his friendship with his younger sister, but also through his friendship with his much older schoolteacher. As in Byron, friendship is "the dear peculiar bond of youth," but for Wordsworth, it doesn't matter how old you are. Everyone is young who is still committed to the special intimacies and intensities of Romantic friendship.

Both Wordsworth and Coleridge invest the word "friend" with special sanctity, utter it with special urgency and passion.[56] Of particular note is the way it is repositioned within the two-volume *Lyrical Ballads*. The reordered first volume features it in four of its first five poems, as if Wordsworth, like Austen in *Emma*, were seeking to redefine and resituate it as a cardinal element of his social imagination. The forsaken Indian woman repeatedly and pathetically calls out to her clan as "My friends . . .

Dear friends" (ll. 28–30), as if there were no closer bond, no dearer name, no higher term of appeal. The poet in "The Last of the Flock" greets the weeping stranger with "My friend, / what ails you?" as the warmest possible earnest of his sympathy (ll. 15).

Friendship, a name applied equally to kin and stranger, thus becomes a flexibly ambiguous or multivalent relationship in just the sense we have been developing. It also becomes a democratic one: that "My friend" in "The Last of the Flock" signals a spirit of equality and a programmatic embrace of humanity that anticipates Whitman. It is in that spirit, of course, that the collection as a whole, with its elevation of the marginal and wretched to literary status, is written. Wordsworth's usage here is thus connected to yet another element within the eighteenth-century complex of ideas about friendship, one that achieved a new relevance around the turn of the nineteenth century: Shaftesbury's notion of social sympathy. This is friendship in its most explicitly political dimension, for sympathy was Shaftesbury's answer, in 1711, to Hobbes's pessimism about human nature, and for well over a century following Shaftesbury, sympathy was understood to rank among the most important bonds that held society together.[57] What is more, as Caleb Crain explains in his study of male friendship in the early American Republic, the replacement of monarchy by democracy in the new nation meant that "friendship in America became charged with a new meaning," as the *only* bond that now held citizens together.[58]

The relevance of this development to the Wordsworth of *Lyrical Ballads*—as he moves from direct political investment in the democratic ideals of the French Revolution toward their embodiment in poetry—need hardly be emphasized. Friendship becomes not only, as in "Tintern Abbey" and the Matthew poems, the ideal of one-to-one relatedness, but also the basis for a revivified human collectivity, a new human community. It is a community that—like the poet and the stranger in "The Last of the Flock'" meeting "[a]long the broad highway" (l. 7), like Wordsworth and his figures in so many of his poems, wanderers all along the broad highway—stands symbolically outside the hierarchical structures of nation and society. Wordsworth thus revolutionizes the classical-romantic tradition of friendship in a second respect. He retains its intensity but discards its exclusivity, calling upon us to bring that kind of presence—erotic in its ardor—to all of our relationships.

That this ideal is indeed made into a moral imperative aimed at his readers Wordsworth makes clear through the sleight-of-hand he performs with the word "friend" in the very first two poems of *Lyrical Ballads'* reordered first volume. While "Expostulation and Reply" is a dialogue between the poet and his "good friend Matthew," Matthew drops out as a speaker in "The Tables Turned," a maneuver that unmistakably puts the reader in his place. The poem's opening address—"Up! up! my friend, and quit your books"—must be read, then, as directed at us (an idea reinforced by the purport of that address, since it is of course we who are reading at that moment). In this, the first of many moves in *Lyrical Ballads* by which Wordsworth signals the kind of reader he wants us to be and the kind of relationship he wants to have with us, he names that relationship as one of friendship—with all the intimacy, ardor, and productive ambiguity that it will later, in "Tintern Abbey" and the Matthew poems, come to imply, but also with the sense of equality and democratic inter-involvement with both the poet and his subjects that it will very soon, in "The Last of the Flock," come to imply.

In *Lyrical Ballads*, as later in *Emma*, we find an artist both seizing upon and adding fresh impetus to the fact that friendship at the turn of the nineteenth century was not only undergoing a rapid expansion of meaning, it was also beginning an enormous elevation in importance. In both Wordsworth and, following him, in Austen, friendship becomes the essential context of the new values of affective individualism, with its drive toward an increased intensity of, esteem for, and mindfulness toward interpersonal relationships.

These, then, are the various streams that fed into the idea of friendship at the time Austen was writing *Emma*: "friends" as elder kin and benefactors; "friends" as neighbors; the (to us) commonsense notion of a "friend" as a familiar companion for whom one feels affection; friendship as the political phenomenon of social sympathy; the conjugal friendship of the companionate marriage, a self-consciously English institution; the classical-romantic tradition of intense nonsexual friendship; and the Romantic inversions of that ideal to make it an experience particular to youth, perhaps prolongable into adulthood with special determination, and universalized into a common human bond.

Now as I already noted, Austen had been familiar with a number of these ideas, and had been working with them in her fiction, since very early in her career. Indeed, critics have noted from the very first that friendship is her highest social ideal, her image of what marriage should be.[59] But in recognizing that, criticism has taken the idea of friendship too much at face value. Yes, Austen valued friendship above all things; the question is—given the rapidly-evolving welter of possibilities available to her, the enormous semantic complexity encoded in that seemingly innocuous word, "friend"—what did she mean by friendship?

She herself seems to have taken the concept for granted before *Emma*, or at least before about the middle of *Mansfield Park*. *Northanger Abbey* balances that commonsense form of friendship, the kind Catherine has with Eleanor Tilney, against a bad form, the faux-sentimental, the kind she has with Isabella Thorpe. *Sense and Sensibility* sets that same good form against another evil alternative, "friends" as unloving and mercenary relations. And both novels, as well as *Pride and Prejudice*, hold out that same good form as the basis of a newly profound version of conjugal friendship, one that begins to develop even before marriage.[60] Then, in *Mansfield Park*, with its musings on "the different sorts of friendship in the world" and its own evident ambivalence about whether Fanny's friendship with Mary is good or not, we find that these certainties begin to get shaken (298).

Finally, in *Emma*—in response, it seems, to the stimulus of Wordsworth's exploration of ambiguous relationships in general and of a reimagined friendship as the radical form of such relationships in particular—Austen starts to take the full measure of the concept's complexity in her time, and of the opportunities inherent in that complexity, starts to put the word "friend" in vigorous motion, forces its incongruous and even contradictory semantic alternatives to confront one another, experiments with what friendship can and ought to be by creating situation after situation that tests and stretches its possibilities.

To begin with, the novel itself arrays its conceptions of friendship along a historical axis. I noted in the second chapter of this study that the community of Highbury experiences slow but steady change throughout the novel, as families like the Coles, Perrys, Eltons, Martins, and Westons gradually rise, and the Bateses gradually sink. What I did not note at the time is that the community is portrayed as being, initially, in a state of senescence. We are told, during Emma and Frank's preparations for the ball, that a large room had been added to the Crown Inn "many years ago for a ball-room, and while the neighborhood had been in a particularly populous, dancing state, had been occasionally used as such" (164). "[B]ut such brilliant days had long passed away," and the room is now employed as a club for "the gentlemen and half-gentlemen of the place." The image is one of youthful vigor and excitement declining into aging indolence, and as such reinforces the impression we have had all along, of a community dominated and, as it were, held in check by the feebleness of its most powerful member, Mr. Woodhouse, and the cramped frugality of its most pervasive presence, Miss

Bates.[61] The two of them, the second also because of her association with her invalid mother, embody the community's past and the attitudes and practices of that past, still maintaining their hold on the present.

One of the most important of those attitudes is the idea of friendship Mr. Woodhouse and Miss Bates share. It is essentially the one that *A History of Private Life* contrasts with the classical ideal: friendship as "everyday social relations"—friends as neighbors—except that it carries a much greater significance than that pallid phrase implies. For these two figures, their neighbors are indeed all friends. It is an attitude that cuts both ways, for while it implies far less intimacy than we normally associate with friends, it implies a great deal more goodwill and sense of mutual responsibility than we associate today with neighbors. Miss Bates, she announces at one point, feels herself most fortunate to be surrounded by "so many good neighbors and friends," a phrase that—given that we have just been told that "[s]he loved every body, was interested in every body's happiness" (20)—signifies the identity of its two terms rather than their difference. Again, as she makes her way into the ball, greeting a whole raft of characters we have never heard of before and will never hear of again, she exclaims in pleasure at "[s]uch a host of friends!" (267).

Mr. Woodhouse's characteristic way of expressing his goodwill toward his neighbors is to refer to them as his "old friends" or even his "very old friends" (143, 317, 320). Of the Bateses he says "[t]hey are some of my very old friends. I wish my health allowed me to be a better neighbor" (241)—a statement that not only reinforces the identity of "friends" and "neighbors" for the community's most conservative members, but confirms that this idea of friendship has the limitation we suggested before. Mr. Woodhouse's practice of friendship is as shallow as it is broad, and it is interesting that we are told that he is "everywhere beloved for the friendliness of his heart," for to say that someone has a friendly heart is not quite the same thing as saying that he is friendly (8). Mr. Woodhouse's friendliness is more a matter of intention than performance.

Into this settled, self-enclosed world irrupt two highly energetic agents of change: Frank Churchill and Mrs. Elton.[62] I will consider Frank below; Mrs. Elton, needless to say, brings to Highbury a new and thoroughly vulgar idea of friendship, one rooted in some of the same soil as Wordsworth's but trained in a very different direction. If Mr. Woodhouse and Miss Bates's way of relating to the people around them is inadequate for being premodern, Mrs. Elton's is all too modern. With everyone she is instantly intimate, as her famous "Knightley" suggests (228). In one respect, this new style seems to resemble the old; like Mr. Woodhouse, she, too, regards her neighbors as friends. But there are two crucial differences. The first is the quality of their respective friendships, the degree of their presumed intimacy, which in Mrs. Elton's case seems to know no bounds. The second is her failure to make distinctions between degrees of friendship. Mr. Woodhouse may regard everyone as a friend, but for that very reason he needs to make distinctions between kinds of friends; there are those, as we have seen, who are his "old friends," and there are those who are not, but whom, like Mrs. Elton herself, he is prepared to accept anyway. Miss Bates, too, has her "steady friend[s]" and "true friend[s]" (313). But not only does Mrs. Elton presume to called Knightley her "good friend" after only a few days' acquaintance (294), she refers to him, speaking to Emma, as "our friend Knightley" (375), as if the two were equally his friend.[63] But why shouldn't they be, since Mrs. Elton requires so little time to form her deepest attachments? "I like [the Westons] extremely," she says, "Mr. Weston seems an excellent creature— quite a first-rate favorite with me already" (228).

Mrs. Elton's hyperventilated rhetoric and lack of emotional decorum recall Austen's adolescent spoof of sentimental friendship ("We flew into each other's arms . . . "). She is no parody figure, however, but one Austen intends as a picture of a real and peculiarly modern kind of monster, one who, in Lionel Trilling's phrase, "cultivates the *style* of sensitivity."[64] There is a direct line from that "Knightley" to the confessionalism of the daytime talk-show. She is affective individualism run wild, and as such, represents the negative image of Wordsworth's ideal. Mrs. Elton wants the thrills and trappings of a general intimacy without doing the work necessary to attain it— the work, as Wordsworth performs it in "The Last of the Flock" and so many other poems, of listening to other people's stories in a spirit of wise passiveness, without seeking to foist his will upon them.

Austen's ideal, or at least a large part of it, is something quite similar, but with an important difference that is characteristic of other differences between the novelist and the poet. As we saw on a number of occasions in considering *Mansfield Park*, their different treatment of the same themes can be traced to the fact that, whereas Wordsworth's figures are solitary, Austen's are firmly embedded in their social matrix. The new human community Wordsworth seeks to forge one encounter at a time "along the broad highway" Austen seeks to construct within the confines of the old, structured community itself. For if Mr. Woodhouse and Miss Bates's kind of neighborly friendship is increasingly anachronistic and increasingly inadequate in an age of affective individualism, with its drive for deeper intimacies, Austen does not for that reason seek to discard it, but rather to preserve and extend it.

We can best see why in an encounter the likes of which can be found in none of her other novels, the conversation between Jane Fairfax and John Knightley during the evening of Emma's dinner for the Eltons at Hartfield. It is uniquely characteristic of *Emma*, and directly related to its interest in the kinds of friendships possible within communities, that the novel shows us this interaction at all, one that takes place away from the main lines of the plot and involves neither the heroine nor the hero. What Jane and John Knightley first talk about, in fact, is "the value of friendship" (241)—Austen announcing the theme of the passage even as she develops it. But more important, for now, than what they say on the topic is the fact that John Knightley refers to Jane as his "old friend"—a surprising enough statement considering the scant amount of time they have likely spent together, but all the more so given that just a page earlier he had thought of her merely as "an old acquaintance." The point is that, in the world of *Emma*, the two things are the same. Mr. Woodhouse and Miss Bates's style of friendship, the norm for all personal relationships at Highbury, gives Jane and John Knightley a share in each other's concerns, creates an assumption of mutual benevolence, and in so doing sets them on the road to an intimacy of which neither Mr. Woodhouse nor Miss Bates is capable but which is nevertheless available for more sensitive, more modern spirits to pursue.

Here, the old style enables John Knightley, speaking as just such a friend, to express a delicately phrased hope on a very personal and poignant subject: "As an old friend, you will allow me to hope, Miss Fairfax, that ten years hence you may have as many concentrated objects as I have [i.e., have a family—a rather unlikely prospect]." He speaks the wish as a friend, and she receives it as one: "It was kindly said, and very far from giving offense." The moment swells with feeling: "a blush, a quivering lip, a tear in the eye." Like the poet consoling the weeping stranger in "The Last of the Flock," albeit in a very different way, John Knightley has listened to another person's story and caught her tears. I noted before that Jane and John Knightley have a relationship for which no name seems to exist; we can now recognize that the name is "friendship." It is a friendship that blossoms almost miraculously between these two rather unlikely intimates: they may never have another exchange like this in their lives, but the old style of Highbury friendship, creating the conditions of its own transcendence, has allowed them to have this one.

And then Mr. Woodhouse himself claims Jane's attention to express solicitude in his own way: "I am very sorry to hear, Miss Fairfax, of your being out this morning in the rain. Young ladies should take care of themselves.—Young ladies are delicate plants." These are formal, even formulaic expressions of goodwill, for this "kind-hearted, polite old man"—"making the circle of his guests," speaking "with all his mildest urbanity"—is performing what amounts to a ceremonial, almost a public function. His insight into Jane's situation and feelings does not remotely approach that of his son-in-law—really, he has none at all—and he does not talk with her so much as at her. And yet she receives his words with equal gratitude: "I am very much obliged by your kind solicitude about me." Part of the value of this old style of friendship, as I suggested before, is that it is itself highly flexible, highly ambiguous in exactly the way we looked at before in examining the scene between Emma and George Knightley. Jane can communicate on one level with Mr. Woodhouse and on an entirely different one with John Knightley, and yet the kind of generalized friendship that prevails in Highbury accommodates the two exchanges equally well. The community's close-knit social structure, in other words—the fact that individuals there typically interact within the context of a larger group, as they do in this scene—does not prevent the development of the kind of higher friendship to which Wordsworth is committed; it enables it.

Indeed, the scene continues with two more people addressing Jane on the matter of her health, Mrs. Elton and Mrs. Weston. The latter "kindly and persuasively" advises her not to go out in the rain (242): after four iterations in less than a page, we cannot by now miss the scene's leading verbal motif—the word "kind." In fact, the word occurs again and again in *Emma* as the hallmark of the novel's sense of a common human community, its belief that we are all of the same "kind." It is a word, then—as these exchanges make very clear—that entails Shaftesbury's notion of social sympathy, one that I earlier connected with the new democratic spirit taking shape both on the far side of the Atlantic and in Wordsworth's poetry.

Emma, of course, like that poetry, was written in a society in which traditional vertical ties still possessed enormous strength. Sympathy—or to revert to the novel's language, kindness—did not need to be relied upon as the sole basis of social relations, as *Mansfield Park* abundantly shows. But as many critics have recognized, *Emma* represents a visionary act of social imagination. Trilling calls it an idyll, quoting Schiller's definition of the genre as one that "presents the idea and description of an innocent and happy humanity."[65] But I do not think that Austen meant us to take her vision as quite so utopian as that, quite so unattainable. She may not have been a democrat, but neither was she the conservative as which she has so often been painted.[66] *Emma*, which stands between *Mansfield Park* and *Persuasion*—a novel oppressed by hierarchical distinctions and another novel that essentially disinherits the aristocracy in favor of a professional class figured as a band of brothers—is an insistently egalitarian work. Everywhere we see class lines being disregarded and crossed: the impoverished Bates visiting Hartfield; Knightley befriending his farmer; "gentlemen and half-gentlemen" playing whist together. One of Emma's most reprehensible faults is her insistence on petty distinctions of class, her fixation on "gradations of rank" (113). *Emma* may not seek to overthrow hierarchical distinctions, but it does seek to ignore them. And this egalitarian impulse is squarely in line with the novel's general interest in the erasure of socially and emotionally confining distinctions. As with the lines drawn by relational terms like "mother and "sister," the novel blurs the boundaries of class, overriding conventional social categories, creating an egalitarian space in which as wide as possible a range of classes can mix freely. Friendship in *Emma*, then, as in Wordsworth's poetry, is a democratizing or leveling relationship. Horizontal ties supersede vertical ones, and the old neighborliness becomes the foundation of an envisioned community of equals.

The idea is underscored by Mrs. Elton's contribution to the scene we have been looking at. While Mr. Woodhouse and Mrs. Weston hope to persuade Jane not to go out again in the rain, Mrs. Elton intends to compel her not to: "Oh! she *shall not* do such a thing again . . . We will not allow her to do such a thing again" (242; emphasis in the original). Her attitude toward other people and their stories is about as far from wise passiveness as can be imagined. Indeed, her whole relationship to Jane is that of a self-appointed "friend" in the John Dashwood sense of the word—a patron who orders destinies by means of the social and financial power at her disposal. "You are extremely kind," Jane responds here, but the word is mere politeness in her use of it—she preserves the forms of neighborliness even if Mrs. Elton does not—and bitterly ironic in the novel's.

Mrs. Elton's own understanding of the word, and her own attitude about class, emerges a few paragraphs later, in connection with the fetching of Jane's letters, when she declares that it would be "a kindness to employ our men." In other words, she will be doing one of her servants a favor by having him go out of his way every day to deliver another household's letters. Which servant? "The man who fetches our letters every morning (one of our men, I forget his name)." Such negligence is a moral lapse of which Mr. Woodhouse, for all his inadequacies, would never be guilty. The "*style of* sensitivity," narcissistic as it finally is, bespeaks an essential disregard for the common humanity—the kind-ness—of others. The villain in this egalitarian novel is that character most insistent on exercising hierarchical power, most careless and unfeeling in its exercise.

To say that friendship forms the basis of an egalitarian community is not, again, to say that all friendships are equal. Indeed, an emphasis on horizontal connections—the rewriting of all relationships as friendships—gives rise, here, to a need for horizontal differentiation. The word "friend" thus attracts, over the course of the novel, a whole host of qualifiers. We're all friends now, so the question is, what kind of friends are you and I? We have already come across "old friends" and "very old friends," "steady friend," "true friend," and "good friend," and we also find "intimate friend" (54), "very warm friend" (55), "very good friend" (94), "but half a friend" (114), "particular friends" (286), "very particular friend" (168), "excellent friend" (182), "best friend" (220), "dear friends" (263), "kind friends" (314), "thorough friends" (318), and "intimate friends" (346).

I noted before that the freedom that Austen introduces into the ordinarily strict system of social roles—creating flexible, ambiguous relationships that make room for improvisation and growth—can be thought of as a form of playfulness or play. So it is here with friendship, the apotheosis of ambiguous relationships. A world in which everyone is a friend rather than a landlord or patron or dependent is one in which relationships are endlessly adjustable and imagination a more important force than convention. That is exactly what we see in the Matthew poems, but while Wordsworth is not normally thought of as a playful poet, everyone recognizes that *Emma* is an exuberantly playful novel, full of riddles and puzzles and games—the most important of which, as I noted in chapter 1, being the game Austen plays with her readers, setting us in search of the clues that will solve her narrative puzzle.[67] As the Wordsworthian allusion I also noted in chapter 1 makes clear, *Emma* does not condemn the imagination, it only condemns its misuse by the heroine. In fact, it celebrates the imagination, and for the same reason as does *Don Quixote*, another novel that at first appears to condemn it: because the imagination is the faculty that enables us to rejuvenate ourselves, our world, and our relationships with others.

So where is Emma in all of this? It is telling that she is silent throughout most of the scene we were just looking at, speaking up only when the conversation turns to Frank, a subject that flatters her vanity, and even then addressing herself only to Mrs. Weston and Knightley, her particular intimates. With the kind of friendship that binds the community together she has as little to do as possible, holding herself aloof from the likes of the Bateses and the Coles, begrudging them her every expression of kindness. It is no wonder that loneliness so threatens her as the novel opens, as it threatens no other Austenian heroine.[68]

The idea, pressed on Emma by her environment, that she ought, as a young person, to cultivate a serious friendship or two—the idea that friendship is "the dear peculiar bond of youth"—reflects Austen's absorption of the Byronic revaluation of the classical-romantic tradition. For despite our general sense that Austen valued friendship very highly, the same-sex friendships that we see in the early novels and in *Mansfield Park* almost always involve disappointment and even betrayal: Elizabeth and Charlotte Lucas, Elinor and Lucy Steele, Catherine and Isabella Thorpe, Fanny and Mary Crawford. But here it is part of what marks Emma as psychically misshapen, part of the disabling legacy of her overindulged childhood, that she seems never to have had a true Byronic friend, an equal with whom to share genuine intimacy.

Of course, the friendship she does soon choose to cultivate perfectly accords with her exalted sense of her place in the world and the splendid isolation in which it keeps her. But Emma was looking for a friendship neither equal nor intimate: Harriet, we are told, is not "exactly the friend Emma wanted," but "exactly the young friend she wanted" (24).[69] And not only is Harriet younger—all of four years younger, a difference Emma stresses at every turn—she is also far less worldly, very less wealthy, and—this seems especially important to Emma—far shorter. She is invariably, not Emma's "friend," but her "little friend" (239) or "poor little friend" (25) or "sweet little friend" (47). If we need any further evidence that this is not a friendship of equals, even to its participants, we may note that while Emma calls Harriet "Harriet," Harriet calls Emma "Miss Woodhouse" (e.g., 220).

In fact, we can see exactly what kind of friend Emma thinks she is to Harriet. As in so many respects, Mrs. Elton holds the mirror up to the heroine's worst qualities; Emma plays for Harriet the self-appointed role of benefactor, of "friend" in the John Dashwood sense—patronizing, overbearing, controlling, and just as misguided and destructive as Mrs. Elton is with respect to Jane. Notwithstanding the observation that she treats Harriet in ways analogous to a wife,[70] there is nothing at all ambiguous about this relationship, nothing playful or flexible or spontaneous. Emma may participate in ambiguous relationships, but in this one of her own devising, she establishes strict roles from the moment she takes Harriet under her patronage and never permits the slightest deviation from her script.

On this score, as on all others, her reformation is a path of many steps. She partly realizes the inappropriateness of her friendship with Harriet by the end of volume I, and it is at this point that the novel first becomes self-conscious about the theme of friendship, its characters first openly struggling over its meaning. Knightley works his own changes on the word in admonishing Emma for trying to raise Harriet out of Mrs. Goddard's set: "Her friends evidently thought this good enough for her; and it *was* good enough . . . Till you chose to turn her into a friend, her mind had no distaste for her own set . . . You have been no friend to Harriet Smith" (54; emphasis in the original). Emma's idea of "friendship," in other words—one in which she falsely tries to substitute for Harriet's real "friends" or benefactors—does not deserve the name. Emma resists Knightley's admonition, but after the Elton fiasco, in a soliloquy that clearly echoes this exchange, she comes to concur at least in part: "I have been but half a friend to her" (114). The assessment is still half-wrong—she hasn't been any kind of friend to her, not in the sense she should have been—but it shows that Emma has begun to think about what friendship ought to mean.

She also eventually realizes, of course, that the friendship she should have been cultivating is with Jane Fairfax.[71] Although she faults Jane for her lack of candor, she is threatened by the prospect of a relationship with her not just because of its inevitable equality, but also because of its inevitable intimacy. For while Emma has never known the intimacy of an equal, Jane has, having been brought up since the age of nine with the daughter of her adoptive parents. It is no surprise that Jane "ha[s] never been quite well since the time of [Miss Campbell's] marriage" (138)—not, as Emma suspects, because of a secret love between her and Miss Campbell's new husband, but rather, we may conclude, because of the loss of so very dear a friend, one who has been, as the narrator of *Emma* might say, almost a sister. (The absence of such closeness between Emma and her own sister is conspicuous.)

Indeed, in Emma's malicious fantasy of a secret affair between Jane and Dixon, there seems more than a little need to denigrate that friendship. Responding to Emma's surprise that Dixon could prefer Jane's playing to that of his fiancée, and to her insinuation that Miss Campbell could not have liked that very much, Frank reminds Emma that Jane is Miss Campbell's "very particular friend." Emma seizes upon the phrase as if it were a snake that had to be crushed: "Poor comfort! . . . One would rather have a stranger preferred than one's very particular friend—with a stranger it might not occur again—but the misery of having a very particular friend always at hand, to do every thing better than one does oneself" (168). Emma does not have a very particular friend and does not like hearing that anyone else does, especially not the woman with whom she is always being unfavorably compared.

Not only does she find Jane's friendship with Miss Campbell threatening, she also finds it incomprehensible, and the first perhaps because of the second. She knows that the two women share something she has never experienced, and she also knows that her inability to understand it, or experience it, reflects the weaknesses of her own character—just as she knows that her resistance to befriending Jane does as well. Her vanity bars her not only from participating in such a friendship of equals, but also from comprehending the nature of its equality—so evidently unrelated to any superficial equality of accomplishment—or of its intimacy—so evidently unthreatened by the inequality of accomplishment that actually exists.

But even while Emma is failing to develop her long-promised friendship with Jane, she is quite unintentionally developing a different one, one that represents the freest and most far-reaching aspect of the novel's experiment in friendship, as well as Austen's fullest exploration of a kind of relationship of which, as we saw, she was the great pioneer: the friendship of men and women outside the boundaries of marriage. It is Emma's friendship with Frank, one that has been greatly if understandably undervalued in the critical literature. Frank's advance billing is admittedly not good, especially with respect to his qualities as a friend. It is of him that Knightley is speaking—he is arguing with Emma about the likely character of the as-yet-unknown young man—when he makes his distinction between the English "amiable" and the French "*aimable*" (124). The first he defines as having an "English delicacy towards the feelings of other people," the second as merely "hav[ing] very good manners, and be[ing] very agreeable," and behind this distinction we can hear the national differences, or at least national stereotypes, we looked at above.

In their own perception, at least, the English valued friendship over sexual love—indeed, dissolved the second into the first, rewriting marriage as friendship—while the French valued love over friendship, keeping the two rigorously separate. To be amiable, in this understanding, is to behave as a true friend, to be *aimable* to make oneself desirable, lovable in the sense of sexual love. In other words, we might say, if "amiable" means "*amis*-able," "*aimable*" means "*aimer*-able," and pointing to the fact that two etymologically identical words have such different meanings is Austen's way of underscoring the difference between national styles of intimacy.[72]

In fact, Knightley's definitions do accurately anticipate Frank's character as it first appears—he is very agreeable, but his pretense with Emma and Jane does show a lack of delicacy toward the feelings of other people. And yet, by the end of the novel, his character has modulated, as a greater delicacy, a greater sensitivity, has gradually emerged; Frank the "Frank" has become Frank the "frank." And in the meantime, a relationship has developed between him and Emma that, while it begins because she finds him so *aimable*, so desirable, a feeling he does everything he can to incite, continues and grows stronger precisely because they come to find each other so amiable. In other words, a very "English" dissolving of love into friendship is exactly what ends up taking place between them—without their having planned it, and perhaps even without Austen having fully planned it, for some of their most significant encounters have an especially improvisatory feeling. Austen is allowing herself to experiment with the possibilities of friendship between an unmarried young man and young woman, and so are they.

The most important of these encounters is Frank's leave-taking at Hartfield right around the middle of the novel. His pretend courtship has not only led Emma to mistake his feelings for her, as he intended, it has led them both into depths of feeling he did not foresee. Emma is wrong to think he is in love with her, but she is not wrong to think that he feels for her very deeply. The misunderstanding is concentrated in a single moment: "He hesitated, got up, walked to a window. 'In short,' said he, 'perhaps Miss Woodhouse—I think you can hardly be quite without suspicion'—" (215). She expects a proposal of marriage, of course, while what he really wishes to divulge—out of a sense of trust and a desire for frankness that are almost enough to make him breech an inviolable secrecy—is his understanding with Jane. Still, with his nervous movements and broken speech, Emma does not mistake the strength of his feelings. Precisely because he has so involved Emma, albeit unbeknownst to her, in his deepest emotions and concerns, his feelings toward her have become those of an intimate friend. It is no wonder that Emma is so confused, after he leaves, about her own feelings. She thinks that she, too, is in love—or rather, thinks "that she *must* be" (216; emphasis in the original). Frank's scheme of obfuscation has caused her to misread her own emotions as well, but again, not their depth. As her continued reflections lead her to see—Emma's emotional honesty always eventually saves her from her worst errors of imagination—the feelings she is feeling and groping to express are also those of an intimate friend. In every scenario she spins out about her future with Frank, "[t]heir affection was always to subside into friendship," "true disinterested friendship" (217, 219).

And that is just what happens, even while Frank maintains his charade of pretend-flirtation, and especially afterward. For we must remember that most of the negative judgments passed on Frank, both before and after the revelation of his true attachment, come from Knightley, who is a far from disinterested witness. In a novel in which even the "good" characters almost all come with large admixtures of negative qualities, Frank is very far from being all bad, and the best thing about him is the relationship he develops and maintains with Emma, unconsciously cooperating with her to move it from the pretend-love in which it begins to the "true disinterested friendship" in which it ends.

And it is precisely the ambiguity of the word "friendship" at that time, the flexibility of the relationship in the contemporaneous English practice of it, that allows them to make the necessary imaginative and emotional transitions. A rigorously "French" segregation of erotic and amicable feelings and bonds would have made that process impossible. Instead, Austen develops potentialities latent in her culture's evolving social practices, especially the practice of the companionate marriage. And yet her development was so far-reaching as to result in a radically innovative type of relationship, the male-female friendship—before, after, or entirely apart from the existence of erotic impulses and possibilities—one that remained otherwise virtually unexampled in the literary record for many years after Austen's day but that is a commonplace of social practice in our own.[73]

The scene of Frank's leave-taking closes with a characteristically English gesture that, as much as the word we have been looking at and in conjunction with the occurrence of one of its forms, encapsulates the ambiguities and possibilities of Emma and Frank's relationship at that moment. The two take their leave with "[a] very friendly shake of the hand." It is remarkable that such different understandings and differently understood emotions are able to meet and find expression in one gesture, and it is also remarkable that the same gesture, with some of the same accompanying language, recurs later in the novel under very different circumstances. Visiting Jane after the revelation of her engagement, and hearing that Mrs. Elton is about to interrupt them, Emma "compress[es] all her friendly and all her congratulatory sensations into a very, very earnest shake of the hand" (371).

Austen has created a physical analogue to the language of friendship, a gestural shorthand, so to speak. That gesture is poignant here in that it is virtually all the friendship that Emma and Jane will ever have, but the retrospective light it throws on that earlier handshake suggests that instead of getting her equal, intimate, flexible, mutually respectful friendship with Jane (and in a devious manner, because of that loss), Emma gets it with Frank. The latter may not be quite as rich and satisfactory as the former would have been, but as we have said, it is far more revolutionary. With it, the novel and its characters cross yet another boundary (that of gender), blur yet another set of socially and emotionally confining distinctions. And again, just as with their crossing of the boundaries of class, the vehicle is friendship. So while Mrs. Elton brings a deplorable new form of friendship to Highbury, Frank, the novel's other bearer of modern tidings, helps create one that Austen means us to value very much. Among other things, it becomes one of the chief constituents of the novel's crowning ambiguous relationship, its crowning friendship.

That relationship, of course, is Emma's with Knightley.[74] We know precisely when she realizes that she loves him, but when does he realize that he loves her? He gives two completely different answers, each time with evident sincerity: "He had been in love with Emma, and jealous of Frank Churchill, from about the same period, one sentiment having probably enlightened him as to the other" (355; the statement is Knightley's, rendered through indirect discourse, not the narrator's), and "I . . . have been in love with you ever since you were thirteen at least" (379). Which account is true? They both are, of course, because Emma and Knightley's sexual attraction is an outgrowth of all the other feelings, all the other modes of relatedness, they share, and so its origin is necessarily obscure. Even more, as Knightley's apparent confusion suggests, its nature keeps changing. Frank's arrival raises Knightley's desire to a sexual boil, but his feelings for Emma had had an erotic component long before that. How else can we explain his otherwise paradoxical statement, very early in the novel, when forced by Mrs. Weston to acknowledge Emma's beauty: "I confess that I have seldom seen a face or figure more pleasing to me than her's. But I am a partial old friend" (34). The avowal borders on the shocking: an "old friend," a "friend of the family" nearly twice her age, taking great "pleasure" from the contemplation of a young woman's figure. But then, with Knightley's "I . . . have been in love with you ever since you were thirteen at least," Austen flirts with outright pedophilia. Like the "incest" in *Mansfield Park*—and indeed, the incest here, in this same relationship—her point is precisely to challenge us into rethinking our conventional compartmentalizations of the different forms of intense affection.[75]

We may be forgiven our obtuseness, however, because these same conventional understandings blind Emma and Knightley themselves, for a long time, to all that they feel for each other. Indeed, one of the novel's pleasures lies in watching both parties come to a full awareness of just what their relationship contains. The ball marks one important stage. After another display of the extraordinary mutual sensitivity that their long and rich history has made possible—"her eyes invited him irresistibly to come to her and be thanked," "[h]e looked with smiling penetration," etc.—Emma asks him to join her in the set: "You have shown that you can dance, and you know we are not really so much brother and sister as to make it at all improper" (273–274). "[N]ot really so much brother and sister" is, of course, exactly the kind of ambiguity the narrator employs in the opening description of Emma's relationship with Miss Taylor. Emma and Knightley are not brother and sister, but then again, in the language of the day, they are. Emma, still oblivious to her sexual feelings, is undisturbed by the ambiguity. But Knightley, already alive to his, is very much disturbed. "Brother and sister! no, indeed," he exclaims—to which the novel ultimately replies, "Brother and sister! yes, indeed." The exchange concludes a chapter—concludes, indeed the whole long episode of the ball—and the effect of this pregnant placement is to make it into a signpost that points us toward Emma and Knightley's climactic encounters.

The physical gesture that accompanies that exchange is again as significant as its play with language, for what do Emma and Knightley do as they prepare to dance, but, as the text tells us, take hands? Emma's handshake with Frank anticipates more than one, indeed more than two subsequent moments of intimacy, but before we can look at the others, we must glance at the scene that precipitates Emma's final recognitions, the outing at Box Hill. To Emma's humiliating witticism there, Miss Bates responds, "I must make myself very disagreeable, or she would not have said such a thing to an old friend" (306). "Old friend," again: Emma's great sin is to have violated, more flagrantly than ever and in the glow of her more intimate connection with Frank, the kind of friendship that binds the community together, that basic sense of equality that expresses itself in an acknowledgment of every person's dignity and without which, as Wordsworth understood, the more exalted reaches of friendship risk becoming no more than a mutual narcissism. In delivering his rebuke, Knightley also speaks as a "friend," even though by doing so, as he knows, he risks alienating the woman he loves (310). Friendship, he implies, means sacrificing oneself for one's friend's sake. His attempt to educate Emma into friendship's responsibilities has thus come full circle, for his reproof here echoes and completes the one he had delivered near the start of the novel, when he told her that she had been "no friend to Harriet Smith" (54).

Austen's rendering of the scene in which Knightley becomes aware that Emma has atoned for her sin strikes all the chords with which we are by now familiar. The information that she has visited the Bateses is communicated indirectly (by Mr. Woodhouse, in fact), and the interchange that follows between Emma and Knightley is both highly complex and entirely silent; in fact, the two do not speak again for the rest of the scene. Emma blushes, looks at him, and it seems "as if his eyes received the truth from her's, and all that had passed of good in her feelings were at once caught and honoured" (317). And then comes "a little movement of more than common friendliness on his part.—He took her hand." Or is it rather that Emma herself makes the first motion? She isn't sure. "More than common friendliness"—their bodies are speaking a language of their own, saying things their possessors do not fully understand: "He took her hand, pressed it, and certainly was on the point of carrying it to his lips—when, from some fancy or other, he suddenly let it go."

The gesture that Austen established those many chapters earlier as a physical sign of friendship's ambiguities she is now, like the word "friend" itself, playing with, stretching, manipulating, making ever more complex and ambiguous. Here the handshake is on the point of turning into a kiss of the hand, a gesture Knightley forswears for a reason the converse of that for which he abjured the label of "brother and sister." That had seemed to preclude eros, this too clearly to speak it. But Emma does not think so; to her it would have spoken "perfect amity" (318). As I discussed in chapter 2, the word "perfect" is ironized nearly every time it appears in the novel, and this instance is no exception. Here, though, the irony points to a state in excess of the indicated perfection, not one that falls short of it. "Perfect amity" is not nearly amity enough; there is more to Emma and Knightley's friendship than mere friendship.

The novel's climactic scene, the marriage proposal, includes yet another variation on the handshake motif, as Emma, walking with Knightley in the shrubbery, suddenly finds "her arm drawn within his, and pressed against his heart" (349). We might recognize by now that all of these takings of hands point to and in a manner pun on the novel's final, implicit one, Emma and Knightley's "joining of hands" in matrimony.[76] But this echoing of gestures is not the only way in which Emma's most important scene with Knightley recalls that earlier one with Frank. There she forestalled a man's avowal of his love for another woman in the mistaken belief that it was to have been a proposal of marriage. Here she forestalls a proposal of marriage in the mistaken belief that it was to have been a man's avowal of his love for another woman. But here she relents the next minute, and precisely out of a sense of what it means to be a friend—indeed, the very sense that Knightley had displayed at Box Hill: "I stopped you ungraciously, just now, Mr. Knightley, and, I am afraid, gave you pain.—But if you have any wish to speak openly to me as a friend . . . as a friend, indeed, you may command me" (352). Given what she thinks he is going to say and what she has already discovered about her own feelings, it is the most self-sacrificing thing she can do.

With it, and with Knightley's response, Austen places the word "friend" at the novel's very fulcrum, reimagining it one final time as the characters reimagine it for themselves, discovering the full significance with which she would have them invest it. Knightley at first recoils from the word: " 'As a friend!'—repeated Mr. Knightley.—'Emma, that I fear is a word—No, I have no wish—'." As with his earlier recoil from "brother and sister," he still believes that one kind of relationship, one set of feelings, precludes another. It is precisely the same blindness that had kept Emma from recognizing her own sexual feelings all along. But then a light dawns: "Stay, yes, but why should I hesitate? . . . Emma, I accept your offer—Extraordinary as it may seem, I accept it, and refer myself to you as a friend." The basis of the love he hopes they will have, he finally sees, is friendship. Loving each other sexually, as husband and wife, would not preclude loving each other as friends in all the ways they always have. Marriage would be not the end of their friendship, but its fulfillment. And so it is as a friend that he is willing to speak, just as it is as a friend that she is willing to listen. Austen constructs the encounter so that friendship becomes the path to its own transfiguration. It is as friends that Emma and Knightley avow their love, and as friends that they will live it.

As in Wordsworth, friendship thus makes possible the transgression of yet another conventional social boundary, that of age. Emma, who had made so much of the four-year difference between herself and Harriet Smith, will marry a man sixteen years her senior. At thirty-seven, Knightley is old enough to be her father, but in contrast to the comparable disparity between Marianne Dashwood and Colonel Brandon, this one is deemphasized as the lovers draw together. Emma herself, at the ball at which Knightley splutters his "no, indeed," laments his "classing himself with the husbands, and fathers . . . so young as he looked! . . . His tall, firm, upright figure . . . there was not one among the whole row of young men who could be compared with him" (269). Youth and age are not to be determined, Austen is telling us, by the calendar. This is a novel, after all, in which the elderly Mr. Woodhouse, "a much older man in ways than in years," is babied by his young daughter (8). Emma and Knightley's marriage is a union, like that of Matthew and the poet, of two young people of very different ages. Indeed, like Matthew and the poet, the two keep each other young, Knightley by releasing Emma from the frozen certainties—including the certainty that she will never marry—that threaten to make her (as Elizabeth Elliot will be of Sir Walter) a carbon copy of her father, Emma precisely by retrieving Knightley from the class of husbands and fathers and drawing him back into the mating dance.

The circumstance suggests an addendum to Brain's dictum about modern friendship: we are friends with everyone now because, while friendship in modernity is the special province of youth, we are all young now, too. Ever becoming, mind ever growing (like Emma, like Wordsworth): the modern individual—or at least the contemporary individual, for Austen is very far ahead of her own time here—is ever young, his or her intimacies always cast in terms of youth's "dear peculiar bond."[77]

To put it another way—for youth and adulthood, as we have been saying, are no longer mutually exclusive categories here—Emma and Knightley's relationship, like that of Matthew and the poet or the poet and his sister in "Tintern Abbey," carries friendship over into adulthood. That friendship can be so carried over is, in fact, exactly the theme of Jane Fairfax and John Knightley's discussion of friendship in the scene we looked at earlier. John Knightley claims, or pretends to claim, that friendship is exclusively an affair of the young, that husbands and fathers can no longer be bothered with it. But as Jane recognizes perfectly well, the very conversation they are having belies his self-consciously world-weary pose (241).

Austen is well known for her commitment to maturity,[78] but she is also—less obviously but quite as much as Wordsworth or Byron—a lover of youth and its ardor. It is a matter, in the sense I developed in chapter 1, of esteeming "Elinor" but loving "Marianne." Adults do not tend to come off very well in Austen's novels, and the young people she likes least—Collins, Mr. and Mrs. Elton—are precisely those who lack true passion. Those she loves most, though—Catherine; Marianne; Elizabeth Bennet, with her bright eyes; Fanny and Anne, with their quiet but powerful feelings; and finally Emma herself—conspicuously display it. Austen believed in growing up, but she also believed in carrying what is most valuable in youth over into adulthood. Here, where youth and adulthood join hands under the aegis of friendship, the distinction between the two is blurred altogether.

And like Emma and Frank, but even more importantly so, Emma and Knightley also blur the boundaries of gender.[79] Just as Austen seeks to level the hierarchy of classes here, so too the hierarchy of husband and wife. That Knightley takes the extraordinary step of moving in to his bride's home is itself quite significant, but there is far more to their equality than that. For equality in friendship, as the relationship between Jane and Miss Campbell has taught us, is not a matter of equal abilities and accomplishments. In that superficial sense, Emma does indeed make an unequal marriage. It is rather a matter of a mutual esteem so deep that it can ignore such differences. By rewriting marriage as friendship, Austen replaces an institutional, legal, hierarchical relationship, one ultimately based on the power of coercion, with an informal, egalitarian, loosely structured one that is ultimately based on autonomy, affection, and trust.

Of course, we must ask by now, of the idea that Austen rewrites marriage as friendship, friendship in what sense? The answer is: in as many senses as possible. As hard as Austen works to create the possibility of pre- or extramarital friendship between men and women through her development of the relationship between Emma and Frank, she knows that such a relationship, by excluding sex, is necessarily limited. By making that relationship a long prelude to Emma and Knightley's, she incorporates this new form of friendship into the sexual union of husband and wife. It is important to emphasize, again, that this does not entail a replacement of sexual love by friendship. It has been said that Austen preferred friendship to sexual love, and in this particular case, that the love of Emma and Knightley is nonerotic.[80] But such judgments proceed from precisely the cultural prejudice that Austen was seeking to overthrow. As Brain points out, it is only in the West that we draw a sharp distinction between eros and friendship at all.[81] Other cultures do not make that distinction, and neither—and this is part of what is so revolutionary about her—did Austen.

Indeed, incorporating friendship into the sexual union of marriage allows her to bring the intensity of same-sex classical-romantic friendship—which is patterned, after all, on the erotic bond—into the kind of male-female friendship she pioneered. But while she is interested in classical-romantic intensity, as we have seen, she has no interest in classical-romantic exclusivity. Emma and Knightley's marriage will honor the ties of neighborly friendship as well, as the novel's closing reference to "the small band of true friends" who witness their wedding suggests (396). The result is a kind of meta-ambiguity, as the hero and heroine's relationship becomes a space in which different forms of friendship, each themselves ambiguous, can meet and combine into ever-new possibilities. The novel begins by asking "what will become" of Emma (35); it ends by inviting us to imagine what will become of Emma and Knightley's friendships—and our own.

CHAPTER FIVE

Persuasion

Widowhood and Waterloo

. . . a state of alteration, perhaps of improvement . . .

Persuasion, it has been noted, is a novel of widows.[1] Sir Walter Elliot, Lady Russell, William Walter Elliot, Mrs. Smith, Mrs. Clay, and the Dowager Viscountess Dalrymple are all literally widowed, as is, by a slight extension of the term, Captain Benwick. Anne, bereaved of Wentworth, is clearly marked as being figuratively so, as is, of course, Wentworth himself. Charles Hayter briefly suffers a similar figurative bereavement at the hands of Henrietta Musgrove, one that, given Wentworth's preference for Louisa, would have insured a complementary fate for Henrietta herself. And once we recognize widowhood as the novel's metaphor for bereavement of all kinds, we see that all three of the Elliot girls, who have lost a mother; Captain Harville, who has lost the sister Captain Benwick was to have married; and Mr. and Mrs. Musgrove, who have lost their son Richard, are all widows, as well.

Austen has shown us widows before, but of a very different kind. Lady Catherine de Bourgh, Mrs. Jennings, Mrs. Norris—widowhood, for these women, has nothing to do with bereavement (remember that Mrs. Norris consoles herself for the loss of her husband "by considering that she could do very well without him" [MP 21]) and everything to do with possessing power, independence, and stature beyond the reach of married women. For them, it is an office of dignity, rather something to be congratulated on than regretted. Nor are Mr. Woodhouse and General Tilney (Catherine's fantasies notwithstanding) any more marked, in their lives or their feelings, by the loss of their wives, whom they never mention nor, apparently, even think of. But in *Persuasion*, widowhood, and all that it implies—grief, memory, wrenching adjustments, the painful attempt to move forward or the refusal to try—becomes the central fact in nearly all the lives of the bereaved, and the novel takes shape as a meditation on its dimensions and implications.[2]

It is no wonder that near the center of the novel we come upon a discussion of two of Byron's Turkish Tales, *The Giaour* and *The Bride of Abydos* (a third, *The Corsair*, is quoted in the following chapter[3]), and two of Scott's verse romances, *Marmion* and *The Lady of the Lake*.[4] For the central theme of each of these bodies of work, the Tales and the romances, is survival: who and what lives on, and on what terms, after the experience of loss—of bereavement, of war, of cultural extinction.[5] That this is true in Scott is less immediately obvious and is a point I will defer until later. That it is true in Byron is most evident in *The Giaour*, the first of the Tales and the one to which *Persuasion* gives special emphasis.

The poem's very form embodies the idea of survival. It is, according to the conceit named in its subtitle, "A Fragment of a Turkish Tale"—or to be precise, a set of fragments, its twenty-six disconnected sections coming to us like so many pieces of narrative flotsam, the sole remnants, the sole evidence, of the explosive passions of which they tell. One of the things that survive a loss, Byron suggests, is stories—just as, by the end of the poem, the Giaour's own story is the only thing he has left to show for his bereavement. But even stories—passing from teller to teller, as this one claims to do, subject to the fallibility of memory and the uncertainties of repetition—provide no guarantee of survival. And therein lies the source of the Giaour's dilemma and of his extreme response to it.

The problem is stated implicitly in the first narrator's remarkable simile of the Greek shore as akin in appearance to a corpse in the first hours after death, its features so beautiful, reposeful, and tender that one bending over them might still fancy them inhabited by life. It is the false hope expressed in these lines to which the Giaour wishes to cling. Having suffered an unacceptable loss, he desires to arrest time at the very moment of that loss, achieving his wish the only way he can, by forcing his own psyche into a state of suspended animation.[6] For the Giaour knows—or least, his poem does—that to move forward emotionally is to subject the dead to a second death, the death of one's own grief. The irony is that grief will die eventually anyway, when the mourner himself dies. Hence the poem's evocation of the cypress as "still sad when others' grief is fled, / The only constant mourner o'er the dead" (ll. 286–287), a sentiment echoed in *The Bride of Abydos*.[7] Hence also the poem's opening glance at the tomb of Themistocles "gleaming o'er the cliff" (l. 3), as well as the fisherman-narrator's description of the Giaour as having a face as "pale as marble o'er the tomb" (l. 238). Cypresses and marble slabs are what people never can be: lasting witnesses to loss.

Still, the Giaour does his best to make himself into a living monument, so that when the fisherman sees him six years later, his face "breathes the same dark spirit now, / As death were stamped upon his brow" (ll. 797–798). An apt figure, this suggestion of a living death, one that reinforces the immediately preceding curse, in which the narrator had foreseen a future for the Giaour as a "Vampire" or "living corse" (ll. 755, 762), and the later simile of the desolate heart as like a sentient corpse that can feel the worms crawling over it in the grave (ll. 945–948). Indeed, death-in-life and life-in-death are the poem's mirror-image master metaphors: the Giaour dies while alive so that Leila may remain alive, for him, in death.[8] Grief, undigested, becomes itself a kind of death, and a willed death, at that, a morbid identification with the lost beloved.

These are the chief concerns Austen takes over from *The Giaour*—and indeed from all four of the Turkish Tales, for *The Corsair* and *Lara*, its sequel, rework these same issues of unacceptable loss and psychic arrest, while *The Bride of Abydos* avoids doing so only by having its lovers die simultaneously, leaving their strangely animate monuments—his wandering marble slab, her eternally blooming rose—to carry on a posthumous love affair. Before the novel even arrives at Anne, it gives a sketch of three psyches arrested in the wake of irreparable loss, albeit under conditions very different from those experienced by the Giaour or Lara. We looked, in chapter 2, at how thoroughly the loss of her mother disrupted Anne's life and damaged her psyche, and by the same arts of subtle but devastating implication, Austen shows us the effect that loss has had on the rest of her family. For the seventeen years of her marriage, Lady Elliot was the rudder that had kept her husband from foundering on his own silliness and conceit, the protector who had "humoured, or softened, or concealed his failings" (36). There is no way of knowing how deep Sir Walter's passion for her had run—given his narcissism, probably not very deep at all—but without her he is lost, and not just financially. Vanity alone does not explain the freeze-dried quality we noted in him in chapter 2, and the mirrors that are his emblem, instruments of sterile repetition, signify more than just the intensity of his self-regard. If we can imagine the suppressed panic that succeeded his wife's loss, we will recognize that while his reasons for wishing to arrest time at the moment of his partner's death may have been very different from the Giaour's, they were no less urgent.

Sir Walter's widowhood is a psychic stasis not of intense passion, but of stunned numbness, and we are pointedly told, right after the account of Lady Elliot's death, that despite everyone's expectations, he "did *not* marry" again (36; emphasis in the original). The woman he "did *not* marry" is Lady Russell, herself a widow—indeed, given her great friendship with Lady Elliot, a widow twice over. There the two abide, Sir Walter and Lady Russell, one at Kellynch-hall, one at Kellynch-lodge, "one remain[ing] a widower, the other a widow," paired remnants of Lady Elliot's demise endlessly mirroring each other in their inability to move forward from that loss (37). (By the end of the novel, Sir Walter will have also not-married Mrs. Clay.) The third member of the trio is Elizabeth Elliot, "still the same handsome Miss Elliot that she had begun to be thirteen years ago," still unmarried, as well, still trapped in the annual cycle of "revolving frosts" and brief social springs (38). Had Lady Elliot lived, and had she been anything like the woman the narrator says she was, Elizabeth would surely have been married long since, and even Sir Walter might well have begun, at age fifty-four, to let go of his youth. Without her, the family comes to a virtual standstill, bearing continuous witness to her death in their lives if not in their hearts.

In the opening chapters, then, her father and elder sister do not serve merely as contrasts to Anne. They also help define and contextualize her own Giaour-like mourning for Wentworth, that state of wan hopelessness and perpetual regret every bit as monastic as the Giaour's and enlivened only by a self-tormenting addiction to the navy lists—a state that, but for the authorial miracle of the Croft-Wentworth coincidence, would undoubtedly have persisted to the grave. In fact, the Elliot family bereavement allows Austen, with her more socially and narratively complex novelistic canvas, to explore dimensions of widowhood unavailable to Byron, with his narrower focus, in all the Tales, on a single character living in self-willed isolation. Widowhood, she shows, is not only a matter of what is lost, but also of what is left behind. In the case of Lady Elliot's death, what is left behind are "[t]hree girls, the two eldest sixteen and fourteen . . . an awful legacy for a mother to bequeath" (36). No wonder Sir Walter has been so much at sea all these years.

Lady Elliot's "legacy" points, in turn, to another aspect of widowhood, one that will assume increasing importance as the novel goes on: how the survivors adjust their relations with one another in the wake of their bereavement, how the family circle reforms itself without its lost link. In the case of the Elliots, not surprisingly, it does not do so terribly well: Lady Russell and Elizabeth each inherit a share of Lady Elliot's role, but Anne is cut out almost entirely. Hence, another aspect of widowhood: with the loss of the loved one come other losses. In Anne's case, these include more or less her entire family. She finally gets a family back only when she finds other people more generous in adjusting to bereavement. After Fanny Harville's death, the young woman's brother and sister-in-law reconstitute their family so as to include Fanny's bereaved fiancé, and notwithstanding Benwick's later departure for Uppercross, the three of them become the nucleus of the extended family that both Wentworth and Anne eventually join.

But long before that, Anne has suffered other losses, other changes. Her mother's death also bereaves her of her home, for she is immediately sent packing to a Bath boarding school for three years, a period of her life she looks back on with something less than fondness. Far more importantly, it is an open question as to whether this first bereavement does not also lead to her next. Would Lady Elliot, "sensible and amiable," have opposed her daughter's marriage to Wentworth, as the somewhat less sensible, because blinded by pride, and decidedly less amiable Lady Russell does (36)? And does Anne yield to Lady Russell's persuasion out of a sense of duty to her dead mother that she can express only through unwavering obedience to her surrogate? Certainly we can see how one widowing rehearses her for the next, each of them isolating her further from those around her, each settling into an unbudgeable despondency.

Anne's grief over Wentworth, however, differs from the Giaour's in one important respect. "[T]ime had softened down much, perhaps nearly all of peculiar attachment to him" (57). In other words, she thinks she's gotten over him. But "down" is exactly where her feelings for him have gone, as she discovers when he returns and they come back up. Austen marshals a new range of Byronic imagery in exploring this aspect of bereavement (memory both mental and physical, and its capacity to astonish and overwhelm), imagery the thrust of which we will be better equipped to understand after examining a different character's act of mourning, albeit one that is generally read as Austen's picture of the wrong way to remember the dead.

The scenes in question are those in which Mrs. Musgrove remembers "poor Richard." On the surface, Austen's only purpose in raising the subject of this long-forgotten son is to ridicule everything connected with him: the boy himself, the selective memory his mother displays in grieving for him so demonstratively after all these years, even the fact that Mrs. Musgrove, as she grieves, is overweight. More than one critic has deplored Austen's infamous gibe at her "large fat sighings," and Austen herself seems to have been ashamed of this breach of decorum, following it with a paragraph of not-very-convincing justification (92).[9] Yet she had been scarcely less excessive, some pages earlier, in heaping scorn on poor Richard himself, essentially declaring that some people are better off dead and do not deserve being mourned for.[10] But these very excesses suggest that something deeper is going on, for it is always Austen's tendency to lose her otherwise fabulous poise when the artist in her has stirred up feelings of which the critic in her disapproves. We see this tendency at work especially in *Sense and Sensibility*, the novel in which she seems most at odds with herself—esteem for Elinor struggling with love for Marianne—as she frequently puts her thumb on Elinor's side of the moral scale, invariably sounding shrill and school-marmish as she does so.

So it is here. There is something powerful about Mrs. Musgrove's grief, something the narrator feels compelled to suppress. We can begin to understand it by noting that poor Richard comes up in conversation just after Wentworth has been talking about his first command, a ship that, as he twice says and a third time implies, almost caused him to "go to the bottom" of the sea (89, 90).[11] Now the sea is not only a crucial and multivalent image in *Persuasion*, it is also the very central, the ubiquitous image in the Turkish Tales.[12] Among other things, it is the home of the dead, the place where both Leila in *The Giaour* and Selim in *The Bride of Abydos* are buried. Leila's burial—burial alive—is pictured in particularly rich detail; of the sack that contains her, recalling how it slipped from view, the fisherman says that "all its hidden secrets sleep, / Known but to Genii of the deep" (ll. 384–385). Such a grave would have been Wentworth's had he "gone to the bottom," and implicitly, such a grave is Richard's, lost some years after he had been "sent to sea" (76).

But if the sea in Byron is a tomb full of hidden, sleeping secrets, so is something else. Says the Giaour: "My memory now is but the tomb / Of joys long dead" (ll. 1000–1001). Memory as a sea: it is at the bottom of that grave, too, that Richard has been lying—hidden, secret, asleep. For it is important to remember that Mrs. Musgrove does not habitually sentimentalize him, does not even voluntarily remember him on this occasion. Instead, in "one of those extraordinary bursts of mind which do sometimes occur," she was "suddenly struck, this very day, with a recollection of the name of Wentworth," and thus also, as a result, with a recollection of her son (77). With Wentworth's return, in other words, her son bursts up at her out of the depths of memory. Her grief may be greater than it was upon first hearing of his death, but it is not therefore the less genuine. That grief can grow rather than diminish through time and forgetfulness, that a chance event can startle it back into consciousness with all its original freshness and more than its original strength, is, after all, the central insight of Wordsworth's "Two April Mornings." Yes, Mrs. Musgrove has forgotten Richard's faults, has even forgotten that she used to call him "Dick"; time has worked a sea change on memory and feeling alike, and even the boy's name has been transformed by its pressure. But the moral of *Persuasion*, after all, is that it's never as good as the second time.

What is more, between the first time Richard is mentioned and the scene in which we watch his mother remember him, a similar and far more important act of memory has taken place.[13] We already examined this scene in chapter 2; it is the one in which Anne's feelings for Wentworth—feelings more powerful, in some respects, than those she had felt eight years earlier—burst up at her out of the depths of her memory (the depths, it seems, of her very body), shocking her out of her Giaour-like stasis. The mere sound of Wentworth's name sends the blood to her cheeks; with his approach, "a thousand feelings rushed on Anne"; and his actual appearance renders her scarcely able to hear, see, or eat (84). Her mind tries to reason down her body's insurrection: "How absurd to be resuming the agitation which such an interval had banished into distance and indistinctness!" (85).

But Anne learns that time is not a road one traverses, leaving the past behind in the distance, it is a sea on which one precariously floats: "Alas! with all her reasonings, she found, that to retentive feelings eight years may be little more than nothing." The perception echoes that of the fisherman (himself a traveler over time and the sea) as he watches the Giaour, standing on shore, lose himself in recollection: " 'Twas but a moment that he stood / . . . / But in that instant o'er his soul / Winters of Memory seemed to roll, / And gather in that drop of time / A life of pain" (ll. 259–264). The present moment may be only a drop, but memory contains the whole ocean of time. And it is from out of that ocean of memory that Anne and Wentworth will ultimately conduct their salvage operation, their resurrection of feeling. But not quite yet, for not everyone's feelings have yet resurfaced: "You were so altered," Mary tells her sister, that "he should not have known you again" (85). Sea changes, after all, are not always for the better, and our heroine knows it: "Anne fully submitted, in silent, deep mortification." Silent, deep: Anne, or at least his feelings for her, still slumbers at the bottom of the sea of Wentworth's memory. She remains in a state of "mortification," dead to him.

Having examined Mrs. Musgrove's style of mourning, we should look at Captain Benwick's, for his is also almost universally regarded as a negative example. A jaundiced view says that his very indulgence in grief and great show of bereavement foretell his rapid inconstancy—that if he had felt more, he would have displayed less and been more true. But this view ignores Anne's own response to her fellow mourner. Yes, she later joins Captain Harville in deploring the rapidity with which Benwick gets reengaged, but she not only recognizes the genuineness of his grief, she had encouraged him to overcome it and had foreseen, with envy rather than condemnation, that he would. "I cannot believe his prospects so blighted forever," she thinks to herself. "He is younger than I am; younger in feeling, if not in fact; younger as a man. He will rally again, and be happy with another" (119). Anne recognizes that it is the very strength of Benwick's passion—the passion of a younger person, in her understanding, and of a man (for elsewhere she avows, whatever we may think of such a judgment, that men's "feelings may be [i.e., are] the strongest" [236])—not its superficiality, that insures that he will soon fall in love again. And she also helps bring that eventuality to pass, not only by "recommend[ing] a larger allowance of prose in his daily study" and supplying the requisite syllabus (122), but much more importantly, by becoming the first woman to arouse his interest since Fanny's death (for there can be little doubt, as Charles Musgrove sees, that she does so). Once those feelings have put forth their first tentative shoots, it is only a matter of time before they come to full flower.

I use a vegetative metaphor here because Austen does ("I cannot believe his prospects so blighted forever"), and in so doing points to the logic that underlies the whole question of widowhood in *Persuasion*—that underlies, indeed, the entire novel: structurally, imagistically, ethically. It is the logic of nature. Mourning, for Austen, is a natural process, with its own cycle of birth, growth, aging, and death. The idea both picks up Byronic language and inverts its logic. The Giaour declares himself "a scattered leaf, / Seared by the autumn blast of Grief!" (ll. 1255–1256), but Austen knows that every autumn is followed by a spring. That is why Anne can call Benwick, as someone recently bereaved, a "young mourner" (128),[14] and it gives a sense to the six-month period of his mourning, born in summer, dying in winter.[15] The mourning that violates nature—the mourning that, if we come to *Persuasion* looking for pictures of right and wrong ways to handle grief, is certainly not the model Austen would have us choose—is Anne's. The narrator makes it clear that her grief at the loss of Wentworth was badly mishandled;

had she been given a proper change of scenery, she would have been able to form a "second attachment, the only thoroughly natural, happy, and sufficient cure, at her time of life" (57). "Natural" is the cardinal adjective here, making possible both happiness and health.

In fact, the theme of sterility, of a violation of nature through the refusal of natural forms of continuity, underlies the entire initial presentation of the Elliot family.[16] It is a presentation that, while demonstrating that Anne has yet to break out of the family pattern of Byronic psychic arrest, differentiates her from her father and elder sister and foretells the later course of her story by placing her on the side of natural growth and decay. Sir Walter's resistance to the aging process, his and others', needs little emphasis. This is someone who thinks that sailors should be "knocked on the head" before their fortieth birthday, so much does their profession age them (50). Nor is his eldest daughter any less disconnected from natural processes of change—"still the same" Elizabeth, "as blooming as ever," her seasons those of the social rather than the natural calendar, her springs those of London rather than the country, and as if perpetually nipped in the bud, only ever a few weeks long (38).[17]

I noted before that Sir Walter is a man of mirrors, his unchanging image endlessly repeated without change, and we may note further that "[v]anity was the beginning and the end of Sir Walter Elliot's character" (36). Its beginning is vanity, in other words, and its end is vanity, and from one end to the other, his character is all unchanging vanity. The novel's opening lines tell us, emblematically, of his contempt for "the almost endless creations of the last century" (35). Creation of any kind, let alone almost endless creation, is Sir Walter's abhorrence. This is the man who wants to preserve his "pleasure-grounds"—preserve their virginity, as it were—from Admiral Crawford's violation (48), and it is a fine irony to have him noticing—in the course of complaining about how old everyone else is "growing" (38)—"the rapid increase" of crow's feet on Lady Russell's temples, as if the deplorable procreative habits of natural creatures were leaving their disfiguring marks everywhere. Sir Walter is a kind of Lord of Sterility, letting copulation die everywhere in the Elliot kingdom. The marriage of his heir, William Walter Elliot, produced no children, and though that of Mrs. Clay produced two, they remain absent and unthought of, essentially erased, for the length of the novel. Even when Elliots do beget, virtually all they can do is repeat themselves. Mary and Elizabeth descend from the long line of "all the Marys and Elizabeths [the Elliot men] had married" (35). The latest Mary, daughter of Walter, marries Charles, son of Charles, and gives birth to one Walter and one Charles. As for Elizabeth, daughter of Elizabeth, her father is delighted to find her "very like himself" (37).

But this vision of continuity as unchanging repetition is precisely what Sir Walter's notion of family entails. As I noted in chapter 2, "family" to him means the Elliot lineage, the unbroken line of eldest sons, and his vision for it is that "[t]he Kellynch estate should be transmitted whole and entire" from generation to generation—the legalistic doubling of adjectives reinforcing the notion of repetition without change (41). This vision is threatened when Sir Walter runs into debt, eating up more then he produces, and the various characters' plans to address the situation exhibit the novel's competing ideas of continuity. Some "retrenchment" is required (we hear the word in one form or another nearly half a dozen times), but while Lady Russell argues for "reductions" and "regulations"—the same style of living, only less of it—Anne hopes for a thorough "reformation"—continuity, yes, but with change. In the event, Sir Walter rejects even Lady Russell's proposals as necessitating intolerable "restrictions," and is forced to accept his lawyer's alternative, "removal" from Kellynch altogether (42–46). As the linguistic pattern suggests, the issue is what kind of "re-ing," of doing again, will enable Sir Walter to redeem himself. We are reminded, once more, that *Persuasion* is a novel of second times.

Anne herself, stuck in a state of mourning though she may be, is the exception to this principle of sterile repetition. Literally the exception: the one Anne, the one variation, that slips in to the production line of Marys and Elizabeths. And while her father may be seen to repeat in her elder sister, in Anne, Lady Russell imagines, her mother "revives" (37). In a novel of deaths and widows, that word carries enormous thematic importance. Lady Elliot lives again in Anne, but to live again is not to live the same way and assume the same form as one had the first time—any more than to grieve again, as Mrs. Musgrove knows, or to fall in love again, as Anne and Wentworth will learn, is to do so the same way one had before. It is telling that Sir Walter, so quick to see Elizabeth's near-identity with himself, completely misses Anne's subtler continuity with his wife. And Austen plays a marvelous linguistic trick around this circumstance. To Sir Walter, Anne is "only Anne," but two sentences later, it is "only in Anne" that Lady Russell can imagine Lady Elliot's revival (37). "Only Anne . . . only in Anne": the phrase, modulating from a context of sterile mechanical repetition to one of procreative natural renewal, becomes pregnant, gets an "in" in it, becomes big with inner possibility.

The novel's and its heroine's attentiveness to nature have been widely commented on, especially with respect to the question of whether *Persuasion* is or is not a "Romantic" novel, but the presence of nature in its pages goes far deeper than a few walks in the grass.[18] The natural world forms the deepest stratum of its imagery, and the natural—not the moral or the Christian as such—provides its normative standards. Nature imagery clusters around Anne in particular. Her loss and retrieval of "bloom"—the possibility that she will enjoy a "second spring" (139)—is, of course, at constant issue. Her disappointment over Wentworth "cloud[s] every enjoyment of youth" (57). Moving to Uppercross, she thinks of herself as being "transplanted," and she eventually learns that she has never been "supplanted" in Wentworth's affections (70, 243). But such imagery does not attach to her alone, and Austen sometimes goes out of her way to make her use of the natural register too obvious to miss. To the scheme of the Elliots' quitting Kellynch, an additional aspect of the plan, the renting of the estate, becomes "engrafted" (45). In a novel in which the social fabric is so clearly fraying, and in which the heroine in particular is largely isolated from the social world, characters are repeatedly set against the kind of monumental natural backdrops—vast meadows, the sea—that mark them as natural creatures rather than social actors. The town of Bath, by contrast, is represented as a place of spiritual oppression and false values.

Of course, this is precisely the way Byron and Scott place their figures in the Tales and the romances—figures whose free and passionate existence draws its energy from, and gives them a creaturely intimacy with, the Greek seas and Scottish mountains, in pointed contradistinction to the stifling confines of Turkish and Scottish courts. (It is no coincidence, as has been widely noted, that English landscape painting was entering its golden age at just this time.) For no one in *Persuasion* is this fact of creatureliness more pronounced than for Anne, as her intense sympathy with the natural world suggests. It is, after all, a "fine wind," not Gowland's lotion, that first restores to her "the bloom and freshness of youth" (125). Perhaps no statement about her is more important than the one in which the narrator sums up the history of her aborted engagement and its aftermath: "She had been forced into prudence in her youth, she learned romance as she grew older—the natural sequel of an unnatural beginning" (58). Anne's troubles begin in a denial of nature, and it is a reembrace of nature that cures them. When the imperatives of the social world run contrary to nature—and they do so here under the aegis of an unnatural, a social, mother—those imperatives are void. Anne's story can be seen as that of a young woman, forced out of her natural patterns of growth, being reclaimed by Mother Nature as her own.

Nature furnishes the novel's main set of images and is the source of its ethical norms, and it also provides the template for an entire system of processes that structure its action. The chief of these is widowhood itself—the process of bereavement and the overcoming of bereavement—as we have already seen in the cases of Benwick and, as yet largely as a negative example, Anne. Mourning, as we said, is for Austen a cyclical natural process: birth, growth, decay, death. But parallel to that process, amplifying and universalizing it, Austen constructs an entire array of others, each implicitly echoing one another and all of them ultimately echoing the cycle of the seasons. Actually, it will be simpler and more accurate to think of these processes as comprising not four stages, but two: growth and decay. This is in part because the initiation of a given process, its "birth," is often incidental, and in part because these processes do not always reach their termination—a fact that, as I will discuss later, assumes enormous importance. Finally, because these processes all begin negatively, it will make more sense to think of their two stages not as growth and decay, but—thinking of widowhood again—as loss and recovery. In terms of the natural cycle, it is simply a matter of starting at a different point: autumn, as the novel's main action itself does, rather than spring.

The most visible of these parallel processes, and the one most commented upon in the critical literature, is illness and recovery.[19] The number of the ill or injured in *Persuasion* nearly matches the number of bereaved: Louisa, of course; Mary, with her sore throats; her son Charles, with his dislocated collarbone; Anne herself, whose sister's family gives her a headache; Sir Walter, whose illness at the time of Viscount Dalrymple's death led to his estrangement from the Viscountess; Richard Musgrove, left ill at Gibraltar; Dr. Shirley, the aging vicar whose curate Charles Hayter hopes to become, taken ill two springs back; Captain Harville, wounded in battle; the gouty Admiral Crawford; his wife, who develops a blister accompanying him on his medicinal walks; the invalid Mrs. Smith; and even, by the days' lights, Mrs. Cornwallis, in the final stages of her confinement. In almost every case, we watch or learn of the entire process of illness and convalescence, and are taught to think of it as a cycle, a complete two-stage process, a worsening and an improving—an autumn and a spring, a loss and a recovery. It is no wonder that the novel is also so well stocked with nurses: Anne herself; Mrs. Harville; her nurserymaid; the Musgroves' old nurse Sarah, who now lives to "dress all the blains and bruises she could get near" (137); and of course, the well-informed and intriguing Nurse Rooke. Indeed, much of the action in the first half of the novel revolves around the increasingly serious illnesses or injuries and increasingly protracted recoveries first of Mary, then of her son, then of Louisa.

Of equal structural and thematic importance is the process of losing and finding a home.[20] The Elliots' loss of a home incites the novel's action—or rather, their loss of a house, for it is Anne alone who feels the surrender of Kellynch as the loss of home, and who wanders homeless from Uppercross to Lyme to Kellynch-lodge to Bath in search of the home she has lost. Her quest parallels—with beautiful aptness, given whom she finally marries—that of the nation's naval officers after the peace, for "[t]hey will all be wanting"— note the exact choice of words—"a home" (47). Once ashore, Wentworth also wanders from home to home, until he and Anne find one in each other. But where and what is it to be? The suitability of naval ships to provide a home is explicitly discussed, but more fundamentally, the novel constitutes an extended exploration of the nature and meaning of home, an essay in comparative domesticity. Nowhere else in Austen's work do the appearance and atmosphere of different domestic settings receive so much emphasis: the boisterous joviality of Uppercross, the coldness of the Elliot lodgings at Bath, the greater fitness of the Crawfords than the Elliots as caretakers of Kellynch, and, most emphatically of all, the Harville lodgings in Lyme, with their lovingly described "ingenious contrivances and nice arrangements" making for a "picture of repose and domestic happiness" (119–120).

In a novel in which homes are so easily lost (by spendthrift baronets and naval officers alike), the ability to make a home away from home becomes a leading mark of character. Mary is conspicuously unable to make a home, or even feel at home, in her new home at Uppercross; she is, as she readily admits, "of no use at home" (82). Anne, by contrast, with her "domestic habits" (57), is justly matched to a member of "that profession which is, if possible, more distinguished in its domestic virtues than in its national importance" (254). But if domesticity is a high virtue in such a world, hospitality is an even higher one. Early on, Anne deplores the Musgrove habit of having to include everyone in whatever anyone is doing, but as the novel unfolds, she— or Austen—learns to love a home where everyone is always welcome, even if things get a little loud. The novel's elect are not the Elliots, with their careful doling out of invitations, but the Harvilles, who "invite from the heart" (119).

The loss and recovery of home is related, not just analogously but also in terms of cause and effect, to an array of subsidiary processes, each of which also represents some form of loss and recovery. The most important of these is exile, or, in the novel's language, "removal." Just as the idea of place is related but not identical to that of home, as we saw in chapter 2, so too are their losses to each other. Naval service constitutes a kind of continual exile from England, as Wentworth's stories of his cruises remind us, and just as that service provides *Persuasion*'s standing symbol of homelessness, so must the novel's other instances of exile be understood in relation to it.

Anne's experience again parallels that of the man she will marry, for she suffers removals after each of her widowings, both times to Bath: after the death of her mother, those three years in boarding school; after her disappointment with Wentworth, a visit with Lady Russell, one during which, as we are told in the kind of savagely bleak understatement Austen employs in the novel's opening chapters, she "happen[ed] to be not in perfectly good spirits" (45). Both removals prefigure her exile in Bath throughout the second half of the novel. Her earlier exiles, like Wentworth's exiles at sea, receive their eventual "springs" of return, but it is not at all certain, despite the hope that Sir Walter will someday clear his debts, that this one ever will. Anne eventually shares her exile with the entire cast of characters, and one might even say that the novel itself goes into exile—or rather, that Austen's entire oeuvre does, an exile that continues in *Sanditon*, a removal from the country estate that (save for her own youthful excursion to Bath in *Northanger Abbey*) is the only world Austen's art has ever really known, and certainly the only one it has ever valued. Austen points her prow to sea and, like Childe Harold, bids her native shore adieu. A beloved place, a beloved England, has been taken leave of—a point I shall return to below.

Mention of Sir Walter's financial troubles alerts us to indebtedness and repayment as another parallel process. A number of Austen's novels include characters who get into debt, as both Willoughby and Wickham do; what entitles us to think of Sir Walter's indebtedness in the way I have outlined is, again, that it is presented as a development that unfolds over time, reaches a nadir (a winter solstice or symbolic death,[21] in this case the crisis that forces him to surrender Kellynch, though in other instances, as we have seen, the crisis can prolong itself into an extended winter of stasis), and finally turns back toward regeneration (in this case, repayment). Akin in content to Sir Walter's financial troubles but in structure more like Anne's bereavements is Mrs. Smith's long gloom of impoverishment, one that is finally redressed through a process of reenrichment.

More immediately related to the cycles of homelessness and exile we were just examining is that of desertion and repopulation. We are told that the Musgroves' nurserymaid dwells in a "deserted nursery"—one that is sure to be repopulated sooner or later—just one page before we see Anne wandering through a Musgrove manor-house that has itself suddenly become deserted (137). And only a few pages after that, once the Musgroves have returned from Lyme, we have Anne, thinking back to that solitary ramble, feeling "that Uppercross was already quite alive again" (148). As that leave-taking shows, exile and return, desertion and repopulation, are also related to isolation and companionship (or resocialization, for lack of a better word—the process of rejoining or being rejoined by others), a process whose systole and diastole make themselves felt throughout Anne's story.

Related in turn is the cycle of parting and reunion, so important to Anne's relationship with Mrs. Smith—and, one might say, with Wentworth, but for that relationship a stronger pair of terms is required: estrangement ("alien-ation," in the novel's language) and reconciliation. It is a process widely dispersed throughout the novel, not only on a small scale in the doings at Uppercross—Charles and Mary Musgrove, Henrietta Musgrove and Charles Hayter, the Cottage and the Great House—but more importantly, in the long-term affairs of the Elliots. Just as the characters' comings and goings in the first half of the novel are largely governed by the cycle of illness and convalescence, so is much narrative energy focused in the second half around Sir Walter's reconciliation, first with William Walter Elliot, then with the Dowager Viscountess Dalrymple. These breakings and reforgings of the Elliot family links may not ultimately matter much to Anne and Wentworth, but they amplify the lovers' own process of rupture and repair, figuring it as a cyclical phenomenon parallel with others and ultimately with the deepest movements of nature.

Finally, Austen works her master pattern of decline and recovery, down and up, into the narrative at the most elementary, physical level, as if to emphasize its fundamentality and drive home its ubiquity. Everywhere in *Persuasion* we find characters literally descending and ascending, be it hills, stairs, or walls—an image-pattern that echoes *The Giaour*'s own landscape, literal and metaphorical, of highs and lows. Hills form an essential part of the topography of all three of the novel's major settings: Uppercross, Lyme, and Bath. The culminating scene at Uppercross is a walk that, as we are frequently reminded, takes the party down and up a series of hills and that itself culminates at "the summit of the most considerable" (108). Just a few pages later, Lyme is introduced with a long (and in Austen, unique) disquisition on its cliffs and the cliffs and chasms of its neighboring villages. The narrative of the characters' arrival and stay in the town makes us continually aware of the fall of the land there—"the long hill into Lyme" (116), "the still steeper street of the town itself" (116), "walk directly down to the sea" (117), "the steps, leading upwards" (124), "as far up the hill as they could" (126)—and that of Anne's return journey to Uppercross is marked by a similar consciousness—"the same hills and the same objects," "going up their last hill"

(136). The same may be said of the chapters in Bath. It is always: "the lower part of the town" (179), "ascending Belmont" (181), "returning down Pulteney-street" (188), "as high as Belmont" (242), "at the bottom of Union-street" (243).

Not all of the novel's descents are voluntary. Little Charles's injury is the result of a fall; Wentworth praises his famous nut for having clung to its high perch "while so many of its brethren have fallen" (110); and even the cliff at Pinney has experienced a "partial falling"—height itself tumbling down (117). But of course, the most important of the novel's falling bodies is Louisa's, the imagery of descent and ascent reaching its apogee of importance at the novel's very pivot-point. Indeed, Louisa's fall is an event that, with her repeated climbings and jumpings, possesses an emblematic significance. What goes up must come down, but by the same token, what goes down eventually comes back up—just as (the pun is inevitable) the season of "spring" inevitably succeeds that of "fall."[22]

But our account of things that fall and rise is not yet complete, and extending it will enable us to see the full complexity and essential unity of the system of parallel cyclic processes around which Austen structures the novel. Two other things that fall and rise are Anne's bloom—no longer, at the novel's outset, at its "height" (37)—and her spirits—after her mother's death, "not high" (165). These are not incidental things, but rather the essential indices, respectively, of the heroine's physical and mental health; as such, their risings and fallings are of persistent concern. And in this novel in which depression is so frequent a psychological peril, the height or depth of other characters' spirits—Louisa's, Benwick's, Mrs. Smith's—is also a matter of frequent comment.

But of course, bloom and spirits rise and fall only metaphorically. These examples show that the novel's many down-and-up processes are not merely analogous, they are mutually interlinked and ultimately mutually identified. The interlinkages are made through metonymy, the identifications through metaphor. The former include the fact that Sir Walter's homelessness is a result of his indebtedness; that his estrangement from the Viscountess is a consequence of his illness; that Mrs. Smith's invalidism is exacerbated by her poverty, in turn a product of her widowhood; that Anne's exiles are consequent on her bereavements; and—a particularly subtle example—that the return of her bloom first becomes apparent as she climbs the stairs from the beach at Lyme. The causal relationships we noted earlier among the processes of homelessness, exile, desertion, isolation, and so forth are also instances of such interlinkages.

The many metaphoric identifications Austen weaves into the novel's linguistic texture include, of course, the very term "bloom" itself. We also find the Musgrove sisters in a "fever of admiration" for Wentworth (105), Anne likening his possible estrangement from Benwick to the "wound[ing]" of their friendship (183), and, as we noted, the fumbled possibility of a "cure" for her loss of the man she loves (57). Illness and injury are indeed, like the natural world itself, among the most common sources of metaphors for other processes; one of Austen's slyest involves the fact that the injury little Charles sustains is a "dislocation"—the very "injury" that universally afflicts the novel's cast of homeless exiles.

We began this chapter by noting that Austen extends the idea of widowhood to include other forms of bereavement; we have seen by now that she ultimately expands it into something in fact far vaster. Widowhood in *Persuasion* becomes the central metaphor for a great array of losses, bereavement and mourning the template for the process of loss and recovery as such. It is a process, as we have seen, that is understood as essentially natural, so that the novel's archetype of the healthy response to loss is the farmer whose presence Anne discerns as the party ascends the final hill during that long walk at Uppercross, the one who has been plowing his fields in the face of the oncoming winter, "meaning to have spring again" (108).

And yet the novel is shadowed from the start by a knowledge of that other natural process, the one form of loss that cannot turn back toward recovery: death itself. Nature as whole may return to life, but natural creatures do not. Two deaths mark the Eliot family in the novel's opening two pages, that of Sir Walter's stillborn son and heir, and that, as we have seen, of his wife. Lady Eliot, we might say, is widowed of life itself, a bereavement from which there is no recovery. So while we have been able to see, with the advantage of hindsight, that the novel's many down-and-up processes ultimately bend back toward "spring," the characters who must endure them, unable to see beyond the present moment, have no such reassuring perspective. Just as it does to the Giaour, loss, to them, feels like death. That is why so many of the novel's metaphors for loss are drawn from the language of death. Anne, as we have seen, submits to Wentworth's judgment on her loss of bloom in silent "mortification" (85, and see also 135). Charles Hayter, bereft of Henrietta, is in danger of "studying himself to death" (105). Wentworth, in his note to Anne, speaks of the end of love as a "death" (240). And not only does Louisa look dead after her fall, so does Wentworth, his face "as pallid as her own" (129). The novel's pivotal event is a symbolic death, as if to reinforce the idea that mortality lurks in every loss, and that every loss is an image of mortality.

A symbolic death, at the novel's center, followed by a symbolic resurrection—a falling to the bottom followed by a raising up. That is also the story of Anne and Wentworth's love; it is no accident that their reunion is figured as a resurrection. Not only, as we have seen, do Anne's feelings for Wentworth resurface out of the depths of her memory. He had been prevented from proposing sooner, he later tells her, because a knowledge of her true character had been "overwhelmed, buried, lost" beneath his feelings of bitterness (246). She had been lying at the bottom of his consciousness—silent, deep, mortified—just as he had been lying at the bottom of hers. Anne and Wentworth recover the future by recovering the past, move forward by moving backward, an idea that pervades the scene in which the two are finally reunited. Not only do they literally walk uphill, "slowly pacing the gradual ascent," as they repeat their vows and avowals; as they do so—the syntax makes the two journeys exactly parallel—they "retur[n] again into the past" (243). The logic of the novel's accumulated imagery could not be clearer: Anne and Wentworth's "many, many years of division and estrangement" are a long downward slope that memory now allows them to reascend.

The past is recaptured, but as always, it has suffered a sea change. As Lady Elliot had "revived" in, not been mechanically repeated by, Anne, so Wentworth now experiences a "revival" of his attachment for his beloved (245). It's never as good as the second time: Anne and Wentworth are now "more exquisitely happy . . . more tender, more tried, more fixed in a knowledge of each other's character, truth, and attachment" than they had been eight years before (243). Nor will memory resurrect the past only; in a novel about death and some dozen analogues for death, recollection will also bestow upon this climactic "present hour" nothing less than "immortality." "[O]f yesterday and to-day," we are told of Anne and Wentworth's retellings of the preceding week's events, "there could scarcely be an end." Past and present are brought forward together, immortal, into the future. Finally, as the scene closes, we read that "[a]t last Anne was at home again" (247). Home—the home she had lost, not half a year before, but eight and a half before—is both Wentworth and the past, the underworld or underwater world into which, Orpheus-like, she had had to descend to retrieve him.

We might pause for a moment to ponder more deeply one of the phrases I just quoted. Austen tells us that Anne and Wentworth, in their reminiscences, "returned again" into the past. The redundancy might mean nothing, or it might be an index of overflowing feeling, but a different passage suggests that something more may be intended. Austen's description of the cliffs and chasms of Lyme and its vicinity constitutes the only passage in her work that seems wholly gratuitous—reason enough to suspect that it is not. The topography of course prepares us for the heights and depths, the fallings and risings, that will be experienced at the place, but the whole momentum of the passage has the effect of propelling us, like the characters themselves—"descending the long hill into Lyme . . . entering upon the still steeper street of the town itself . . . passing down . . . and still descending"—to the sea (ll. 116–117).

Given the sea's symbolic importance in the novel, this passage down to it is no incidental event, and the narrator herself calls our attention, obliquely, to its importance: "The party from Uppercross . . . soon found themselves on the sea shore . . . lingering . . . as all must linger and gaze on a first return to the sea, who ever deserve to look on it at all." Only those who recognize the power of the sea, in all its meanings, deserve to look—to read—at all. But why "first return"—an apparent oxymoron that closely anticipates "returned again"? Doesn't the narrator mean "first visit"? Or is that first visit itself a return—as it is if the sea is the past, but as it is anyway if one understands Austen to have a national rather than a personal bearing in mind. England is an island; the English people perforce came from across the sea, so that any visit to the sea is necessarily a return.

That it is appropriate to read this larger dimension into the passage—that such ideas are close to the novel's mind, that the sea is paid homage to here not just for reasons of natural beauty or symbolic importance, but also because of its role in the life of the nation—is an argument to which I will return in a moment. For now, let us note that the logic that makes a first visit into a return picks up language from earlier in the passage, where the narrator had declared that the wonderful and lovely places she has just enumerated "must be visited, and visited again, to make the worth of Lyme understood" (117). No single visit, no matter how extensive, no single experience, is sufficient for understanding. True knowledge, for us as for Anne and Wentworth (and as, for that matter, for Wordsworth[23]), is a product of layered associations, a function of seeing with the eyes of memory as well as of the body. It is not that a first visit is a return, but that only a return is a true visit. Understanding, like the landscape of England itself—for "many a generation must have passed away since the first partial falling of the cliff"— is a work of time. Anne and Wentworth return again to the past, and they will continue to return to it again and again.

Yet for all that Anne and Wentworth's reunion strikes so many of the novel's most prominent imagistic and symbolic chords, it fails to strike the one that is most obvious and most easily struck. The novel's main action begins in autumn, and given its underlying seasonal logic, nothing would have made more sense than for Austen to have set its climactic events in spring. Instead she sets them in late winter—February, to be exact.[24] Why? To answer this question is to reveal an entirely new range of reference and meaning, that national and historical dimension I just alluded to, one that, for all that recent criticism has done to uncover the extent to which Austen's novels engage contemporaneous social and political debates, is still largely regarded as beyond her interest and even her grasp.

Persuasion begins in the aftermath of Napoleon's surrender in the spring of 1814, and although she leaves the exact dates somewhat vague, she runs its concluding events right up to the end of the following February.[25] Now the very end of February 1815 is the exact time of Napoleon's flight from Elba—he escaped from the island on February 26 and landed on the mainland on March 1.[26] Subtly, covertly, without announcing as much, Austen makes the events of the novel coincide precisely with the period of Napoleon's first exile. To put it differently, *Persuasion* is a novel that takes place in the shadow of Napoleon's return—the shadow of Waterloo.

Lest anyone doubt that Waterloo was at the forefront of Austen's mind as she wrote the novel, we have only to consult her letters. Prior to 1815, her engagement with the war seems to have been minimal. In May 1811, we find her responding to news of the Battle of Albuera with, "How horrible it is to have so many people killed!—And what a blessing that one cares for none of them!"[27] In October 1813, in the midst of Napoleon's collapse, she writes, "I am tired of lives of Nelson, being that I never read any. I will read this [Southey's] however, if Frank is mentioned in it."[28] But in November 1815 we find her thanking her publisher, John Murray, for sending, at her request, a copy of Scott's *Field of Waterloo*, and in the letter that accompanies her return of that volume three weeks later, she is asking—"supposing you have any set already opened"—for *Paul's Letter to His Kinfolk*, which gives the same author's impressions of conditions in France in the wake of Waterloo and includes a detailed account of that battle.[29] In her very next letter, she happily reports that Murray has supplied not only the Scott, but also Helen Maria Williams's *Narrative of the events which have taken place in France, from the landing of Napoleon Bonaparte on the first of March, 1815, till the restoration of Louis XVIII*. More than a year later, her appetite is still keen: "We have been reading the 'Poet's Pilgrimage to Waterloo' "—by Southey, an author she does not ordinarily like very much—"& generally with much approbation."[30]

But surely the most telling evidence that Austen was obsessed with the final acts of Napoleon's drama is the fact, mentioned in chapter 1, that she took the trouble to copy out Byron's dramatic monologue "Napoleon's Farewell"—even making a few modifications as she did so, as if to turn the poem into a statement of her own—when it first appeared in periodical form on July 30, 1815. (On July 24—the event that clearly inspired the poem—the British warship on which Napoleon was imprisoned had "arrived off the English coast and tourists flocked out to see the fallen Emperor."[31]) *Persuasion* was begun nine days later.[32]

So while there are symbolic implications to *Persuasion*'s failure to reach its promised spring, as I will discuss below, the first ramification of its chronology is to synchronize the novel's personal drama of loss and love with the national drama of war and peace. And it is here that we begin to see the relevance of Scott. I noted before that the overriding theme of his verse romances, as it is that of the Turkish Tales, is survival after loss. In Scott's case, that means, first and foremost, national survival and national loss. Those themes are only residually present in the main plots of *Marmion* and *The Lady of the Lake*, the two romances *Persuasion* mentions by name, but it is a conspicuous fact about these works—as well as about the one that precedes them, *The Lay of the Last Minstrel* (the three together comprising the first and most celebrated of Scott's half-dozen efforts in the form)—that their framing devices are as important as the stories themselves. The six cantos of *Marmion*, for example, are each prefaced by lengthy introductions that together account for some one-fourth of the entire work.

The purpose of these frames, as is often the case, is to give the poet an opportunity to reflect upon both the story and his telling of it. The frames, in other words, tell the story of the story. And the story of the story is, in each case, the story of the senescence of Scottish literary traditions and their laborious revival at the poet's own hands. This, of course, is always Scott's story, Scott's question: how can the past be restored—not relived, but remembered? How can the lost be recovered, the nation put in contact again with its own spirit? "Harp of the North!" (I.1), *The Lady of the Lake* begins:

> O wake once more! how rude soe'er the hand
> That ventures o'er thy magic maze to stray;
> O wake once more! though scarce my skill command
> Some feeble echoing of thine earlier lay.
>
> (I.19–22)

Marmion's sense of belatedness is everywhere implicit in the time of year at which each canto's introduction is set. Though Scott claims, in the fourth, that the composition of the poem has occupied more than a year, the five whose seasons are specified are all written in late autumn or early winter—the poet, looking about him, forever reflecting on scenes of desolation, and only the final introduction, set at Christmas, offering symbolic hope of "salvation" (VI.49). The same imagery continues in *The Lord of the Isles*—one of the later romances and the last to be published before Austen started work on *Persuasion*—which begins with an extended metaphor of the poet as still, even after autumn's departure, "a lonely gleaner" "Through fields time-wasted, on sad inquest bound, / Where happier bards of yore have richer harvest found" (I.34–36). Like Anne after her loss of Wentworth, traditional Scotland's spiritual date is a perpetual December.

But Scott's fullest embodiment of his sense of the state of Scottish cultural traditions and of his status relative to them is the authorial figure of the "last minstrel" himself, that founding image of Scott's vast corpus. "[I]nfirm and old" (I.2), without peers or progeny, he haltingly attempts a "long forgotten melody" that finally emerges after great effort (I.83).[33] As will be the case in Austen, memory is the vehicle of resurrection, and as selective as that faculty sometimes is in *Persuasion*, it is far more so when the survival of cultural rather than personal memories is at stake: "Each blank, in faithless memory void," we are told at the work's outset, "The poet's glowing thought supplied" (I.97–98). It is a striking acknowledgment on Scott's part: he will recover of his nation's legends and ballads as much as he can, but what he cannot recover, he will make up. Still, the poem communicates the sense of urgency that drives him to such expedients. When a poet dies, we are told:

> the stream, the wood, the gale,
> Is vocal with the plaintive wail
> Of those, who, else forgotten long,
> Liv'd in the poet's faithful song,
> And, with the poet's parting breath,
> Whose memory feels a second death.
> (V.ii.3–8)

As in *The Giaour*, the dead die a second time with the death of those who remember them. If Scott does not get his material down on paper now, it will be lost forever.

The relevance to *Persuasion* of this question of cultural memory will become clear below. For now, it is worth noting that the same issues of national death and resurrection are present throughout the Turkish Tales as well as *Childe Harold* I–II, published the year before the first of the Tales, except that in Byron the nation in question is not the poet's own, but his adopted one, Greece. The opening of *The Giaour*, as we saw, strikes this very note, with its description of the Greek shore as a corpse in the first moments after death: "'Tis Greece, but living Greece no more!" (l. 91). The land of ancient heroes, having descended into servility and dependence, exists, as it were, in a state of living death, and the poet calls upon his Greek contemporaries to revive it by honoring the memory of their forebears and rising up against the foreign oppressor:

These scenes, their story not unknown,
Arise, and make again your own;
Snatch from the ashes of your Sires
The embers of their former fires[.]
(ll. 104–107)

As in Scott, Byron's introductions tend to lengthen themselves into digressions that reveal the larger issues occupying the poet's mind—the stories that his stories are really about. Canto II of *Childe Harold* both begins and ends with extended lamentations over the ruins of ancient Greek glory. Canto II of *The Bride of Abydos* opens with a meditation on the Hellespont, the tale's setting, and thence on Troy—an implicit exhortation to present-day Greeks to emulate their ancestors' fabled defeat of an Asian power (just as the tale itself, like *The Giaour* and *The Corsair*, allegorically enacts a Greek assertion of freedom from the Turkish overlord). And Byron, like Scott, is also vexed by the problem of cultural memory, of keeping alive even the knowledge of ancient glory. Both *The Giaour* and *Childe Harold* elaborate a conceit the effect of which is that even if those who now inhabit the land of heroes have forgotten their sires along with their sires' virtues, and even if the very memorials of those virtues are now gone, the land itself remembers.[34] But at other moments—those when he laments the destruction of ancient monuments or bewails the fact that only visiting foreigners now recognize the places of glory—Byron implicitly acknowledges that the land cannot speak for itself, but only voice the words its beholders put in its mouth.

Memory, again, embodied in story, depends on the rememberer; the dead are invariably threatened with a second death. But as we saw at the start of the chapter, that is the theme not only of *The Giaour*'s framing meditation, but also of the poem itself. Byron juxtaposes there the questions of personal and national bereavement—loss, melancholy, memory, revival—and he does so again in *The Bride of Abydos*, implicitly in *The Corsair* (given the allegorical dimension I noted above), and also in *Childe Harold* II, which ends with an extended lamentation on an unnamed "more than friend" (II.xcvi.6) that immediately follows ("Thou too art gone, thou loved and lovely one!" [II.xcv.1]) his elegy on Greek glory.

And this juxtaposition is exactly what Austen accomplishes in *Persuasion* by synchronizing the personal story of Anne and Wentworth with the national story of war and peace—which is, of course, no less a story of death and life, bereavement and recovery. War and peace, that is to say, comprise another one of the novel's down-and-up processes, but one that possesses a special status. Not only does it work itself out on a national scale, but we might suspect, given that it does, and given Austen's obsession with Waterloo and the end of the war during the months she was composing the novel, that the national story is in fact the genesis of the personal one. This story of widows, in other words, was written as a way of addressing the fact that England itself had been widowed—widowed thousands of times over—and was now trying to understand, after twenty years of war, how to move forward, how to live again, in the aftermath of bereavement.

But before we explore Austen's great intertwining of these personal and national stories, we should note that her most important source for the idea of this juxtaposition—both in general and in the specific context of the Napoleonic War—is not Byron, but Scott. The first and most prominent of *Marmion*'s introductions, the one that heads the poem as a whole, mourns the deaths of Nelson, Pitt, and Fox, Britain's chief military and political leaders during this time of crisis. The passage bemoans the same tragic circumstance we looked at with respect to *Persuasion* and Lady Elliot: that although Nature is reborn each spring, individuals once dead are dead forever. But Scott also makes a further leap. The deaths of individuals, or at least of great individuals, threaten national survival, as well:

> To mute and to material things
> New life revolving summer brings;
> . . . .
> But oh! my country's wintry state
> What second spring shall renovate?

What powerful call shall bid arise
The buried warlike and the wise[?]
(I.53–54, 57–60)

The life of a country and the lives of its countrymen are inextricably inter-twined, and war imperils both.

Marmion was written in the dark days of 1808, but we find the same logic, only now applied to the "up" phase of the cycle, in the romance Scott com-posed the year the war drew to its first close, *The Lord of the Isles*. The poem intertwines the story of Robert the Bruce's liberation of Scotland with that of the thwarted love of Edith of Lorn, daughter of a nobleman who has sided with the English, and Ronald, "Lord of the Isles," one of the vassals who has remained loyal to Bruce. Edith renews her vows to Robert—the poet speaks of her love as "reviv[ing]" (VI.ix.6)—at the same time Lorn repledges his alle-giance to Bruce, and the poem ends with a service that functions at once as noble wedding and national thanksgiving. Personal and national intertwine, and the story, as Scott makes sure to tell us, possesses a more than antiquar-ian interest. The introduction to the final canto explicitly likens the breath-less pace of Bruce's campaign of reconquest to that of the closing period of the Napoleonic war. The analogy is strengthened by Scott's headnote to the poem, which calls Bruce "the restorer of Scottish monarchy."[35] "Restoration" was no innocuous word in 1814: Bruce restored the Scottish monarchy just as the allies restored the French. The identity of the personal and the national at this time of great crisis is again affirmed. The fate of the country is the fate of its countrymen. One can well imagine, and Austen clearly did imagine, the number of men (like Robert, like Wentworth) who were return-ing to wives, fiancées, or lovers in 1814—and the number who were not.

Waverley was already in press when *The Lord of the Isles* was being written; Scott had by now hit upon the device, central to his development of the his-torical novel, of setting his narratives at moments of historical crisis, transi-tions from one social order to another.[36] Bruce's conquest was one, Napoleon's defeat, implicitly, a second. That Austen saw the latter likewise, that she recognized the end of the war as a profoundly significant historical turning point, has been noted before, though it bears further discussion.[37] But she also, with the example of Scott before her, saw it in larger terms, as analogous to other historical turning points, moments when old orders gave way to new or when, on the contrary, historical change was impeded or reversed.

That this is so is not obvious, for she encodes these analogies in a passage the likes of which she had never attempted before, one that seems to contain a great deal of surplus information. It is the Elliot family's entry in the Baronetage—*Persuasion*'s shadow-text, the book in which the book itself is mirrored—a passage that stands at the novel's very head:

Walter Elliot, born March 1, 1760, married, July 15, 1784, Elizabeth, daughter of James Stevenson, Esq. of South Park, in the county of Gloucester; by which lady (who died 1800) he has issue Elizabeth, born June 1, 1785; Anne, born August 9, 1787; a still-born son, Nov. 5, 1789; Mary, born Nov. 20, 1791. (35)

The key to unraveling the information encoded in this passage actually comes a few lines later, as the narrator paraphrases the rest of the entry, which tells of "the history and rise of the ancient and respectable family" and which includes the information that the Elliots were elevated to the "dignity of baronet, in the first year of Charles II." The family as a whole, and Sir Walter in particular, is thus associated with the Stuart Restoration, the turning back of the historical clock in 1660—fittingly so, since Sir Walter is so unyielding a reactionary, so staunch an opponent of social change.

But the historical associations only begin there. Sir Walter's daughters are Elizabeth and Mary, themselves the latest, as we know, in the long line of "Marys and Elizabeths" the Elliot men have married. Elizabeth and Mary are the queens of the Tudor-Stuart monarchy, the one superseded in 1689 by the Glorious Revolution. For Austen, Britain's one queen since then had, of course, been Anne. Sir Walter also marries the daughter of a James, one of the Stuart male names, and marries his own daughter to a Charles, the other. As Anne represents the new order among the female Elliots—remember that she urges "reformation" on her father—William Walter Elliot represents it among the males.[38] And lest we miss this second association with the post-Revolutionary settlement, Austen tells us that during the period of his estrangement from Sir Walter—the period of his most complete apostasy from aristocratic values—William Walter drops his middle name, becoming simply "William." Furthermore, that Sir Walter is the last of his breed, that he represents an order that is passing from the historical stage, is signified, as in the case of Scott's last minstrel, by the death of his son. And this blow to his lineage is delivered on none other than Guy Fawkes Day, the day of the Gunpowder Plot that sought to overthrow the first of the Stuart kings, and in the year that marked the start of the French Revolution, a more successful attempt to overthrow an old monarchical order.

But old and new are relative terms; what was new becomes old. Sir Walter, born in 1760, is also associated with George III, the king who ascended the throne that year and who had become, by 1815, the very embodiment of senescence, superseded, while still alive, by his own son. 1660 and 1760, two signposts of old orders—Austen could not have failed to see, and did not fail to make use of, that historical rhyme, just as she also implicitly calls our attention to a complementary one: 1689 and 1789, the two revolutions. Lady Elliot, like her husband, embodies the old, dying in 1800—for people had not yet forgotten in Austen's time that a new century begins in the year '01—and it is interesting that Austen seems to have changed her mind at some point as to whether Anne's mother belongs to the party of the new or the old, for she later tells us that "[t]hirteen years had passed away since Lady Elliot's death" when the novel begins in 1814 (37).[39] Finally, to bring us back to Waterloo, Sir Walter's association with everything old receives one more confirmation in the fact of his being born on March 1—the day, as we noted, that Napoleon landed in France. Old and new are relative terms, and the resurrection of Britain's archenemy was a particularly horrible example of the return of an "old" that was thought to be dead and gone—a fact of enormous importance to the novel and one that I will return to shortly.[40]

Reformation, revolution; restoration, return. In this coded manner, right at the outset, Austen announces the scope of her ambitions for the novel. It is to be a story of the great historical transition England was living through, and even more, a meditation on historical transitions as such. But how to write such a story—to write, in other words, in the epic mode? Again, Byron and Scott had wrestled with the same questions in the Turkish Tales and the verse romances. Over and over we find them forswearing the lofty, heroic strain as, in Byron's case, no longer feasible, and in Scott's, above his powers. *The Giaour*, with its opening glance at the tomb of Themistocles—"When shall such Hero live again?" (6)—and its lament on the servility of present-day Greeks, is self-consciously non-epic or even anti-epic. For while the poem features a variety of epic devices—epic similes, women-stealing, a Homeric battle—it remains resolutely a private tale only, a romance.

Indeed, throughout his early narrative verse, Byron struggles continuously with the shadowing presence of the epic possibility. Troy, the epic subject *par excellence*, cuts athwart the romance plot, as we have seen, at the start of canto II of *The Bride of Abydos*, as if every time the poet paused for breath, the longing for epic, pressing always on his mind, came flooding back. The root of Byron's struggle, it seems, is precisely that he knew himself to be living in epic times yet no longer believed in the possibility of epic poetry. *Childe Harold* I, which has been called an "unepical modern epic," deliberately swerves from the subject matter of the Peninsular War, traversing the same ground, surveying the scenes of battle, but returning quickly to its private tale.[41] What we might call the poem's anti-invocation tells the Muse that the poet will *not* be calling on her, precisely because she has been, since her glory days, "shamed full oft by later lyres." In any case, he adds, he has no right to ask "the weary Nine / To grace so plain a tale—this lowly lay of mine" (I.i.3, 8–9). Of course, *Don Juan* will constitute Byron's greatest exercise in anti-epic, one that begins by announcing that the so-called heroes of the Napoleonic age are, in fact, unworthy of epic treatment.

Scott, however, does not at all think them unworthy of such treatment, he just does not think himself worthy to attempt it. *Marmion*'s opening elegy for Nelson, Pitt, and Fox ends with the poet confessing his inability adequately to treat such a theme. Better for him to "Essay to break a feeble lance / In the fair fields of old romance" (I.286–287)—to stick, in other words, with the "lowly lay." Again, in *The Vision of Don Roderick* (1811), a retelling of Spanish history in the guise of the prophetic dream of the country's last pre-Moslem Christian king, he opens by pronouncing Wellington's deeds a theme fit for Homer or Milton, but unfit for "we, weak minstrels of a laggard day" (I.iii.1). Near the poem's end, when the narrative reaches the contemporary events of the Peninsular War, he waves away his governing conceit altogether, for "shall fond fable mix with heroes' praise? / Hath fiction's stage for truth's long triumphs room?" (II.lxi.5–6).

But by 1814—*Waverley* and *The Lord of the Isles*—he has devised a way of bringing "truth's long triumphs" onto "fiction's stage"—that is, of writing in the epic mode. It is a solution we noted, in a different context, above, another key element in Scott's creation of the historical novel: he focuses the national story through the lives of ordinary, "unheroic" individuals, who nevertheless, under the stress of great events, find themselves capable of heroic action.[42] And this is precisely the model that Austen takes over from Scott, only with two differences.[43] Undoubtedly out of a sense that to do so would cheapen them in just the way he worried about at the end of *The Vision of Don Roderick*, Scott never did apply his method to the great events of his own time. But Austen did; *Persuasion* is Austen's history of the present. But it is also—for Austen appropriated this new novelistic form by fitting it to the one she had already perfected—history told from the opposite perspective. *Middlemarch* may be George Eliot's "home epic," but *Persuasion* is Austen's. It is an epic of the present told from the perspective of Penelope.

The Homeric allusion is not adventitious. *Persuasion* actually contains a Penelope—Mrs. Clay—not to signal that the novel rewrites Homer in any direct, Virgilian way, but to alert us to the fact that it takes Homeric materials and reorders them for its own purposes. We have a Penelope, and we have a different woman who plays the role of Penelope, and we have a warrior and sailor who returns to her from across the sea after many years of absence and uncertainty to resume their life of love and domesticity. But the roles of the principals are in some ways reversed: it is she who has changed beyond recognition, he who is beset by suitors. Still, their relationship is marked by *homonoia*, like-mindedness, that intuitive mutual understanding that is in Homer the mark of a good marriage, for Anne instinctively knows what is going through Wentworth's mind at any number of moments.

Other Homeric virtues are represented by Captain Harville, with whom Wentworth divides the role of Odysseus. It is he, as we noted above, who embodies the *Odyssey*'s great value of *xenia*, hospitality, and it is he, with his "ingenious contrivances and nice arrangements," including "some few articles of a rare species of wood, excellently worked up," who inherits Odysseus's skill as a craftsman and imagination as a domestic architect (119–120). In fact, Austen's sailors unite the same two qualities that make Odysseus the hero of Homer's epic of homecoming, those celebrated in the novel's last sentence: "domestic virtues" and martial valor (254). Indeed, as sea-fighters—warriors and wanderers at once—they unite the heroism of the *Iliad* and the *Odyssey*.

They are the men who saved the nation, Austen clearly believes, and it is her aim in *Persuasion*, to the extent that her form permits, to be the bard of their glory, to get their story down on paper—like Scott that of old Scotland's—before it passes from memory. For already the nation was forgetting:

"And who is Admiral Croft?" was Sir Walter's cold suspicious inquiry . . .
"He is rear admiral of the white. He was in the Trafalgar action." (51)[44]

This is one of the reasons for the novel's allusions to Byron and Scott. Austen's form does not permit her to recount the Navy's exploits directly, but she can point her readers to contemporaneous writers who have described comparable scenes of valor. The poetic material, like Wentworth's insouciant references to his dangers and triumphs, gestures toward the other half of the novel's story, the one that has taken place on another, wider stage and that Austen wishes to install as an ever-looming presence in our minds. And then there is the testimony of Anne, the "last minstrel" through whose voice Austen sings:

> You have difficulties, and privations, and dangers enough to struggle with. You are always laboring and toiling, exposed to every risk and hardship. Your home, country, friends, all quitted. Neither time, nor health, nor life, to call your own.   (237)

Domestic virtues and martial valor: the sailors unite in their person the novel's two intertwined strands, the national story and the personal story. Just as Anne's salvation comes from the sea, so does Britain's—both during the war and after. The officers released onto land in the summer of 1814 fertilize social as well as individual rebirths. Anne's reaction upon seeing Wentworth's note held out before her is a "revolution" (239). At the small scale, so at the large.

This is the historical transition Austen is describing, the movement from an old order to a new: from a society led by the nobility to one led by the professions.[45] Like Scott, Austen believed that the decline of the hereditary aristocracy made way for a natural aristocracy to rise.[46] The one group stands on nothing but its own sense of entitlement, the other on "toil" and "labour," as Mrs. Clay's inventory of the professions suggests (50). The novel takes its own inventory, Austen contriving to exhibit in its pages not only a gaggle of naval officers, but precisely one each of army officers, lawyers, clergymen, surgeons, and professional nurses. The contrast with the nobility is drawn all through the work: the Baronetage versus the Navy list; the "tax" of worldly prominence paid by "consequence" versus "the tax of quick alarm" (47, 254); the fact that the Crofts are fitter stewards of Kellynch than are the Elliots. Anne enunciates this last assessment—"she could not but in conscience feel that they were gone who deserved not to stay, and that Kellynch-hall had passed into better hands than its owners" (141)—and of course, the statement is emblematic. Like *Howards End*, in Lionel Trilling's well-known phrase, *Persuasion* asks the question, "Who shall inherit England?"[47]

But for all that Austen celebrates the new professional spirit and the emerging society of careers open to talent, where a young man with "nothing but himself to recommend him" (55) can rise in the world, that question does not receive so clear or so hopeful an answer. Indeed, in the narrower sense, the person who will inherit Kellynch is William Walter Elliot, and possibly also, as his wife, Mrs. Clay. The same world that gives opportunities to stalwart professionals also gives them to smiling hypocrites. Nor are the two groups as distinct as we would wish. Mr. Shepherd, "a civil, cautious

lawyer" and father of Mrs. Clay (42), makes use of Sir Walter's two most valued adjectives, but with a twist: "Many a noble fortune has been made during the war," he says (47), and soon reports of Admiral Croft, that he has
"acquired a handsome fortune" (50). Nobility and handsomeness now
belong only to money. But aside from drawing a subtle but pointed contrast
with Sir Walter, who likes to pretend that the cash economy does not even
exist, Mr. Shepherd's words remind us that being a naval officer is also about
making money, especially for the officers themselves. In fact, Wentworth
describes his career in precisely those terms.

It is in introducing the Musgroves, parents and children, that Austen speaks
of "the Old English style" and "the new," but what she says about the family—
and again, emblematically, about their houses—is that they are "in a state of
alteration, perhaps of improvement" (67). Austen is profoundly ambivalent
about England's future—given what would come next, in *Sanditon*, one might
even say more pessimistic than not. Like Scott, she observed historical change
without rooting for it.[48] England's future is Anne and Wentworth, but it is also
William Walter Eliot and Mrs. Clay. Critics have been too eager to see *Persuasion* as prophetic of the decades to follow, even of the entire rest of the century.[49] But Austen could only begin to intimate what was coming. All she could
be certain of was that the old England of the country estates—her England, the
England of her first five novels—was giving way to something very new.

Or was it? We asked why, if Austen is telling a story of death and revival,
she ends the novel in late winter rather than spring. Now we must ask why,
if she is telling the story of the postwar transition and the emergence of a new
society, she sets the novel in the period between Napoleon's abdication and
return rather than beginning it after Waterloo. In order to answer this question, we must imagine the shock and horror that return must have aroused.
Bonaparte: the great enemy, the great scourge, the great devil, the man who
had brought to the Continent fifteen years of war and had once stood on the
point of invading England, the specter that would haunt the English imagination for generations to come, was now suddenly, appallingly, risen from the
grave.[50] Death itself had come back from the dead—literally so, for the thousands who would be killed at Waterloo in one final bloodbath. Imagine Hitler
having pulled off the same feat—captured in 1945, let us say, rather than
dead, and escaped a year later to lead a rerisen Third Reich back into war—
and we have some sense of what that crisis must have been.

A war that had to end twice, an ending that turned out to be no ending at
all—a false resurrection, a lying spring. It was this, remember, not the war's
first end, that fired Austen's imagination—it was Waterloo that she was

reading about so compulsively as she began work on *Persuasion*. And it was this uncanny procession of events, finally, that provided the novel's master pattern.

For while every one of the novel's many "downs" is eventually answered by a corresponding "up," every loss by a recovery, it is also true that in the most important instances that recovery is either never full or never permanent.[51] That is another reason the novel never reaches its promised spring.[52] No end is final, and some never arrive at all. Again, the Regency: a beginning that was no beginning, for an end that was no end—forward motion held in check. The novel's very last paragraph tells us that Mrs. Smith experiences merely an "improvement of income, with some improvement of health," never becoming again the well-off, healthy woman she once was (253). Whether Sir Walter pays off his debts and returns to Kellynch is left an open question. Captain Harville remains disabled; Louisa's fall has robbed her forever of her liveliness and good cheer. The novel's abundance of nurses is suggestive, as is the fact that Louisa is nursed by the same woman who had nursed her as a baby. We are all convalescents, the implication is—nursed once as children, we will be nursed again on our deathbed.

As for bereavement itself, memory, the same faculty that allows Anne and Wentworth to return to their love, will keep bringing the bereaved, as Mrs. Musgrove knows, back to their loss. And as for homelessness, though it is true that Anne and Wentworth find a metaphorical home in each other, it is quite striking, given how careful Austen normally is to settle her heroines in specific and appropriate dwellings, that she never even hints as to where these two will finally live. Indeed, given the characters' earlier discussion about the suitability of ships as homes, she clearly means to tell us that their home will remain, precisely, unsettled, a home that is no home—that like Cain, Anne and Wentworth will settle in the land of Wandering.[53]

And the novel's final reference to "the tax of quick alarm," the ever-present possibility of a future war—aside from being an enormous and bitter irony given what we have seen about the story's chronological structure—reminds us of a further and even sadder irony to which the novel's profusion of widows should already have pointed us (254). Anne and Wentworth have found each other again, but some day, sooner or later, war or no war, they will also lose each other again. One of them is going to die first, leaving the other a widow in a sense not merely metaphoric. Whatever Austen may have said about the "immortality" of that glorious hour of reunion, nothing human really lasts forever. That Austen herself was soon to be bereft of life she may have realized by the time she came to the novel's end, and is the final irony that history wrote into her story.

Notes

CHAPTER 1: Introduction

1. J. E. Austen-Leigh, *A Memoir of Jane Austen* (1870), in Jane Austen, *Persuasion* (London: Penguin, 1965), p. 374.

2. According to the memorandum made by Cassandra Austen after her sister's death, as the Penguin editor points out (*Persuasion*, p. 399 n. 40), the manuscript of *Susan/Northanger Abbey* was completed in 1799.

3. Norman Page notes that "as early as 1870 we find the more rigorous critic distinguishing between the earlier trilogy . . . and the later" ("Orders of Merit," in *Jane Austen Today*, ed. Joel Weinsheimer [Athens: University of Georgia Press, 1975], p. 99). Page is referring not to Austen-Leigh's *Memoir*, but to Richard Simpson's celebrated review of the same year. Echoing the language of the *Memoir*, the publication of which occasioned the review, Simpson remarks that "[m]any readers must have felt tempted to consider the latter trilogy a kind of reproduction of the former, in the light of a mature knowledge . . . In the former set the art is simpler, less concealed, more easily discovered: in the latter, both passion and humour are rather more developed" (in *Jane Austen: The Critical Heritage*, ed. B.C. Southam [London: Routledge and Kegan Paul, 1968], pp. 253–254). Among other critics who mention the distinction, see George Whalley, "Jane Austen: Poet," in *Jane Austen's Achievement*, ed. Juliet McMaster (London: Macmillan, 1976), p. 127; Alastair M. Duckworth, who calls *Pride and Prejudice* the "culmination of her early mode" (*The Improvement of the Estate* [Baltimore: Johns Hopkins University Press, 1971], p. x); and Avrom Fleishman, who remarks that "whereas Elizabeth Bennet ends a century, Fanny Price begins one" (*A Reading of Mansfield Park* [Minneapolis: University of Minnesota Press, 1967], p. 73). *The Cambridge Companion to Jane Austen* (ed. Edward Copeland and Juliet McMaster [Cambridge: Cambridge University Press, 1997]) further consolidates this taxonomy by covering the novels under two entries, one for each "trilogy."

While these and many similar references are scattered about the critical literature, however, in no case does the difference between the two trilogies or modes or phases receive more than a few sentences of discussion. (I summarize those brief discussions at the start of chapter 2.) In fact, as Page points out, criticism is far more apt to see Austen's corpus as "[a] small, compact, homogenous body of work, capable of being discussed as an entity, in which the recurrence of themes and character types is somehow more significant than the structural and tonal contrasts between novels" (p. 93). And indeed, to a first approximation, Austen's half-dozen novels do all look and sound more or less the same— marriage stories told in a finely ironic style. Thus, the typical study of her work consists of six chapters, one for each novel, each discussing its respective novel in reference to the same general theme or ideological question. This approach has produced a great deal of valuable criticism, to be sure, but because it cuts each of the novels to the same measure, it tends to minimize differences among them, forestalling questions of periodization or categorization together with any account of systematic growth or change.

4. Biographical details taken from Deirdre Le Faye, "Chronology of Jane Austen's Life," in *Cambridge Companion*, pp. 1–11. The account I have sketched implies a particular position on the most vexed question about Jane Austen's life, that of the apparent hiatus in her literary production. Did she indeed essentially stop writing between 1799 and 1809—no revisions, no new projects except the abandoned *Watsons* in 1805 or thereabouts—and if so, why? I discuss the issue of revisions more fully below, but I take the majority view that the theories of continuous revision put forward by Q. D. Leavis and others are exceeded in their ingenuity only by their incredibility. (See Q. D. Leavis, "A Critical Theory of Jane Austen's Writing," *Collected Essays*, 3 vols. [Cambridge: Cambridge University Press, 1983], I:61–146.) As to why so immensely energetic and gifted a writer, one who moreover seemed to take such pleasure in the act of composition, should have abandoned her literary habits so thoroughly for so long, one can only conjecture. Surely the failure of *Susan* to see print, as well as of *First Impressions* even to get a reading from a publisher, must have been very discouraging. These disappointments, together with the fact that her writing had been so intimately bound up with her place as a girl and young woman in a particular family circle, might have convinced her, after the breakup of that circle, to put her literary pursuits behind her, as an enthusiasm of youth. As for *The Watsons*, I think Virginia Woolf was mistaken in believing that "the stiffness and the bareness of the first chapters prove that she was one of those writers who lay their facts out rather baldly in the first version and then go back and back and back and cover them with flesh and atmosphere" (Virginia Woolf, "Jane Austen," *The Common Reader* [New York: Harcourt Brace, Jovanovich, 1984], pp. 137–138). *Sanditon* suggests otherwise, that the feebleness of *The Watsons* proves rather that Austen was experiencing a dearth of energy and inspiration at that point in her career, midway through the great hiatus. For while *The Watsons* peters out, *Sanditon* breaks off in mid-stride.

5. According to Marilyn Butler, "Romantics" as a name for Wordsworth, Coleridge, Blake, Scott, Byron, Shelley, and Keats emerged in the 1860s (Scott, of course, has long ago ceased to be regarded as a major Romantic poet), while analytic discussions of "Romanticism" did not begin until the twentieth century (*Romantics, Rebels, and Reactionaries* [New York: Oxford University Press, 1981], p. 1). For a discussion of more recent shifts in the Romantic canon, see Harriet Kramer Linkin, "The Current Canon in British Romantics Studies," *College English* 53 (1991): 548–570.

6. The best evidence of the extent to which these poets were known by educated middle-class readers, as well as of what the makers of middle-class taste thought of their work, comes from the literary reviews. That Austen was such a reader—that she read avidly and widely in poetry, fiction, and other genres, and that her reading was impeccably up-to-date—both her novels and letters abundantly attest. (See Margaret Anne Doody, "Jane Austen's Reading," in *The Jane Austen Companion*, ed. J. David Grey [New York: Macmillan, 1986], pp. 347–363.) The reviews, which had proliferated from the mid–eighteenth century, had by 1800 long since become the medium by which middle-class British readers kept themselves informed about the latest literary developments.

Indeed, the reviews reached a new height of sophistication and importance at just this time, with the inauguration in 1802 of Francis Jeffrey's *Edinburgh Review*. (See Marilyn Butler, "Culture's Medium: The Role of the Reviews," in *The Cambridge Companion to British Romanticism*, ed. Stuart Curran [Cambridge: Cambridge University Press, 1993], pp. 120–147.)

Lyrical Ballads was reviewed widely from its first publication (Butler, *Romantics, Rebels, and Reactionaries*, p. 62). For a partial list of reviews, see John E. Jordan, "The Novelty of *Lyrical Ballads*," in *Bicentenary Wordsworth Studies*, ed. Jonathan Wordsworth (Ithaca: Cornell University Press, 1970), pp. 344–345; Jordan also mentions several reviews of Wordsworth's 1807 *Poems in Two Volumes*. For excerpts from a number of these reviews, see *Romantic Bards and British Reviewers*, ed. John O. Hayden (Lincoln: University of Nebraska Press, 1970), pp. 3–38. Jordan reviews the critical environment and critical reception more generally in *Why the* Lyrical Ballads? (Berkeley: University of California Press, 1976), pp. 53–83, elsewhere noting that "much of the verse of the time, including Wordsworth's, achieved a wide circulation in magazines . . . there were between 1798 and 1802 twenty-three reprintings of fifteen different poems from the *Lyrical Ballads*" (*Why the* Lyrical Ballads?, p. 113). One review of the 1798 *Lyrical Ballads* that was particularly likely to have caught Austen's eye appeared in the *Monthly Review*; its author was Dr. Charles Burney, father of Fanny Burney, one of Austen's favorite novelists and most important influences (Mary Jacobus, *Tradition and Experiment in Wordsworth's* Lyrical Ballads [Oxford: Clarendon Press, 1976], p. 160). In 1807, in the course of his attack on *Poems in Two Volumes*, Jeffrey noted that "[t]he *Lyrical Ballads* were unquestionably popular; and, we have no hesitation in saying, deservedly popular" (*Romantic Bards and British Reviewers*, p. 11).

Indeed by then, if not earlier, Jeffrey's own campaign against *Lyrical Ballads*, Wordsworth, and the Lake Poets had made those poets notorious (Butler, *Romantics, Rebels, and Reactionaries*, p. 63). In 1808, the anonymous *Simpliciad* satirized Wordsworth as the founder of the "Simple School" (Jordan, "Novelty of *Lyrical Ballads*," pp. 84–86). In 1809, Southey, Wordsworth, and Coleridge yielded place only to Scott at the head of Byron's dishonor roll in *English Bards, and Scotch Reviewers*. At the same time, however— as Byron's ranking suggests—Wordsworth and his fellow avant-gardists were steadily moving from notoriety to centrality. According to René Wellek, by late in the first decade of the nineteenth century, the Johnsonian narrative of English poetry as a steady development to Dryden and Pope was being rewritten to make the Augustan period a dark age, with the return to feeling and nature seen as having begun with James Thomson in *The Seasons* (1746) and Wordsworth recognized as the head of a great new school ("The Concept of Romanticism in Literary History," in *Romanticism: Points of View*, ed. Robert Gleckner and Gerald Enscoe [2nd ed.; Englewood Cliffs, N.J.: Prentice-Hall, 1962], pp. 196–197). Southey articulated such judgments as early as 1807, Leigh Hunt in 1814, and Hazlitt definitively crystallized the new critical orthodoxy in his *Lectures on English Poets* in 1818. That Southey himself was made Poet Laureate in 1813 constituted additional confirmation of the Lakists' centrality.

7. Le Faye, "Chronology of Jane Austen's Life," p. 5.

8. Studies of Austen's relationship to her predecessors and contemporaries include

Henrietta Ten Harmsel, *Jane Austen: A Study in Fictional Conventions* (The Hague: Mouton, 1964), which concentrates on Richardson and Burney; Frank W. Bradbrook, *Jane Austen and Her Predecessors* (Cambridge: Cambridge University Press, 1966), which covers a range of eighteenth-century literature, including periodical essays, conduct books, the literature of the picturesque, drama, poetry, and, especially, fiction; Kenneth L. Moler, *Jane Austen's Art of Allusion* (Lincoln: University of Nebraska Press, 1968), which is organized thematically rather than by genre, but which concentrates on conduct books and the novel; Jocelyn Harris, *Jane Austen's Art of Memory* (Cambridge: Cambridge University Press, 1989), which focuses on Richardson; and Mary Waldron, *Jane Austen and the Fiction of Her Time* (Cambridge: Cambridge University Press, 1999), which focuses on the didactic novel. Enumerations of Austen's major influences include Johnson and Cowper (Mary Lascelles, *Jane Austen and Her Art* [Oxford: Clarendon Press, 1939], p. 43); Shakespeare, Cowper, and Crabbe (Q. D. Leavis, *"Mansfield Park," Collected Essays*, I:167); Richardson and Fielding (Ian Watt, *The Rise of the Novel* [Berkeley: University of California Press, 1957], pp. 296–299; and Joseph Wiesenfarth, *The Errand of Form* [New York: Fordham University Press, 1967], p. ix); and Milton, Richardson, Shakespeare, Chaucer, Locke, Cowper, and Thomson (Jocelyn Harris, "Jane Austen and the Burden of the [Male] Past: The Case Reexamined," in *Jane Austen and the Discourses of Feminism*, ed. Devoney Looser [New York: St. Martin's, 1995], pp. 87–100).

9. Not even Crabbe's impact has been investigated, though a leading critic counts him as one of her three major influences (see Leavis, previous note) and her love for his poetry is well known (see *Jane Austen's Letters*, ed. Deirdre Le Faye [Oxford: Oxford University Press, 1995], p. 243 [21 Oct. 1813] and elsewhere, and Austen-Leigh, *Persuasion*, p. 331). Bradbrook spends only a few sentences on Crabbe. For the other half-dozen very brief treatments in the critical literature of the last half-century, see Barry Roth and Joel Weinsheimer, *An Annotated Bibliography of Jane Austen Studies, 1952–1972* (Charlottesville: University Press of Virginia, 1973); Barry Roth, *An Annotated Bibliography of Jane Austen Studies, 1973–83* (Charlottesville: University Press of Virginia, 1985); and Barry Roth, *An Annotated Bibliography of Jane Austen Studies, 1984–94* (Athens: Ohio University Press, 1996). The fact that the great majority of Crabbe's work began to appear only in 1807 does not seem to be the sole reason for this neglect. Even Cowper, whom virtually everyone acknowledges as a major influence, has scarcely ever been investigated as such. (The only study listed in the aforementioned bibliographies is John Halperin's brief essay on the quotation from *The Task* that appears in *Emma*, "The Worlds of *Emma*: Jane Austen and Cowper," in *Jane Austen: Bicentenary Essays*, ed. John Halperin [Cambridge: Cambridge University Press, 1975], pp. 197–206.) The bias seems to be against any consideration not only of the literature of Austen's adulthood, but also of poetry as such. Waldron's study is an exception to the former prejudice, but the didactic fiction she discusses is hardly representative of the new currents in English literature, and in fact her point is that Austen introduced the moral complexity of nineteenth-century fiction into didactic fiction's simplistic paradigms—again leaving open the question of where she absorbed the new elements from.

10. For an example of the old view, see Q. D. Leavis, "Jane Austen: Novelist of a Changing Society," *Collected Essays*, I:58–59. For examples of the more recent one, which

sees her novels as combining elements of both centuries, see Julia Prewitt Brown, *Jane Austen's Novels: Social Change and Literary Form* (Cambridge, Mass.: Harvard University Press, 1979), pp. 38–39; and Patricia Spacks, "Muted Discord: Generational Conflict in Jane Austen," in *Jane Austen in a Social Context*, ed. David Monaghan (Totowa, N.J.: Barnes and Noble, 1981), pp. 159–179.

11. Susan Morgan discusses this long-standing critical posture, and the prejudices that underlay it, in "Jane Austen and Romanticism," *Jane Austen Companion*, pp. 364–368. To cite the opinions of three venerable critics of the first half of the twentieth century: for A. C. Bradley, Austen is not Romantic at all: she appreciates nature, but we detect in her none of the "new modes of feeling" toward it ("Jane Austen," *A Miscellany* [London: Macmillan, 1929], p. 42); according to C. S. Lewis, "[i]n her we still breathe the air of the *Rambler* and *Idler*" ("A Note on Jane Austen," in *Jane Austen: A Collection of Critical Essays*, ed. Ian Watt [Englewood Cliffs, N.J.: Prentice-Hall, 1963], p. 28); and for Leavis, while Austen "shows she knew the work of the Romantic poets and novelists," she was "unimpressed" by it, remaining thoroughly eighteenth century in her view of human nature, her approach to depicting it, and her language ("Jane Austen: Novelist of a Changing Society," pp. 58–59). For a later assertion of this view in response to early claims of Austen's affinity with the Romantics, see Robert Langbaum's contribution in Karl Kroeber, Jerome J. McGann, and Robert Langbaum, "British Romanticism and British Romantic Fiction: A Forum," *Wordsworth Circle* 10 (1979): 139–146.

12. Needless to say, this does not devalue such studies. Examples include Anne K. Mellor, *Romanticism and Gender* (New York: Routledge, 1993); Harris, "Jane Austen and the Burden of the (Male) Past"; Glenda A. Hudson, "Consolidated Communities: Masculine and Feminine Values in Jane Austen's Fiction," in *Jane Austen and the Discourses of Feminism*, pp. 101–114; Beth Lau, "Jane Austen, *Pride and Prejudice*," in *A Companion to Romanticism*, ed. Duncan Wu (Oxford: Blackwell, 1998), pp. 219–226; and Susan J. Wolfson, "Romanticism and Gender," in *A Companion to Romanticism*, pp. 387–396. See also Linkin, "The Current Canon in British Romantics Studies."

13. See Robert Kiely, *The Romantic Novel in England* (Cambridge, Mass.: Harvard University Press, 1972); Joseph Kestner, "Jane Austen: The Tradition of the English Romantic Novel, 1800–1832," *Wordsworth Circle* 7 (1976): 297–311; Butler, *Romantics, Rebels, and Reactionaries*, pp. 55–73; Gary Kelly, "Romantic Fiction," *Cambridge Companion to British Romanticism*, pp. 196–215; and John Sutherland, "The Novel," in *A Companion to Romanticism*, pp. 333–344. Jay Clayton, *Romantic Vision and the Novel* (Cambridge: Cambridge University Press, 1987), sees *Mansfield Park* as articulating an opposition to Romantic desires for vision or transcendence (pp. 61ff.).

14. For Karl Kroeber, both Austen and Wordsworth reject conventionality through a critical engagement with convention ("Jane Austen, Romantic," *Wordsworth Circle* 7 [1976]: 291–296). Kroeber delineates further parallels between Austen and the poets in his contribution to "British Romanticism and British Romantic Fiction: A Forum." Stuart Tave discusses a number of affinities between Austen and Wordsworth, including their shared interest in common subjects and familiar language, in "Jane Austen and One of Her Contemporaries," in *Bicentenary Essays*, pp. 61–74. For Susan Morgan, Jane Austen shares the Romantic poets' epistemological concerns: "The subject of Austen's fiction,

like that of the major poets of her time, is the relation between the mind and its objects" (*In the Meantime* [Chicago: University of Chicago Press, 1980], p. 4). Morgan delineates further parallels in "Jane Austen and Romanticism." Larry J. Swingle incorporates Austen into a number of studies in which he has sought to reconceptualize British Romantic literature. In "The Poets, the Novelists, and the English Romantic Situation," *Wordsworth Circle* 10 (1979): 218–228, Austen's other novels, particularly *Emma* and *Persuasion*, exemplify the observation that "achieved unions of the Romantic period tend to take place in contexts of division that expose barriers" (p. 220), a line of thinking Swingle had developed earlier in "The Perfect Happiness of the Union: Jane Austen's *Emma* and English Romanticism," *Wordsworth Circle* 7 (1976): 312–319. In "The Romantic Emergence," in *Romantic Poetry: Recent Revisionary Criticism*, ed. Karl Kroeber and Gene W. Ruoff (New Brunswick, N.J.: Rutgers University Press, 1993), pp. 44–59, Swingle uses Austen and others to develop the related idea that Romanticism is characterized by an interest in occupying the middle ground between competing systems. In "Jane Austen and the Romantic Imprisonment," Nina Auerbach argues that Austen's depiction of the "tension between the security of a restricted world and its unrelenting imprisonment" aligns her with the Romantics (*Jane Austen in a Social Context*, p. 10). Martin Price sees Austen as valuing the cultivation of what Wordsworth calls "wise passiveness" ("Austen: Manners and Morals," in *Jane Austen*, ed. Harold Bloom [New York: Chelsea House, 1986], p. 178). Marshall Brown points out that Austen's heroines, like the Romantic poets, come to know themselves by remembering past experience ("Romanticism and the Enlightenment," in *Cambridge Companion to British Romanticism*, p. 43). Clifford Siskin argues that in both Austen and Wordsworth the idea of "development" is used to legitimize, by naturalizing, social change—particularly social change in the direction of hierarchical differentiation ("A Formal Development: Austen, the Novel, and Romanticism," *Centennial Review* 28–29 [1984–1985]: 1–28). William Galperin sees in the narrator's defense of novel-writing in *Northanger Abbey* a covert gesture toward the male Romantic poets—an "alliance," he says, "that dare not speak its name" (*The Historical Austen* [Philadelphia: University of Pennsylvania Press, 2003], p. 84; and see also his "What Happens When Jane Austen and Frances Burney Enter the Romantic Canon?," in *Lessons of Romanticism: A Critical Companion*, ed. Thomas Pfau and Robert F. Gleckner [Durham: Duke University Press, 1998], pp. 376–391). Clara Tuite, in *Romantic Austen* (Cambridge: Cambridge University Press, 2002), undertakes a different kind of project: rather than looking at Austen's work in the light of that of specific contemporaneous authors, she seeks to set it within the context of Romantic-era cultural formations—especially what she calls "Romantic organicism" (p. 11)—as a way of understanding issues of "genre, national culture and canon-formation" (p. 2), particularly "the history of the canonical production of Austen" (p. 3). More generally, Rachel M. Brownstein sees women's courtship novels—in their stress on individual choice, sentiment, and subjectivity—as playing a crucial role in the Romantic revolution in culture ("*Northanger Abbey, Sense and Sensibility, Pride and Prejudice*," in *Cambridge Companion to Jane Austen*, pp. 32–57).

15. Significantly, these observations almost always concern one of the last three novels; they tend, however, to be made in passing and to reflect, in their diversity, the lack of critical consensus over what constitutes the "Romantic." Thus, for example, Fanny Price

seems to be Austen's most Romantic heroine in her least Romantic novel. Harold Bloom sees Fanny as Wordsworthian ("Introduction," *Jane Austen*, pp. 7–8), while Nina Auerbach sees her as a monstrous and marginal Romantic figure akin to Wordsworth's leach-gatherer or Coleridge's ancient mariner ("Jane Austen's Dangerous Charm: Feeling as One Ought About Fanny Price," in *Jane Austen: New Perspectives*, ed. Janet Todd [New York: Holmes and Meier, 1983], pp. 208–223). For *Mansfield Park* as Austen's least Romantic novel, see Galperin, "What Happens When Jane Austen and Frances Burney Enter the Romantic Canon?" Whether *Emma* is Romantic depends on what one sees as the novel's final judgment on the value of the imagination—"Imagination" being, along with "Nature," one of the two abstractions to which Romanticism is most often reduced. For *Emma's* imagination as Romantic, see A. Walton Litz, *Jane Austen: A Study of Her Artistic Development* (New York: Oxford University Press, 1965), p. 135; and Moler, *Jane Austen's Art of Allusion*, pp. 156–157. If "Imagination" is most often invoked in discussions of the Romantic in *Emma*, "Nature" is indeed the key term in analogous discussions of *Persuasion*. See, for example, Litz, *Jane Austen*, p. 153, and "*Persuasion*: Forms of Estrangement," in *Bicentenary Essays*, p. 228. Litz writes in the former study that "Nature has ceased to be a mere backdrop; landscape is a structure of feeling which can express, and also modify, the minds of those who view it. In their quiet and restrained fashion [*Persuasion* and *Sanditon*] are part of the new movement in English literature." The latter is one of several studies that see Anne's solitary leave-taking of Uppercross, in its mixing of natural observation with recollection, as the novel's most Romantic scene; others point to the first part of the walk to Winthrop (pp. 106–107). For *Persuasion* as Romantic for reasons other than its attention to nature, see Karl Kroeber, *Styles in Fictional Structure* (Princeton: Princeton University Press, 1971), p. 83; and Harris, "Jane Austen and the Burden of the (Male) Past," p. 95. That the novel is Austen's most Romantic has become common wisdom of late: see Juliet McMaster and Bruce Stovel in their introduction to *Jane Austen's Business* (New York: St. Martin's, 1996), p. xix. For Anne as Austen's most Romantic heroine, see Joseph Wiesenfarth, "*Persuasion*: History and Myth," *Wordsworth Circle* 2 (1971): 164. For readings that reject the characterization of the novel as Romantic, or see it as itself involving a rejection of the Romantic, see John Halperin, *The Life of Jane Austen* (Brighton, Sussex: Harvester Press, 1984), pp. 302–303; Laura G. Mooneyham, *Romance, Language, and Education in Jane Austen's Novels* (Houndmills, Basingstoke, Hampshire: Macmillan, 1988), pp. 152–153; and Lorrie Clark, "Transfiguring the Romantic Sublime in *Persuasion*," in *Jane Austen's Business*, pp. 30–41. For a critique of facile labelings of Austen as un-Romantic or the later Austen as incipiently Romantic, see Swingle, "The Poets, the Novelists, and the English Romantic Situation," p. 218.

16. See Peter Knox-Shaw, "*Persuasion*, Byron, and the Turkish Tale," *RES* 44 (1993): 47–69; Keith G. Thomas, "Jane Austen and the Romantic Lyric: *Persuasion* and Coleridge's Conversation Poems," *ELH* 54 (1987): 893–924; and Jane Millgate, "Prudential Lovers and Lost Heirs: *Persuasion* and the Presence of Scott," in *Jane Austen's Business*, pp. 109–123.

17. A question so famously vexed in the study of the literature of the period as to constitute a virtual subspecialty. See, among others, Arthur O. Lovejoy, "On the Discrimination of Romanticisms," in *English Romantic Poets*, ed. M. H. Abrams (2nd ed.; New York: Oxford

University Press, 1975), pp. 3–24; Wellek, "Concept of Romanticism"; Morse Peckham, *The Triumph of Romanticism* (Columbia: University of South Carolina Press, 1970); M. H. Abrams, *Natural Supernaturalism: Tradition and Revolution in Romantic Literature* (New York: Norton, 1971); Anne K. Mellor, *English Romantic Irony* (Cambridge, Mass.: Harvard University Press, 1980); Jerome J. McGann, *The Romantic Ideology* (Chicago: University of Chicago Press, 1983); Mellor, *Romanticism and Gender*; and Swingle, "The Poets, the Novelists, and the English Romantic Situation" and "The Romantic Emergence."

18. For the pitfalls involved in trying to address the question of whether Jane Austen is a Romantic—the lack of consensus about how Romanticism ought to be defined, the superficiality of the "checklist" approach, the dubious value of declaring Austen a Romantic in any case—see Morgan, "Jane Austen and Romanticism," p. 364.

19. On the matter of influence and of Austen's relationship to these male poets, I should say at the outset that I will not be proposing a gendered reading of that relationship. While feminist criticism has contributed enormously valuable insights to the study of Jane Austen over the last several decades—has, indeed, revolutionized the field to become the major framework through which she is read today—and so has shaped my understanding of her work in ways too numerous and too deeply assimilated to enumerate, I have not found gender to be the first or most urgent line of questioning that has presented itself to me in the course of this investigation—have not found Austen's response to these poets to have been inflected by her female subject position. In this respect my approach is no different from the great bulk of the many influence studies that have been written about Austen's reception of Richardson, Johnson, and other earlier male authors. Nor have I chosen these four poets, as my inclusion of Scott indicates, for their canonical (or formerly canonical) status, but rather, as I show below, because Austen herself signals their importance to her through allusion and reference. Thus, while I hope the conclusions I set out here will be found valuable to the feminist conversation about Austen, as food for future thought, I have developed them within a differently oriented critical framework.

20. It should be said that the attempt to read Austen against these poets presupposes an affirmative answer to a more fundamental question: is it ever legitimate to make arguments of influence across generic lines? The belief that it is not, at least with respect to Austen, is the reason, as I suggest above (note 9), that we have so very few studies of Austen's reception of Cowper or Crabbe. And yet we don't hesitate to accept such arguments with respect to other novelists; no one disputes, for example, that Wordsworth had a profound impact on George Eliot, or that Shakespeare influenced just about everybody. Course syllabi that include both poetry and fiction, once unthinkable, have become common in recent years. And yet, as some of the responses to this study in manuscript suggest, we still resist arguments of influence that cut across the grain of formal and other differences, whatever the demonstrable affinities of theme and concern between the works in question—a resistance that only reinforces the generic boundaries that have made such arguments, at least in Austen's case, lamentably scarce.

21. Austen's exposure to German Romanticism—at least until the appearance of the translation of Mme. de Staël's *De l'Allemagne* in 1813, quite late in the period in question and only an indirect exposure—was almost certainly limited to the plays of Kotzebue and Schiller and, among Goethe's work, *The Sorrows of Young Werther*, mentioned in the juve-

nilia (*The Juvenilia of Jane Austen and Charlotte Brontë* [London: Penguin, 1986], p. 114). For the popularity of Kotzebue and Schiller and the relative obscurity of Goethe in England at this time, see Frederick Ewen, *The Prestige of Schiller in England* (New York: Columbia University Press, 1932). While the impact on Austen of Schiller's plays, in particular, deserves investigation, there seems little evidence that he was a major influence. The impact of Rousseau is another question worthy of study.

22. Examples of this position include Leavis, "Jane Austen: Novelist of a Changing Society," quoted above, and Auerbach, "Romantic Imprisonment": "Jane Austen regarded the poetry of her Romantic contemporaries with a certain lofty and sardonic mistrust, if she regarded it at all" (p. 11).

23. Henry Austen, "Biographical Notice of the Author," *Persuasion*, p. 33.

24. *Persuasion*, p. 331.

25. Jane Austen, *Lady Susan/The Watsons/Sanditon* (London: Penguin, 1974), p. 184.

26. For a review of several of the more prominent expressions of this opinion with respect to Byron—in an article that emphatically does not share it—see Knox-Shaw, "*Persuasion*, Byron, and the Turkish Tale," p. 47 n. 2 and n. 4.

27. *Letters*, p. 131 (20–22 June 1808).

28. *Letters*, p. 257 (5–8 March 1814).

29. *Letters*, p. 164 (10–11 Jan. 1809), and p. 201 (29 Jan. 1813).

30. *Letters*, p. 277 (28 Sept. 1814).

31. *Letters*, p. 323 (16–17 Dec. 1816), p. 295 (3 Nov. 1815), and p. 297 (23 Nov. 1815).

32. As discussed in Brian Southam, "Was Jane Austen a Bonapartist?," in *Report for the Period 2000* (Alton, Hampshire: Jane Austen Society, 2000), p. 30. Southam, who seems to have no doubt that Austen was an admirer of Byron's work (p. 29), adds that "[w]hatever it was about the poem that impressed [her], she was at pains to copy it out in her finest copper-plate hand" (p. 30). His article reproduces Byron's original version side-by-side with the manuscript, which is in the University of Southampton Library.

33. For mocking references to the taste for the picturesque in nearly all her novels, see John Dixon Hunt, "The Picturesque," in *Jane Austen Companion*, pp. 326–329. A number of critics have also argued that the handling of Mr. Darcy in *Pride and Prejudice* constitutes a satire of *Sir Charles Grandison* and the Grandisonian "patrician hero" (e.g., Moler, *Jane Austen's Art of Allusion*, pp. 75–108).

34. Marvin Mudrick, *Irony as Defense and Discovery* (Princeton: Princeton University Press, 1952). See also Jane Nardin, *Those Elegant Decorums* (Albany: State University of New York Press, 1973), p. 2, who speaks of the "double vision in her art" whereby Austen ridicules values and institutions to which she gives her approval as a moralist.

35. For her admiration of Pope, see *Letters*, p. 245 (26 Oct. 1813): "There has been one infallible Pope in the World."

36. See note 6 above.

37. *Persuasion*, p. 33.

38. Austen's most up-to-date readers include Fanny, who reads Crabbe and Scott, and Anne, who, like Benwick, reads Scott and Byron. Scott, as I noted above, was also inserted into Marianne Dashwood's syllabus during the Chawton revision to keep her reading current.

39. That Austen mentions Wordsworth explicitly only in a very late manuscript and Coleridge not at all is, of course, the strongest support for the argument that she did not read them, or at least not with any particular interest. The argument from silence must be treated very cautiously, however, especially with respect to a writer about whose intellectual life our knowledge is so clearly incomplete. Doody relies on it repeatedly in making the most systematic recent survey of Austen's reading, a choice that leads her to conclude, quite unacceptably, that "[w]e can doubt if [Austen] ever read Spenser" and "[t]here is no hint that this last of the Augustans had ever read Dryden" ("Jane Austen's Reading," p. 356). The same logic would force us to conclude that Austen knew nothing of Schiller, either, even though his plays were widely translated, reviewed, and performed from the early 1790s (see Ewen, *Prestige of Schiller in England*, pp. 9–26).

40. Coleridge's contributions to *Lyrical Ballads* consist of "The Rime of the Ancient Mariner," "The Nightingale," "The Foster-Mother's Tale," "The Dungeon," and (from 1800 onward) "Love." Other important poems Austen would likely have seen by 1812 include "The Eolian Harp" (first published in *Poems on Various Subjects*, 1796), "This Lime-Tree Bower My Prison" (*Annual Anthology*, 1800), the Dejection Ode (*Morning Post*, 1802), and "Frost at Midnight" and "Fears in Solitude" (*Poetical Register*, 1808–1809 [1812]). "Christabel" and "Kubla Khan" did not appear until late May of 1816, less than three months before the completion of *Persuasion* (though Harris seems right that "Pinney, with its green chasms between romantic rocks" [*Persuasion*, p. 117] alludes to the "deep romantic chasm" of "Kubla Khan" [l. 12] [*Jane Austen's Art of Memory*, p. 195 and "Jane Austen and the Burden of the (Male) Past," p. 94]).

41. Jane Austen, *Mansfield Park* (London: Penguin, 1996), p. 127 (hereafter cited parenthetically). Critics who see these references as Wordsworthian include Bradbrook, *Jane Austen and Her Predecessors*, p. 50; Tave, "Jane Austen and One of Her Contemporaries," p. 70; Litz, "*Persuasion*: Forms of Estrangement," p. 226; Clayton, *Romantic Vision and the Novel*, p. 68; and Galperin, "What Happens When Jane Austen and Frances Burney Enter the Romantic Canon?," p. 380.

42. It is also worth noting, as further evidence of Wordsworth and Coleridge's prominence by this point, that in *Waverley*, published the same year as *Mansfield Park*, Scott casually quotes both "The Rime of the Ancient Mariner" and "The Idiot Boy" (both of which had as yet appeared only in *Lyrical Ballads*), in each case clearly expecting his audience—that is, the great mass of the reading public—to recognize the passage without the aid of either title or author (*Waverley* [London: Penguin, 1985], pp. 432, 439).

43. The *Poems* did not come out until after the manuscript of *Emma* was complete, but *The Excursion* came out early in its drafting, presumably long before Austen wrote the passage in chapter 41 that contains the allusion.

44. Jane Austen, *Emma* (London: Penguin, 1996), p. 284 (hereafter cited parenthetically). The phrase comes from William Cowper, *The Task* (1785), IV.290.

45. Wordsworth's lines, by his own acknowledgment, more closely echo a phrase from Young's *Night Thoughts*, "Senses . . . half create the wondrous world they see" (see William Wordsworth, *Poems*, vol. 1 [London: Penguin, 1977], p. 954), but by 1798 the *Night Thoughts* (1742–1745), while still read, lay more than fifty years in the past, while *The Task* (1785) remained the most beloved work of England's most prominent poet and

Wordsworth's most important "pre-Romantic" predecessor. That Wordsworth was not reworking Cowper's line at least unconsciously, given the closeness in subject matter of the two passages, is hard to believe.

46. Marilyn Butler, "Jane Austen's Sense of the Volume," in *Jane Austen in a Social Context*, p. 63.

47. The ensuing discussion draws on the following sources: R. W. Chapman, *The Novels of Jane Austen*, 5 vols. (Oxford: Clarendon Press, 1923) II:xi–xiii ("Introductory Note") and II:400–407 ("Chronology of *Pride and Prejudice*"); B.C. Southam, *Jane Austen's Literary Manuscripts* (London: Oxford University Press, 1964), pp. 52–62; P. B. S. Andrews, "The Date of *Pride and Prejudice*," *Notes and Queries* 213 (1968): 338–342; A. Walton Litz, "Chronology of Composition," in *Jane Austen Companion*, pp. 47–52; and Jo Modert, "Chronology Within the Novels," in *Jane Austen Companion*, pp. 53–59.[47]

48. But as noted above, see Leavis, "A Critical Theory of Jane Austen's Writing," for the late novels as the result of continuous revision dating back to very early in Austen's career.

49. Reproduced in Southam, *Jane Austen's Literary Manuscripts*, p. 53. The omitted portion reads:

> Mansfield Park, begun somewhere
> about Feby 1811—finished soon after
> June 1813
> Emma begun Jany 21st 1814, finished
> March 29th 1815
> Persuasion begun Augt 8th 1815
> finished Augt 6th 1816

50. *Persuasion*, p. 339.

51. *Letters*, p. 202 (29 Jan. 1813).

52. Quoted in Southam, *Jane Austen's Literary Manuscripts*, p. 54.

53. In the view of D. W. Harding, "[t]he story that *Sense and Sensibility* existed first in the form of letters is improbable; it derives solely from a note made at the age of 64 by a niece who was not born until 1805" ("Introduction" to *A Memoir of Jane Austen, Persuasion*, p. 269).

54. Jane Austen, *Northanger Abbey* (London: Penguin, 1995), p. 11 (hereafter cited parenthetically).

55. *Letters*, p. 333 (13 March 1817).

56. Le Faye, "Chronology of Jane Austen's Life," p. 11.

57. *Northanger Abbey* and *Persuasion* were published together some nine months later, five months after Austen's death. The final title was in both cases supplied by Austen's brother Henry. Austen had intended to call *Persuasion The Elliots* (Brown, *Jane Austen's Novels*, p. 145).

58. But see Butler, *Romantics, Rebels, and Reactionaries*, p. 106, who dates Henry Tilney's reference to "a mob of three thousand men" to the latest of the three periods in question and claims that the novel's portrait of General Tilney "reflect[s] the national concerns of the second half of 1816." And see Margaret Anne Doody, "The Short Fiction," in *Cambridge Companion to Jane Austen*, pp. 84–99, who argues that major revisions were made on

all three of the early novels to bring them in line with the more conservative tastes of the Regency.

59. It is one of the ironies of this story that of the letters that were spared by Cassandra during her destruction of her sister's correspondence, none survive from the first twenty-two months of the family's residence in Chawton—the period, and more, that Austen-Leigh gives for the revision of *Sense and Sensibility* and *Pride and Prejudice*—or from the nineteen months preceding the publication of *Pride and Prejudice*—the period given for the revision of that novel by most scholars. There are also no letters for the period from late May, 1801, to late August, 1804—the time during which *Susan/Catherine/Northanger Abbey* was "finished"—nor from mid-September, 1796, to early April, 1798—the time during which *First Impressions* was written and the revision of *Elinor and Marianne* into *Sense and Sensibility* begun, if not also completed. And those hiatuses are the only four such in the correspondence, which begins in January, 1796—after the drafting of *Elinor and Marianne*.

60. Chapman, *Novels of Jane Austen*, II:407.

61. Woolf, "Jane Austen," pp. 136–137.

62. Chapman, *Novels of Jane Austen*, II:400. A full date is one that includes both the day-month date and the day of the week.

63. Discussed in Modert, "Chronology Within the Novels," p. 56.

64. It is, for example, the dating to which Modert gives pride of place. See also Katie Trumpener, *Bardic Nationalism* (Princeton: Princeton University Press, 1997), p. 177, where that dating becomes the basis of the argument that Austen set the novel at a very particular moment in the evolution of the debate over slavery and the slave trade.

65. Modert, "Chronology Within the Novels," p. 56.

66. Crabbe's great popularity is attested by the fact that in *Waverley*, published the same year as *Mansfield Park*, Scott is able to refer to him, without mentioning his name, as "our English Juvenal," clearly confident that his readers will recognize the allusion (*Waverley*, p. 479).

67. A few chapters before the mention of the *Tales*, we find the company at Sotherton "loung[ing] away the time as they could with . . . Quarterly Reviews" (87). The *Quarterly Review* did not begin publication until 1809.

68. Chapman, *Novels of Jane Austen*, II:13.

69. Chapman, *Novels of Jane Austen*, II:401–402.

70. Chapman, *Novels of Jane Austen*, II:406.

71. Andrews, "Date of *Pride and Prejudice*," p. 339.

72. Andrews, "Date of *Pride and Prejudice*," p. 340.

73. "It seems to me incredible that the gay and young-in-heart *Pride and Prejudice*, and the mature and bitter *Mansfield Park*, can really be simultaneous productions of the same stage in the author's development" (p. 339).

74. It should be mentioned that Chapman's theory has been so widely accepted in part because it dovetails with another, later, theory about the evolution of the *Pride and Prejudice* manuscript, one that is similarly widely accepted and similarly without evidentiary foundation: that *First Impressions* was, like *Elinor and Marianne* (in Caroline Austen-Leigh's account), an epistolary novel. The idea was first floated by Southam (*Jane Austen's*

Literary Manuscripts, pp. 58–59), who reasoned that the relative weakness of *Sense and Sensibility* as compared with *Pride and Prejudice* must be due to its having been Austen's first effort in direct narrative. But Southam admitted that there is "no evidence" for such a conjecture and acknowledged that "we might expect some remark in the family biographies . . . had *First Impressions* been an epistolary novel" (p. 58). And other, equally plausible explanations of *Sense and Sensibility*'s relative weakness are not hard to imagine, starting with the difficulty of transforming an existing epistolary manuscript, if such *Elinor and Marianne* was, into the direct mode. Or it may simply be that Austen wrote a weaker novel after having written a stronger one. As John Halperin asks, why must we assume that writers always get steadily better, especially when so many artistic careers (George Eliot's, for example) display a more complex trajectory (*Life*, p. 66)?

75. For John Halperin, "[t]here can be little doubt that Jane Austen had [*Pride and Prejudice*] down in fairly finished form by the time her father offered it to a London publisher . . . on 1 November 1797" (*Life* , p. 65); Jan Fergus also sees little significant revision at Chawton (*Jane Austen: A Literary Life* [Houndmills, Basingstoke, Hampshire: Macmillan, 1991], pp. 81–82); and Clare Tomalin writes, in reference to both *Pride and Prejudice* and *Sense and Sensibility*, that "the central characters and plot structures were in place by 1800 . . . and that although she did work on them, they were substantially the books we know" (*Jane Austen: A Life* [London: Viking, 1997], pp. 154–155).

76. J. F. Burrows's statistical analysis of linguistic patterns also affirms this conclusion (*Computation Into Criticism: A Study of Jane Austen's Novels and an Experiment in Method* [Oxford: Clarendon Press, 1987], pp. 132–133).

77. In fact, though the juvenilia are remembered for their brief, high-spirited burlesques, they end with a number of extended attempts at more serious narrative forms—most important, *Lady Susan*—ones that clearly show Austen working toward *Elinor and Marianne* and *First Impressions*. So it is not wrong to see the first of the novel manuscripts as continuous with the last of the juvenilia, as long as we are clear what each of those things were.

78. Indeed, the order in which Austen's first three novels are conventionally enumerated itself constitutes an argument about the significance of the later revisions of *Sense and Sensibility* and *Pride and Prejudice*. The way we think about each of those books, as well as about the shape of the first half of Austen's career, would be very different if we enumerated them, as I think we should, as *Pride and Prejudice*, *Sense and Sensibility*, and *Northanger Abbey*. As for the insistence that *First Impressions* could not be much like the *Pride and Prejudice* we know, since no one, having written a novel like that, would go on to write one like *Northanger Abbey*—that, too, is a circular argument. Who is to say what kind of novel naturally follows any other kind? Does *Mansfield Park* naturally follow *Pride and Prejudice*? Does *Emma* naturally follow *Mansfield Park*? Besides, it is not at all implausible that Austen, having written two straightforward narratives, would wish to cleanse her palate with a sophisticated meta-fictional entertainment like *Northanger Abbey*. There is also a more mundane argument for the plausibility of this order of composition: *First Impressions* was rejected by a publisher sight unseen. Austen immediately set about rewriting *Elinor and Marianne* but was presumably dissatisfied with the results, since as far as we know, she did not even bother sending it out for publication. She may simply have sought to

make her next project more saleable—as it proved to be, even if, once sold, it was not published.

79. Tomalin, *Jane Austen: A Life*, p. 155.

CHAPTER 2: Early Phase Versus Major Phase: The Changing Feelings of the Mind

1. *Letters*, p. 99 (8–11 April 1805).

2. John Wiltshire, "*Mansfield Park, Emma*, and *Persuasion*," in *Cambridge Companion to Jane Austen*, p. 58.

3. John Wiltshire, *Jane Austen and the Body* (Cambridge: Cambridge University Press, 1992), p. 9.

4. Jane Nardin, "Jane Austen and the Problem of Leisure," in *Jane Austen in a Social Context*, p. 123.

5. Mary Poovey, *The Proper Lady and the Woman Writer* (Chicago: University of Chicago Press, 1984), pp. 208–209.

6. Litz, *Jane Austen*, p. 153.

7. Marilyn Butler, *Jane Austen and the War of Ideas* (Oxford: Clarendon Press, 1975), p. 123.

8. Warren Roberts, *Jane Austen and the French Revolution* (New York: St. Martin's, 1979), p. 105. To these more recent characterizations we can add the inaugural ones of Austen-Leigh—"a greater refinement of taste, a more nice sense of propriety, a deeper insight into the delicate anatomy of the human heart" (*Persuasion*, p. 374)—and Simpson—"in the former set the art is simpler, less concealed, more easily discovered: in the latter, both passion and humour are rather more developed" (in *Jane Austen: The Critical Heritage*, ed. Southam, pp. 253–254).

9. Although the ensuing discussion will cite specific works as points of reference, I will not be discussing poets or poems at any length. Apart from considerations of space, the characteristics in question are too well known as elements of Wordsworth's or the other poets' work to require additional demonstration, and the kind of influence I am considering here (as opposed to in my later chapters) is not such as is visible in one-to-one correspondences—allusions, echoes, rewritings—but rather involves the absorption of fundamental orientations.

10. Whether this also makes them "Romantic" I will leave the reader to decide, being anxious, for reasons I explained in the previous chapter (see notes 17 and 18), to avoid that term.

11. In making this argument, I will be drawing my lines of classification athwart those of Julia Prewitt Brown and Susan Morgan, who have articulated two of the most valuable taxonomies of Austen's work. Brown, focusing on narrative structure, divides the novels into works of ironic comedy, *Northanger Abbey*, *Pride and Prejudice*, and *Emma*, and works of satiric realism, *Sense and Sensibility*, *Mansfield Park*, and *Persuasion*, identifying the former with the eighteenth century, the latter with the nineteenth (*Jane Austen's Novels*, pp. 37–45). I have no quarrel with this classificatory scheme, not even with Brown's assignment of each novel to its respective century, not only because she clearly does not mean

us to take her temporal classifications literally (*Emma* is of course not literally a work of the eighteenth century) but also because her criteria relate not to the kinds of questions I will be taking up, but to unconnected matters of social setting and narrative dynamics (pp. 38–39). Morgan, focusing on modes of cognitive development, divides the novels into stories of crisis, *Northanger Abbey*, *Pride and Prejudice*, and *Emma*, and stories of passage, *Mansfield Park* and *Persuasion*. *Sense and Sensibility* splits between the two categories: Marianne's story is one of crisis, Elinor's one of passage (*In the Meantime*, pp. 7–8). Again, I have no quarrel with this. Still, it is worth noting that both Brown's and, to a slightly lesser extent, Morgan's groupings differ from mine with respect to the same two novels, *Sense and Sensibility* and *Emma*. These are indeed the two that present the most difficulty in seeing Austen's earlier work as uninfluenced by the Romantic poets and her later work as decisively shaped by them. *Sense and Sensibility*, to a cursory glance, does seem to present "Romantic" characteristics, while *Emma* seems to present few or none. I will accordingly focus on these two works whenever possible in the ensuing discussion.

12. The handling of nature in the late works has been discussed mainly in connection with *Persuasion*, though also occasionally with *Mansfield Park*. See chapter 1, note 15.

13. Jane Austen, *Sense and Sensibility* (London: Penguin, 1995), p. 85 (hereafter cited parenthetically).

14. Jane Austen, *Pride and Prejudice* (London: Penguin, 1996), p. 129 (hereafter cited parenthetically).

15. Jane Austen, *Persuasion* (London: Penguin, 1965), p. 107 (hereafter cited parenthetically).

16. Litz, "*Persuasion*: Forms of Estrangement," in *Bicentenary Essays*, p. 228.

17. As discussed, classically, in M. H. Abrams's "Structure and Style in the Greater Romantic Lyric" (in *From Sensibility to Romanticism*, ed. Frederick W. Hilles and Harold Bloom [New York: Oxford University Press, 1965], pp. 527–560). This is not to say that this or any scene in Austen reproduces the structure or possesses all the features of Abrams's model. But by the same token, many of Wordsworth and Coleridge's nature poems that also do not fully fit the model exhibit the dialectic in question, which is indeed fundamental to their approach to the perception of nature.

18. Litz, *Jane Austen*, p. 153. See also his "*Persuasion*: Forms of Estrangement," p. 228.

19. See especially ll. 91–99 and 146–166.

20. Though, as Litz points out, it shows a much greater sensitivity toward the natural world than any of the early novels, working the annual cycle into the fabric of the narrative by keying Emma's moods to the passage of the seasons, so that, to take only the most obvious examples, her frosty reception of Elton's proposal accords with the weather outside the carriage, while she and Knightley declare their mutual warmth on a midsummer afternoon (*Jane Austen*, p. 151).

21. Much of Wordsworth's most important poetry of place not having yet been published, the most obvious example available to Austen would have been "The Brothers," in which this theme is central. It is also essential to "Tintern Abbey," of course, as well as to Coleridge's peroration in "Frost at Midnight" ("For I was reared . . . ," ll. 51ff.). In Scott's verse, the theme receives its most emphatic expression in the title character of "The Lady of the Lake"; in his early fiction, in the figure of Brown in *Guy Mannering*, especially upon

that character's return to Ellengowan at the start of vol. III. But it is also an idea that, in an expanded form, informs virtually everything Scott wrote: that national character—whether of Highlanders, Lowlanders, or Englishmen—is shaped by the land in which it took root.

Wiltshire, as I noted above, also mentions the idea of place as among the differences between the first and last three novels (*"Mansfield Park, Emma,* and *Persuasion,"* p. 58). For the view that character is formed in relation to place in all six of the novels, see Ann Banfield, "The Influence of Place: Jane Austen and the Novel of Social Consciousness," in *Jane Austen in a Social Context,* pp. 28–48.

22. Byron expresses the sentiment in two early poems on his school days, "On a Distant View of the Village and School of Harrow on the Hill, 1806," and "Lines Written Beneath an Elm in the Churchyard of Harrow," but his fullest expression of it is negative: Childe Harold's self-tormenting self-exile from his native land.

23. For Elinor's love for Marianne as the emotional center of the novel, see Eve Sedgwick, "Jane Austen and the Masturbating Girl," *Critical Inquiry* 17 (1991): 818–837; and George E. Haggerty, *Unnatural Affections* (Bloomington: Indiana University Press, 1998), pp. 72–87. The passage in question reads, "among the merits and the happiness of Elinor and Marianne, let it not be ranked as the least considerable, that though sisters, and living almost within sight of each other, they could live without disagreement between themselves, or producing coolness between their husbands" (322–323).

24. Gene W. Ruoff discusses the tendency of the last three novels to be about "coming home," as opposed to going out ("The Sense of a Beginning: *Mansfield Park* and Romantic Narrative," *Wordsworth Circle* 10 [1979]: 184–185).

25. Austen did not know *The Prelude,* of course, but she would have known any number of Wordsworth's other poems that show the self as formed during childhood, most obviously the Intimations Ode and "My heart leaps up when I behold," which makes explicit the doctrine that "The Child is father to the Man."

26. In Ruoff's words, "Elizabeth seems in some peculiar fashion to have been born yesterday" ("Sense of a Beginning," p. 178).

27. Wiltshire traces this shaping of character by upbringing in the cases of Fanny and Mary (*"Mansfield Park, Emma,* and *Persuasion,"* pp. 59–66).

28. That Anne was her mother's favorite is implied by the fact that she becomes Lady Russell's, her mother's closest friend's, but even more by the fact that "it was only in Anne that [Lady Russell] could fancy the mother to revive again," for it is a rule in Austen's world that a parent will love the child most like them, as Mr. Bennet does Elizabeth, Mrs. Bennet Lydia, Mrs. Dashwood Marianne, and Anne's own father his Elizabeth.

29. The novel's opening also sketches the histories of several other characters in such a way as to show that their present patterns of behavior are the outgrowth, if not of their childhoods, then still of their pasts. Mr. Weston and Miss Taylor/Mrs. Weston are thus characterized in chapter 2, Miss Bates in chapter 3. Emma's argument to Knightley about Frank in chapter 18 rests on the same logic.

30. Any number of examples may be cited, including "We are Seven," "The Idiot Boy," "Anecdote for Fathers," "Lucy Gray," "Alice Fell," and Coleridge's "The Foster Mother's Tale."

31. Morgan, *In the Meantime,* p. 134.

32. Another, silent example is the gap between the reception of Collins's initial letter, dated 15 October, and his arrival a month later on 18 November, an interval indicated by nothing more than a paragraph break. It took me many years to notice just how long this gap is, probably because, as is not the case with these other two intervals, it does occur at a point in the plot when something important is supposedly in progress, Jane's romance with Bingley. Nevertheless, this interval, too, remains blank, devoid of development.

33. Two peripheral figures, Mr. Norris and Dr. Grant, die during the course of *Mansfield Park*. It is no coincidence that Mrs. Churchill's death precipitates the cascade of changes that results in the novel's culminating unions by releasing a whole raft of characters from the situations in which they had been frozen: Frank and Jane, Emma and Knightley, Harriet and Robert Martin—even, in a comic touch, Mr. Churchill himself, finally able to pay his very old friend the visit he had been promising these ten years.

34. I am indebted to Karl Kroeber for this insight.

35. Lionel Trilling, "*Emma*," *Encounter* 8 (June 1957): 53.

36. The same is also true, more massively and emphatically than ever before in Austen's work, for *Sanditon*.

37. For a different view, see Trumpener, *Bardic Nationalism*, p. 179, who argues that his experiences in Antigua leave Sir Thomas a fundamentally changed man.

38. Particularly illustrative is his remark to Fanny during their dialogue about Henry's proposal, where he rails against the "willfulness of temper, self-conceit and . . . tendency to that independence of spirit, which prevails so much in modern days, even in young women" (262–263).

39. For a reading of this visit that sees it as implicitly critical of Emma's contempt for the poor, see Brown, *Jane Austen's Novels*, pp. 114–117.

40. This development is clearly related to Wiltshire's observation that the later novels undertake a much broader and deeper social critique (see note 2 above). Mary Evans, arguing that Austen criticizes capitalist morality in all her novels, notes that they all present pictures of desperate or potentially desperate financial circumstances (*Jane Austen and the State* [London: Tavestock Publications, 1987], pp. 4–7). (For a similar view, see Judith Lowder Newton's reading of *Pride and Prejudice* in *Women, Power, and Subversion: Social Strategies in British Fiction, 1778–1860* [Athens: University of Georgia Press, 1981], pp. 55–85.) But there is an important difference between a desperate situation and one that is merely potentially so. It is worth noting in this connection that while all three of Brown's "ironic comedies" maintained their lightness of tone by shielding their heroines from financial pressures, *Pride and Prejudice* and *Northanger Abbey* simply wave those pressures away (her mother may worry about the future, but Elizabeth doesn't, and neither does the narrator), whereas in *Emma* the importance of money is confronted squarely, the heroine simply being fortunate enough to have a lot of it.

41. *Lady Susan/The Watsons/Sanditon*, p. 168.

42. I regard Marianne's story as *Sense and Sensibility*'s principal narrative line, with Elinor present mainly to provide contrast and a point of view.

43. *Rambler* 41, *The Yale Edition of the Works of Samuel Johnson*, 16 vols., ed. W. J. Bate (New Haven: Yale University Press, 1969), III:223.

44. For a discussion of the difference between the Johnsonian and Wordsworthian

conceptions of memory very much along these lines, see Margery Sabin, *English Romanticism and the French Tradition* (Cambridge, Mass.: Harvard University Press, 1976), pp. 78–80.

45. Stuart M. Tave provides the most extensive analysis heretofore of the theme of memory in *Mansfield Park*, primarily comparing Fanny's strong memory to the Crawfords' weak ones (*Some Words of Jane Austen* [Chicago: University of Chicago Press, 1973], pp. 194–204). For other discussions, see my chapter on the novel.

46. "The Two April Mornings" presents a particularly complex intertwining of past and present moments through the uniting power of memory. In a striking effect not dissimilar from what we see here, Matthew recollects how, coming upon his daughter's grave some time after her death, he "loved her more, / For so it seemed, than till that day / [he] e'er had loved before" (ll. 38–40). The key to this striking statement seems to be the fact that Matthew had come upon the grave inadvertently; as in Fanny's experience with her mother, memory acts the more powerfully when acting unexpectedly.

47. In one of Wordsworth's most striking images of the power of memory over the body—its physical dwelling within it—the priest says of James that "often, rising from his bed at night, / He in his sleep would walk about, and sleeping / He sought his brother Leonard" (ll. 351–353).

48. Austen is driving home here the closeness of the word "feeling" 's two senses, just as Wordsworth, in Karl Kroeber's account, "prefers the word 'feeling' to 'emotion,' in part because he wants to exploit the dual relevance of 'feeling,' which by its ambiguity emphasizes the inseparableness of emotion and sensation" (*Romantic Landscape Vision* [Madison: University of Wisconsin Press, 1975], p. 35).

49. As Ruoff puts it in connection with *Mansfield Park*, "[l]ife is continuous, without sharply demarcated beginnings and endings; revelations are not sudden, and genuine turning points are not dramatically vivid" ("Sense of a Beginning," p. 181). Thus, "[i]n place of a mode of romance that had enhanced dramatic occurrences—first meetings, flirtations, misapprehensions, quarrels, and conquests—we must substitute one that exemplifies continuity of feeling, the growth of emotion so slow that its very stages are virtually undetectable" (p. 183).

50. Litz notes that Emma's reformation occupies the entire course of the novel, contrasting it to Elizabeth Bennet's (*Jane Austen*, pp. 133–134), while Brown remarks that "Emma has had three enlightenments, and we expect that she will experience more" (p. 123).

51. In Karl Kroeber's analysis, "[f]or the romantics, the highest human achievement is to achieve and sustain intensely contradictory feelings" (*Ecological Literary Criticism* [New York: Columbia University Press, 1994], p. 5). Examples from Wordsworth include the "aching joys" of "Tintern Abbey" (l. 84), the "discontent / Of pleasure" of "To the Daisy" (ll. 2–3), and "That sweet mood when pleasant thoughts / Bring sad thoughts to the mind" of "Lines Written in Early Spring" (ll. 3–4); from Coleridge, the disposition of Genevieve in "Love," who "Loves me best, whene'er I sing / The songs that make her grieve" (ll. 19–20); from Scott, his claim that "When, musing on companions gone, / We doubly feel ourselves alone, / Something, my friend, we yet may gain; / There is a pleasure in this pain" (*Marmion*, Introduction to canto II). For Byronic instances, see the following note.

52. For Byron, see Know-Shaw, "*Persuasion*, Byron, and the Turkish Tale," p. 69, who gives examples of "feelings that simultaneously smart and enchant." For Keats and Shelley, see Nina Auerbach, *Romantic Imprisonment* (New York: Columbia University Press, 1985), p. 54.

53. As Ruoff notes of *Mansfield Park*, "[I]n conventional terms Edmund begins to love Fanny three pages from the end of the story—so much, the novel tells us, for those conventional terms" ("Sense of a Beginning," p. 185).

54. Austen's intended title for *Persuasion*, *The Elliots*, also fits this model, especially when understood as referring not just to the nuclear family of Sir Walter and his daughters, but, as the opening paragraph makes clear it should be, to the family conceived of as a lineage. *Catherine*, her title for *Northanger Abbey*, is clearly a parody of such titles as "Cecilia, or Camilla, or Belinda" (34) rather than a field-of-possibility title like *Emma*.

55. See Peckham, "Toward a Theory of Romanticism" in *Triumph of Romanticism*. See also Peter Thorslev, "German Romantic Idealism," in *Cambridge Companion to British Romanticism*, who remarks that for Wordsworth and Hegel, to modify Pope, "Whatever's about to be is right" (p. 82).

56. Butler, *Jane Austen and the War of Ideas*, p. 261. Butler cites studies by Howard Babb (*Jane Austen's Novels: The Fabric of Dialogue*), K. C. Phillips (*Jane Austen's English*), Kroeber (*Styles in Fictional Structure*), and Page (*The Language of Jane Austen*).

57. In "The Two Voices of Fanny Price," Moler notes how inarticulate Fanny is in the face of passion (*Jane Austen: Bicentenary Essays*, pp. 172–179). In this "schoolgirlish" voice, among other things, "sentences are often loosely structured. Thought is lost and caught up with by means of repetition, left incomplete, revised in mid-sentence" (p. 175).

58. Know-Shaw speaks of "[a]n unusually direct registration of thought and emotion" in *Persuasion*, noting that Anne's feelings "are given comparatively raw, and seem to belong to the moment" ("*Persuasion*, Byron, and the Turkish Tale," p. 53).

59. As Geoffrey Hartman puts it in reference to Wordsworth, "here is a man whose mind moves as he writes, who thinks aloud in verse" (*Wordsworth's Poetry: 1787–1814* [New Haven: Yale University Press, 1964], p. 209). In "Nature and the Humanization of Self in Wordsworth," Hartman further remarks that Wordsworth's was a radically new "consciousness of consciousness," for he shows us feeling moving in "natural rather than fictionally condensed time" (in *English Romantic Poets*, ed. M. H. Abrams [2nd ed.; New York: Oxford University Press, 1975], p. 125). In Kroeber's formulation, Wordsworth's "attitude toward language is apparent in his characteristically long sentences of loose syntactic structure, which permit development of thought, expansive treatment of emotion, and—above all—a fluid interplaying of perceptual fact with mental fancy" (*Romantic Landscape Vision*, p. 128). Hartman and Kroeber clearly have in mind such explicitly introspective first-person poems as "Tintern Abbey," "Resolution and Independence," and the Intimations Ode (as well as *The Prelude*), to which we can of course add Coleridge's conversation poems, but some of the same characteristics—thought moving in real time as emotion finds itself through language—can be seen in such Wordsworthian "dramatic monologues" as "The Complaint of the Forsaken Indian Woman," "The Affliction of Margaret—," and "The Emigrant Mother." For Byron, see Jerome J. McGann, "On Reading Childe Harold's Pilgrimage," where McGann discusses how the poem's tonal

fluctuations trace the moment-by-moment reactions of the poet's mind (in *Critical Essays on Lord Byron*, ed. Robert F. Gleckner [New York: Maxwell Macmillan International, 1991], pp. 33–36).

60. As Know-Shaw notes, "Elinor's feelings are mediated to the reader through the measured language of the narrator, or frequently through a reflective kind of self-report" (*"Persuasion*, Byron, and the Turkish Tale," p. 53).

61. According to Kroeber, all six canonical Romantic poets "tended to regard thought as constituted of emotions" (*Ecological Literary Criticism*, p. 5).

62. Mary Poovey, as I mentioned above, does indeed see the late novels as insisting more on the claims of desire (see note 5). Know-Shaw, citing Thomas Lockwood, argues that "there is truth in his contention that Jane Austen exposes the chasm that separates reason from the life of feeling in *Persuasion*, setting their respective claims at jar" (*"Persuasion*, Byron, and the Turkish Tale," p. 53).

63. Fanny must surrender her desires in nearly every other respect, as I will discuss in detail in my chapter on *Mansfield Park*, but that she must do so is presented as a deplorable consequence of the nature of the novel's social world, not as something endorsed by Austen as ethically desirable. As for Emma, it is not her feelings that are wrong, but her imagination; if anything, as Trilling notes, her feelings tend to set her right after she has seen what her imagination has led her into (*"Emma*," p. 55). And as for her desires—again, it is a matter of discovering what they are rather than what they ought to be.

64. Roger Sales notes that all three novels have unresolved endings (*Jane Austen and the Representation of Regency England* [London: Routledge, 1994], p. xxi). For discussions of individual novels, see below. For the view that all six of the novels resist closure, see Richard Handler and Daniel Segal, *Jane Austen and the Fiction of Culture* (2nd ed.; Lanham, Md.: Rowman and Littlefield, 1999), pp. 130–134, who argue that all of them call into question any one construction of reality by characters or author; Robin Grove, "Austen's Ambiguous Conclusions," in *Jane Austen*, ed. Bloom, pp. 179–190, who claims that, contrary to popular opinion, Austen never takes clear moral positions, that her endings are always qualified or ironic or self-conscious; and also, of course, D. A. Miller, *Narrative and Its Discontents: Problems of Closure in the Traditional Novel* (Princeton: Princeton University Press, 1981), pp. 3–106.

65. None of the early novels exhibits any of these forms of resistance to closure, with one obvious exception. The forced marriage of Marianne to Brandon at the end of *Sense and Sensibility* arouses as much readerly dissatisfaction as does the marriage of Fanny to Edmund. But by the same token it serves to point out the difference between the early and late works. While the late Austen goes out of her way to incite questions about the ending of *Mansfield Park*, as we will soon see, the younger one does her best to shove the ending of *Sense and Sensibility* down our throats. Austen deliberately designed *Mansfield Park* to create interpretive indeterminacy, but *Sense and Sensibility*, her weakest novel in quite a number of ways, simply seems to have gotten away from her. The moral implicit in its ending—and none of her other novels comes close to being as didactic—is at odds with the readerly emotions and desires that had been aroused up to that point. To use terms I developed in the previous chapter, while Austen loved Marianne, she only esteemed Elinor, and so while the novel quite effectively makes us love Marianne as well,

makes us wish to see her as happy at the end of the novel as she had once been with Willoughby, it does not move us to assent to the triumph of Elinor's way of being in the world. Our minds may be convinced, but our hearts aren't persuaded—just as is the case with Marianne herself. (For a different discussion of the problem of closure in the novel, see Laura Mooneyham White, "Jane Austen and the Marriage Plot: Questions of Persistence," in *Jane Austen and the Discourses of Feminism*, pp. 77–78.)

66. Trilling, "*Emma*," p. 51.

67. Along these lines, Claudia L. Johnson argues that Emma is "*not* fully contained within the grid imposed by the courtship plot" (*Equivocal Beings* [Chicago: University of Chicago Press, 1988], p. 195; emphasis in the original), while Brown notes that Emma's dialectical relationships—with herself, with Knightley, and with Highbury—never move to "the death of total resolution" (p. 106).

68. A feeling so widespread in the critical literature as to make particular citation arbitrary. Even George Levine, who believes the novel to be teleological, acknowledges that the ironies of the happy ending represent a tug against telos (*Darwin and the Novelists* [Cambridge, Mass.: Harvard University Press, 1989], p. 69), while Ruth Bernard Yeazell suggests that even Fanny's final happiness is meant to be taken ironically, as a "fiction" (*Fictions of Modesty* [Chicago: University of Chicago Press, 1991], p. 168).

69. We find the same apparent ambivalence and same rare appearance of the first-person pronoun in another passage that bespeaks the possibility of Fanny's ultimate attachment to Henry. Mortified at running into her vulgar father on their walk through Portsmouth, Fanny laments that Henry will undoubtedly "soon give her up, and cease to have the smallest inclination for the match; and yet, though she had been so much wanting his affection to be cured, this was a sort of cure that would be almost as bad as the complaint; and I believe, there is scarcely a young lady in the united kingdoms, who would not rather put up with the misfortune of being sought by a clever, agreeable man, than have him driven away by the vulgarity of her nearest relations" (p. 333).

70. For an extensive discussion of this negativity, see Brown, *Jane Austen's Novels*, pp. 127–150.

71. Swingle, though arguing that this famous final phrase should be taken without irony, sees the ending as "a sort of miracle": "We see a fragile construct, which our sense of the laws of life (at least the novel's laws of life) tells us should not be able to exist, but it is existing" ("Perfect Happiness of the Union," p. 318).

72. For other discussions of the notion of perfection in *Emma*, see Joseph Litvak, "Reading Characters: Self, Society, and Text in *Emma*," in *Jane Austen's* Emma, ed. Harold Bloom (New York: Chelsea House, 1987), p. 134, and Tave, *Some Words of Jane Austen*, p. 241.

73. *Letters*, p. 335 (23 March 1817).

74. Ruoff makes this point about *Mansfield Park* ("Sense of a Beginning," pp. 184–185).

CHAPTER 3: *Mansfield Park*: Substitution

1. For other discussions of this scene, see Barbara Hardy, "Properties and Possessions in Jane Austen's Novels," in *Jane Austen's Achievement*, ed. Juliet McMaster (London:

Macmillan, 1976), p. 96, and "The Objects in *Mansfield Park*," in *Bicentenary Essays*, pp. 185–187, where she notes that Fanny "is qualified for brooding by the powers of memory, like the hero of Wordsworth's *Prelude*" (p. 86); Galperin, "What Happens When Jane Austen and Frances Burney Enter the Romantic Canon?," p. 380; David Monaghan, "Structure and Social Vision," in *Jane Austen's* Mansfield Park, who calls the transparencies "Romantic" (p. 91) and sees them as "an emblem of [Fanny's] private world" (p. 92); Duckworth, *Improvement of the Estate*, pp. 73–74, who regards Fanny's retreat to her room as a "strategic withdrawal of the moral self from the corruption of its environment" and "a search inwards for a purity of moral intention"; Tave, *Some Words of Jane Austen*, p. 200; and Litz, "Forms of Estrangement," p. 226, who sees Fanny's transparencies as a Wordsworthian reference but argues that they illustrate differences between novelist and poet. Most relevantly, Clayton sees the East room as being like an embodiment of Keats's "Chamber of Maiden-Thought," the stage of life that Keats himself identifies with "Tintern Abbey." "The room is in fact a microcosm of consciousness, and a retreat to her room is equivalent to a retreat into herself," Clayton says, going on to point out the presence in the room of the Tintern Abbey transparency (*Romantic Vision and the Novel*, p. 68).

2. Carl Woodring cites Arthur Beatty as noting that the three life-stages of Wordsworth's poem correspond to Hartley's mid–eighteenth-century classification (*Wordsworth* [Boston: Houghton Mifflin, 1965], p. 60). Harold Bloom cites J. H. van den Berg as arguing that the Romantic discovery of childhood also created adolescence as a bridge between child and adult ("The Internalization of Quest Romance," in *The Ringers in the Tower* [Chicago: University of Chicago Press, 1971] , p. 32).

3. Albert O. Wlecke, *Wordsworth and the Sublime* (Berkeley: University of California Press, 1973), pp. 22–23.

4. For discussions of the role of memory in "Tintern Abbey," see, among many others, Harold Bloom, *The Visionary Company* (rev. ed.; Ithaca: Cornell University Press, 1971), pp. 131–140, who discusses memory's redemptive function; Stuart M. Sperry, "From 'Tintern Abbey' to the 'Intimations Ode': Wordsworth and the Function of Memory," *Wordsworth Circle* 1 (1970): 40–49, who notes that memory helps Wordsworth "reexperience the past as a vital and constitutive element within present awareness" (p. 41) and that it has the power to help constitute identity by "fus[ing] past and present into a larger continuity, experienced as a kind of similitude-in-dissimilitude persisting through time" (p. 42), observations equally apposite to Austen's scene; and Marshall Brown, "Romanticism and the Enlightenment," who notes that the poem charts a movement from youthful empiricism to the half-creation of memory and imagination (pp. 40–41). For the difference between Wordsworth's conception of memory and that of Rousseau, see Sabin, *English Romanticism*, pp. 78–102. For the difference between Wordsworth's conception and that of Johnson, see chapter 2 of this study.

5. The principle is especially obvious in the "Poems on the Naming of Places," which as Jonathan Bate argues, "have a profound doubleness: they register loss—the moment recorded in the poem . . . is irredeemably past—but they simultaneously serve as acts of recovery" (*Romantic Ecology: Wordsworth and the Environmental Tradition* [London: Routledge, 1991], p. 93). The idea, Bate continues, may be generalized; for Wordsworth, every poem he writes is "gained out of the loss of a person, a moment, a feeling." Bate is draw-

ing here on Geoffrey Hartman's essay on Wordsworth and the inscription, where Hartman argues that the poet characteristically reads landscape itself as if it were a monument or a grave, so that "[a] secondary consciousness of death and change associates itself with the very act of writing" ("Wordsworth, Inscription, and Romantic Nature Poetry," in *From Sensibility to Romanticism*, p. 401). For the idea of the poem in Wordsworth as a replacement for or final location of what has been lost, see also David Simpson, *Wordsworth and the Figurings of the Real* (London: Macmillan, 1982), p. 41, and Paul H. Fry, *A Defense of Poetry* (Stanford: Stanford University Press, 1995), p. 178.

6. Woodring argues that Wordsworth mentions the Abbey in the title because it was a standard subject of both the picturesque and the sublime, both of which the poem seeks to redo ("The New Sublimity of Tintern Abbey," in *The Evidence of the Imagination*, ed. D. H. Reiman et al. [New York: New York University Press, 1978], pp. 89ff.). Mary Jacobus, *Tradition and Experiment*, sees the poem as moving from picturesque scene-painting to the creation and contemplation of an inner or internalized landscape of memory (p. 110).

7. Paul H. Fry notes "Fanny Price's Cowperian love of the Picturesque" ("Georgic Comedy: The Fictive Territory of Emma," in Emma, ed. David Monaghan [Houndmills, Basingstoke, Hampshire: Macmillan, 1992], p. 176). For discussions of the picturesque in Jane Austen's novels in general and *Mansfield Park* in particular, see Hunt, "Picturesque," and Jill Heydt-Stevenson, "Liberty, Connection, and Tyranny: The Novels of Jane Austen and the Aesthetic Movement of the Picturesque," in *Lessons of Romanticism*, pp. 261–279.

8. William Gilpin, *Observations on the River Wye and Several Parts of South Wales, etc., Relative Chiefly to Picturesque Beauty; Made in the Summer of the Year 1770* (2nd ed.; London, 1789), p. 47. Emphasis in the original.

9. Henry Austen, "Biographical Notice of the Author," *Persuasion*, p. 33.

10. See Brown, who notes similarly that "[i]n the opening of *Mansfield Park*, the voice speaking is that of the neighborhood itself, and the irony is the kind of smirking irony the neighborhood enjoys" (*Jane Austen's Novels*, p. 83).

11. *Letters*, p. 203 (4 Feb. 1813).

12. See Trumpener, *Bardic Nationalism*, and Margaret Kirkham, "Feminist Irony and the Priceless Heroine of *Mansfield Park*," in *Jane Austen's* Mansfield Park, pp. 117–133.

13. I owe this insight to a former undergraduate of mine, Caroline Simons.

14. For a discussion of the novel's use of litotes along different lines, as a mode of narratorial humor, see Eileen Gillooly, *Smile of Discontent: Humor, Gender, and Nineteenth-Century British Fiction* (Chicago: University of Chicago Press, 1999), pp. 103–104.

15. As pointed out by Maija Stewart, *Domestic Realities and Imperial Fictions* (Athens: University of Georgia Press, 1993), p. 7.

16. As Terry Eagleton says, "Samuel Richardson must have known that the saintly Clarissa was a bore, just as the creator of Emma Woodhouse must have seen that the virtuous Fanny Price was hardly a bundle of fun; but both Austen and Richardson are challenging us to imagine how virtue, in such predatory social circumstances, could ever be anything else" (*Figures of Dissent* [London: Verso, 2003], p. 21).

17. Hartman, *Wordsworth's Poetry: 1787–1814*, pp. 118ff.

18. Hartman, *Wordsworth's Poetry: 1787–1814*, p. 143.

19. Freud, *Three Essays on the Theory of Sexuality*, trans. James Strachey ([no city]: HarperCollins, 1962), p. 20. For Freud's principal discussion of the fetish as a perversion of the sexual instinct, see "Fetishism," in *Sexuality and the Psychology of Love* (New York: Macmillan, 1963), pp. 214–219.

20. Quoted from *Three Essays on the Theory of Sexuality*, p. 43 n. 1. The passage is from scene 7; the translation is by Bayard Taylor.

21. According to Neil McKendrick, "[T]he first of the world's consumer societies had unmistakably emerged [in England] by 1800" ("The Consumer Revolution of Eighteenth-Century England," in *The Birth of a Consumer Society: The Commercialization of Eighteenth-Century England*, ed. Neil McKendrick, John Brewer, and J. H. Plumb [Bloomington: Indiana University Press, 1982], p. 13). In his analysis, "the later eighteenth century saw such a convulsion of getting and spending, such an eruption of new prosperity, and such an explosion of new production and marketing techniques, that a greater proportion of the population than in any previous society in human history was able to enjoy the pleasures of buying consumer goods. They bought not only necessities, but decencies, and even luxuries" (p. 9). The imaginative and affective dimension of this revolution can be encapsulated in a single word: fashion. According to McKendrick, "[f]ashion in hats and hair styles, dresses and shoes and wigs and such like, arguably reached even greater extremes than ever before and certainly changed more rapidly and influenced a greater proportion of society" (p. 11). See also Maxine Berg and Helen Clifford, eds., *Consumers and Luxury: Consumer Culture in Europe, 1650–1850* (Manchester: Manchester University Press, 1999), especially pp. 1–16, 63–85, and 208–227.

22. One may cite her long descriptions, to her sister Cassandra, of the latest in ladies fashions, the fun she repeatedly pokes at women's obsession with those fashions in *Northanger Abbey*, Robert Ferrars's deliberations over the purchase of a toothpick case, Emma and Harriet's shopping trip to Ford's, and so forth.

23. David Simpson, *Fetishism and Imagination* (Baltimore: Johns Hopkins University Press, 1982), pp. 20–30. The phrase is from Godwin (quoted in *Fetishism and Imagination*, p. 27). For this definition of the fetish, see p. xiii. Marx also employs the term "fetish" in his theory of commodity fetishism, but while the phrase suggests the kind of phenomenon in question here, it refers to the more general tendency within the bourgeois economy to regard all commodities as possessing value in themselves rather than as deriving their (exchange) value from the human labor that went into their production. For Marx, commodities are fetishized regardless of the psychic energy invested in them simply by virtue of being treated as autonomous agents capable of entering into relations of exchange with one another. (See *The Marx-Engels Reader*, ed. Robert C. Tucker [New York: Norton, 1978], pp. 319–329 [*Capital*, part I, chapter I, section 4].)

24. *Wordsworth and the Figurings of the Real* (London: Macmillan, 1982), p. 41. The complementary risk is a "complete loss of all object-focus, and consequently of all self-identity, in a pantheistic oneness wherein there is no function for consciousness" (p. 41).

25. Similarly, Fry speaks of the "epitaphic moment" as widely diffused in Wordsworth, the distinction between epitaph and elegy being, as Fry develops it, that the former keeps up the appearance that the past—lying right before our eyes, written upon—remains necessarily present (*A Defense of Poetry*, p. 163).

26. *Persuasion* also features a fetish in the form of Captain Benwick's picture. Austen clearly continued to find the phenomenon interesting, but in the later two novels it becomes peripheral to her main concerns.

27. Wiltshire discusses Fanny's use of the cross and chain as a safeguard against the act of appropriation that is "coming out" (*Jane Austen and the Body*, pp. 98–100).

28. Claudia L. Johnson also discusses this idealization in *Jane Austen: Women, Politics, and the Novel* (Chicago: University of Chicago Press, 1988), pp. 115–116.

29. Daniel Cottom also discusses what he calls "supplantments" of one person by another, though he goes considerably farther than I do both in seeing them as significantly present in all of Austen's novels and in concluding that Austen "completely transfers desire from the realm of individual expression and spontaneous affinity . . . to a realm where it is little more than the intersection . . . of a great host of vagrant attachments and supplantments," becoming the product of social forces in a process "destructive of individual identity and of individual expression" (*The Civilized Imagination* [New York: Cambridge University Press, 1985], p. 105). So too, Brownstein sees *Sense and Sensibility* as containing "[t]he suggestion that people may be substituted for one another" ("*Northanger Abbey, Sense and Sensibility, Pride and Prejudice*," p. 47). But for the difference between Marianne's "acceptance" of Colonel Brandon and Edmund's of Fanny, see below.

30. Hartman, *Wordsworth's Poetry: 1787–1814*, p. 160. The two poems Hartman has in mind are undoubtedly "The Two April Mornings" and "The Fountain." In the first, Matthew recalls standing by his daughter's grave and turning to see "A blooming Girl . . . so very fair," but, he says, "I looked at her, and looked again: / And did not wish her mine!" (ll. 43–56). In the second, the poet himself is refused: " 'And, Matthew, for thy children dead / I'll be a son to thee!' / At this he grasped my hand, and said, / 'Alas! that cannot be' " (ll. 61–64). For a similar discussion of "The Two April Mornings," see Richard E. Matlak, "The Men in Wordsworth's Life," *Wordsworth Circle* 9 (1978): 391–397.

31. Frances Ferguson, *Wordsworth: Language as Counter-Spirit* (New Haven: Yale University Press, 1977), pp. 49–51.

32. For a related comment on this scene, see Misty G. Anderson, " 'The Different Sorts of Friendship': Desire in *Mansfield Park*," in *Jane Austen and the Discourses of Feminism*, p. 172.

33. For analyses of this relationship, see Anderson, " 'The Different Sorts of Friendship,' " pp. 167–183, and Janet Todd, *Women's Friendship in Literature* (New York: Columbia University Press, 1980), pp. 246–274. Also relevant are discussions of homoerotic impulses in Austen's fiction, including Sedgwick, "Jane Austen and the Masturbating Girl"; Haggerty, *Unnatural Affections;* and Terry Castle, "Sister-Sister," *London Review of Books* 3 Aug., 1995, pp. 3–6.

34. For the most thorough discussion of incestuous energies in Austen's work, see Glenda A. Hudson, *Sibling Love and Incest in Jane Austen's Fiction* (London: Macmillan, 1992). For discussions that focus on *Mansfield Park*, see Johanna H. Smith, " 'My Only Sister Now': Incest in *Mansfield Park*," *Studies in the Novel* 19 (1987): 1–15, and Kirkham, "Feminist Irony," pp. 128–129. For the displacement of incestuous feelings onto Edmund, see also R. F. Brissenden, "*Mansfield Park*: Freedom and the Family," in *Bicentenary Essays*, p. 166, and Anderson, " 'The Different Sorts of Friendship,' " pp. 170–171.

35. For the marriage of Fanny and Edmund as narcissistic, see Smith, " 'My Only Sister Now,' " Brown, *Jane Austen's Novels*, p. 98, and Handler and Segal, *Jane Austen and the Fiction of Culture*, p. 83 n., who cite a number of studies. Incestuous energies are found, of course, throughout English Romantic poetry. See Peter L. Thorslev, "Incest as a Romantic Symbol," *Comparative Literature Studies* 2 (1965): 41–58; and Alan Richardson, "The Dangers of Sympathy: Sibling Incest in English Romantic Poetry," *SEL* 25 (1985): 737–754. For a defense of the novel's investment in incestuous feeling as in line with what we find in Wordsworth and other British Romantic authors, see Ruoff, "Sense of a Beginning," pp. 183–184.

36. For other discussions of this blurring of conjugal and fraternal impulses, see Hudson, *Sibling Love and Incest*, p. 17, Claudia L. Johnson, *Jane Austen: Women, Politics, and the Novel*, pp. 116–120, and Ruoff, "Sense of a Beginning," pp. 183–184. We will see a great deal more of this and other kinds of blurring in discussing *Emma*'s "ambiguous relationships."

37. For "Tintern Abbey" as a poem of crisis, see Abrams, *Natural Supernaturalism*, p. 92, and Bloom, "To Reason with a Later Reason," in *Ringers in the Tower*, p. 17.

38. For an illuminating discussion of these matters, see Brown, *Jane Austen's Novels*, pp. 92–97.

39. This is not to say that substitution never occurs in Austen's other novels: Mr. Collins's replacement of Elizabeth by Charlotte, Emma's of Mrs. Weston by Harriet, and Anne's of her mother by Lady Russell are all examples; a less obvious but more important one is Miss Bates's whole approach to life, which as I noted in chapter 2 in discussing *Emma*'s manipulation of the word "happy," involves exactly the kind of making-do we are calling by that term. The difference between these examples and what we find in *Mansfield Park* is one of pervasiveness or pattern: *Pride and Prejudice*, *Emma*, and *Persuasion* may contain isolated instances of substitution, but none of those novels is governed by that mechanism in the way that *Mansfield Park* is.

40. Trilling, "Mansfield Park," in *Jane Austen: A Collection of Critical Essays*, p. 133.

CHAPTER 4: *Emma*: Ambiguous Relationships

1. Handler and Segal note that Emma quasi-incestuously replaces her mother (*Jane Austen and the Fiction of Culture*, pp. 41–42).

2. Hudson also notes this multiplicity of roles (*Sibling Love and Incest*, p. 50).

3. As has been pointed out by Claudia L. Johnson, *Equivocal Beings*, p. 196, and Todd, *Women's Friendship in Literature*, p. 277. The observation is based, in part, on Knightley's remark to Mrs. Weston that "you were receiving a very good education from *her*, on the very material matrimonial point of submitting your own will, and doing as you were bid; and if Weston had asked me to recommend him a wife, I should certainly have named Miss Taylor" (33; emphasis in the original).

4. In *Persuasion*, as Handler and Segal note, Elizabeth Elliot also quasi-incestuously replaces her mother (*Jane Austen and the Fiction of Culture*, p. 42).

5. As discussed by Ruoff, "Sense of a Beginning," p. 184, who cites examples from Wordsworth ("The Mad Mother" and *The Prelude*), Coleridge ("Dejection"), Percy Shel-

ley ("Epipsychidion"), and Mary Shelley (*Frankenstein*). For an extended discussion of the way Wordsworth's several "loves" for Dorothy, for Coleridge, and for nature and the objects of nature blend together in *The Prelude*, very much along the lines of the kind of ambiguity I am tracing here in Austen, see Sabin, *English Romanticism*, pp. 33–47.

6. For a discussion of Emma's playfulness, see Tony Tanner, *Jane Austen* (Houndmills, Basingstoke, Hampshire: Macmillan, 1986), p. 199.

7. I am indebted to Karl Kroeber for this insight.

8. Robert Brain, *Friends and Lovers* (New York: Basic Books, 1976), pp. 15–16.

9. Brain, *Friends and Lovers*, p. 258.

10. For the movement from vertical ties toward horizontal ones—from "filiation" to "affiliation," in his terms—see Edward W. Said, *Beginnings: Intention and Method* (2nd ed.; New York: Columbia University Press, 1985), pp. xiii–xiv. Franco Moretti also speaks of "the strengthening of bonds within generations" as characteristic of modernity (*The Way of the World: The Bildungsroman in European Culture* [London: Verso, 1987], p. 5). For the movement from strong, stable social structures toward looser, more temporary ones, see my article on "Conrad's *Lord Jim* and the Transformation of Community," *Raritan* 20 (fall 2000): 71–72.

11. For a discussion of the "spectrum of relationships designated in the eighteenth century as 'friendship,' " see Naomi Tadmor, *Family and Friends in Eighteenth-Century England: Household, Kinship, and Patronage* (Cambridge: Cambridge University Press, 2001), pp. 167ff. Tadmor reviews the historiographic literature on these various types of relationships (pp. 169–170), then goes on to provide a detailed case study of their appearance within the life of the eighteenth-century shopkeeper and diarist Thomas Turner (pp. 171–236).

12. Richard Simpson, in his famous appraisal of 1870, notes that "in her idea love was only an accident of friendship, friendship being the true light of life, while love was often only a troublesome and flickering blaze which interrupted its equable and soothing influence" (in *Jane Austen: The Critical Heritage*, ed. Southam, p. 246), an idea implicit in Scott's remark, in his review of *Emma*, that "at Highbury Cupid walks decorously, and with good discretion, bearing his torch under a lanthorn, instead of flourishing it around to set the house on fire" (in *Jane Austen: The Critical Heritage*, p. 67). For Allan Bloom, the "expectation of [Austen's] novels is that one's beloved will be one's best friend or that marriage is itself the essential friendship" (*Love and Friendship* [New York: Simon and Schuster, 1993], p. 196).

13. Lawrence Stone, *The Family, Sex, and Marriage in England, 1500–1800* (New York: Harper and Row, 1977). Stone's chronology has the Open Lineage model in play from 1450 to 1630, the Restricted Patriarchal from 1550 to 1700, and the Closed Domesticated from 1640 to the end of the period covered by his study.

14. For an example of such criticism, see Alan Macfarlane's review of *The Family, Sex, and Marriage*, *History and Theory* 18.1 (Feb. 1979): 121–122, one of the most important critiques of Stone's work. Macfarlane also cites Stone's qualifications of his chronology (p. 121).

15. Stone, *Family, Sex, and Marriage*, p. 5. Tadmor also discusses this sense of the word (*Family and Friends in Eighteenth-Century England*, pp. 167–168) as well as citing earlier studies that take it up (pp. 169–170).

16. Stone, *Family, Sex, and Marriage*, p. 98. See also Tadmor, *Family and Friends in Eighteenth-Century England*, pp. 167 and 169.

17. Stone, *Family, Sex, and Marriage*, p. 98. His citation from the 1820s, which has "friends" in the plural, "is evidence," Stone says, "of how long the old usage persisted, long after 'friend' in the singular had taken on its modern meaning" (p. 98). But the singular usage also appears in *Sense and Sensibility*, as we will see. The OED is even more behindhand, dating its latest citation for "friend" (sense 3): "kinsman or near relation," to 1721.

18. Stone, *Family, Sex, and Marriage*, pp. 221ff. Again, Stone has been roundly criticized for arguing that affection scarcely existed as a factor in English social relations before the eighteenth century (Alan Macfarlane, review of *The Family, Sex, and Marriage*), but the concept of affective individualism doesn't stand or fall on that question, but rather on the centrality of the affections to an individual's self-conception. Macfarlane convincingly argues that both affection and individualism existed in England before the eighteenth century, but an increasingly strengthened and increasingly important ideology of the individual, increasingly centered on the affections, did emerge during that century and through the period we have come to call the Romantic era, as evidenced in part by the material from Shaftsbury, Wollstonecraft, and Wordsworth that I discuss below. In these writers and others, and especially in Austen, the affections come to be regarded, for the first time, as the principal ties that bind individuals in society as well as the principal way that individuals define themselves. This, as we will see, is what sets us on the road to the situation in which, as Brain says, "We are friends with everyone" (*Friends and Lovers*, p. 258).

19. Stone, *Family, Sex, and Marriage*, p. 97. Stone is quoting Johnson's dictionary. Again, we must hedge Stone round with qualifications. Not only is Johnson's definition a too-simple characterization of the word's modern semantic complexity, as we are saying, it also can't in any sense be called exclusively modern (being present, as we will see, as far back as Aristotle). Still, the definition is useful in denoting the term's meaning within the system of values Austen champions here, one that is presented as nascently modern.

20. As Tadmor argues, the same two notions of friendship struggle, in something like the same way, in *Clarissa* (*Family and Friends in Eighteenth-Century England*, pp. 265–268). We can mark the half-century's distance between the two novels by noting that it is only in the later work that the idea of friend-as-intimate, championed by both writers, can win.

21. According to *A History of Private Life*, "no historian and few anthropologists before Robert Brain have studied friendship for itself" (ed. Roger Chartier, trans. Arthur Goldhammer [Cambridge, Mass.: Harvard University Press, 1989], III:450), and again, "[h]istorians have paid too little attention to friendship" (ed. Michelle Perrot, trans. Arthur Goldhammer [Cambridge, Mass.: Harvard University Press, 1990], IV:562). The *History* itself does only a little to redress the omission, devoting less than twenty-five pages to the topic in the first cited volume, only four in the second, and none at all in the work's final volume (vol. 5, eds. Antoine Prost and Gérard Vincent, trans. Arthur Goldhammer [Cambridge, Mass.: Harvard University Press, 1991]). Brain himself notes that any number of Western thinkers have written treatises on friendship, including "Plato, Aristotle, Ovid, Cicero, St. Francis, Bacon, Montaigne, Thomas More, Descartes, Pascal, Jeremy Taylor, and Adam Smith," but "[m]ost of these literary attempts to portray, explain, or analyze friendship . . . are necessarily ethnocentric . . . We have studies by Freud and Malinowsky, Havelock Ellis and Kinsey on sex, a host of volumes on kinship and marriage, several scientific and not so scientific studies of aggression, refined analyses of romantic

passion, and delicately wrought accounts of amity in the androgynous Bloomsbury set. But we have no modern theorist of love and friendship" (*Friends and Lovers*, p. 12). While Tadmor, as noted, cites a number of studies in which friendship is discussed, none is a study of friendship. Her book, of course, begins to redress this gap.

22. Stone, *Family, Sex, and Marriage*, p. 328.

23. Alan Macfarlane, *Marriage and Love in England: Modes of Reproduction, 1300–1840* (Oxford: Basil Blackwell, 1986), pp. 154–159. Many of Macfarlane's sources express this ideal in the language of friendship, as do many of Stone's.

24. Mary Wollstonecraft, *A Vindication of the Rights of Women* (New York: Norton, 1988), pp. 30ff.

25. Stone, *Family, Sex, and Marriage*, p. 328.

26. Lillian Faderman, *Surpassing the Love of Men* (New York: Morrow, 1981), p. 91.

27. Stone, *Family, Sex, and Marriage*, p. 329. Macfarlane, for once, concurs, noting that "[e]ven the French, within the European marriage pattern, found the system odd" and citing to this effect not only the same passage from the Duc de La Rochefocauld but also ones from Taine and Cobbett (*Marriage and Love in England*, p. 156).

28. Sabin, *English Romanticism*, pp. 23–24, 35–39. Sabin contrasts the definitions of love given in the *Encyclopédie* and Johnson's *Dictionary*.

29. Sabin, *English Romanticism*, p. 26. Her translations are those of the Penguin edition (trans. J. M. Cohen).

30. Sabin, *English Romanticism*, p. 28.

31. Allan Bloom, *Love and Friendship*, p. 147 (the words are Bloom's). But see Faderman, *Surpassing the Love of Men*, pp. 78–79, for a discussion of the friendship between Julie and Claire in the latter work, a bond that "threatens to overshadow the very passionate heterosexual relationships in the story" (p. 78). The two positions can be reconciled with Faderman's observation that, while eighteenth-century society distrusted strong expressions of friendship between men as evidence of or a prelude to homosexual involvement, they had no such corresponding fears about female friendships—women were presumed to be able to control themselves—and indeed often approved of them as evidence that the young women would be equally passionate and loyal in marriage (p. 75). I consider such romantic friendships below.

32. She quotes a string of La Bruyère's maxims to this effect, including "Love and friendship exclude one another" (Sabin, *English Romanticism*, p. 25).

33. *A History of Private Life* III:450.

34. For discussions of the classical tradition, see Allan Bloom, *Love and Friendship*, pp. 401–428, and Faderman, *Surpassing the Love of Men*, pp. 65–67. For friends as neighbors, see also Tadmor, *Family and Friends in Eighteenth-Century England*, p. 169.

35. Leading examples of the latter include Achilles and Patroklos, Socrates and Alcibiades, and Virgil's Nisus and Euryalus. Allan Bloom sees Falstaff and Hal as a comic version of the same paradigm (*Love and Friendship*, pp. 399–428). The friendships mentioned in Cicero all involve adults, as does Montaigne's with Etienne.

36. "Perfect friendship is the friendship of men who are good, and alike in virtue . . . Love and friendship therefore are found most and in their best form between such men. But it is natural that such friendships should be infrequent; for such men are rare" (1156b;

Nicomachean Ethics VIII.3; *Introduction to Aristotle*, ed. Richard McKeon [New York: Modern Library, 1947], p. 475). The complete discussion occupies Books VIII and IX.

37. Cicero, *de Amicitia*, section 21 (*Two Essays on Old Age and Friendship*, trans. E. S. Shuckburgh [London: Macmillan, 1927], pp. 188–189).

38. Allan Bloom, *Love and Friendship*, p. 411. For Socrates's refusal of sexual contact, see Plato, *Symposium*, trans. Alexander Nehemas and Paul Woodruff (Indianapolis: Hackett, 1989), pp. 68–71 (217a–219d).

39. "Of Friendship," in Michel de Montaigne, *The Complete Essays of Montaigne*, trans. Donald M. Frame (Stanford: Stanford University Press, 1957), p. 136.

40. This is consistent with what we saw above about the strict separation of friendship and sexual love in the French tradition. Rousseau, of course, reverses Montaigne and the rest of the classical tradition's valuation of the former over the latter. To Allan Bloom, this is a crucial step in the history of friendship: "For Aristotle, the exchange of speeches, *logoi*, is the ground of friendship and, at the same time, it grows out of man's *natural* spirituality, which is reason. But for Rousseau all meaningful speeches refer back to ultimately bodily sentiments or feelings . . . This is the source of the enduring modern problem of explaining friendship, and perhaps even of practicing it" (*Love and Friendship*, pp. 147–148; emphasis in the original).

41. Montaigne, *Essays*, p. 136.

42. Faderman, *Surpassing the Love of Men*, pp. 65–73.

43. Faderman, *Surpassing the Love of Men*, pp. 74–75.

44. Faderman, *Surpassing the Love of Men*, pp. 76–84, 103ff.

45. Faderman notes that the literature of romantic friendship itself sometimes made a point of distinguishing between true and false manifestations, those based on genuine sentiment and those merely based on the fashion for lofty expression (*Surpassing the Love of Men*, pp. 81–84).

46. *Juvenilia of Jane Austen and Charlotte Brontë*, p. 107.

47. Byron's early poems on friendship include "To E—," "To D—," "Epitaph on a Beloved Friend," "The Cornelian," "Childish Recollections," "To George, Earl Delawarr," "The Episode of Nisus and Euryalus," "The Death of Calmar and Orla," "To Edward Noel Long, Esq.," "To the Duke of Dorset," "To the Earl of Clare," "To a Youthful Friend," and "L'Amitié est L'Amour sans Ailes," not published until 1832. But the pairing of love and friendship as life's two supreme experiences—the love of women and the loving friendship of men—can be found throughout his early verse.

48. See Louis Crompton, *Byron and Greek Love* (Berkeley: University of California Press, 1985), pp. 71–81, for the question of whether any of his "fervid schoolboy friendships" involved sexual activity (p. 75). Crompton's discussion relies on Faderman's delineation of the nature of romantic friendships.

49. He even goes so far, in his paraphrase of Virgil's episode of Nisus and Euryalus, as to turn Nisus, as well, into a youth. Euryalus is still the younger man, but Nisus is referred to as "the Dardan boy" and addresses Euryalus as "the comrade of my youth," which suggests a rough equality of ages (ll. 38, 58). So much did Virgil's story possess Byron's imagination that he rewrote it twice, the second time in a prose version in imitation of "Ossian," "The Death of Calmar and Orla," that makes the denouement even more

self-sacrificing. Calmar, the Nisus figure, survives the bloody encounter and is found by his comrades, but insists on dying and being buried with Orla anyway.

50. Though the same may be said of Rousseau, we have already seen how very different is his conception of friendship as something that arises only in the wake of sexual maturation.

51. For the idea of youth as the Byronic Eden, see Robert Gleckner, *Byron and the Ruins of Paradise* (Baltimore: Johns Hopkins University Press, 1967), pp. 5ff.

52. Though the poem of that name, written around the very same time, was not published until after his death, Byron supplies the original of the proverb in a note.

53. For the early poems' idealization of love and friendship as that which "heaven and paradise" are associated with, see Gleckner, *Byron and the Ruins of Paradise*, pp. 4ff.

54. See "To a Lady, On being asked my Reason for quitting England in the Spring," "Fill the Goblet Again," and "Stanzas to a Lady, on leaving England."

55. We also find the same complex of ideas in Scott. In *The Lady of the Lake*, one of the verse romances named in *Persuasion*, we read that in James's dreams, "Again returned the scenes of youth, / Of confident undoubting truth; / Again his soul he interchanged / With friends whose hearts were long estranged" (I.xxxiii.17–20).

56. Note Coleridge's uses of the word in "This Lime-tree Bower my Prison" (ll. 6, 16, 20, 37) and "The Nightingale" (ll. 40, 110). It is not for nothing that he named his short-lived journal *The Friend*.

57. Caleb Crain, *American Sympathy* (New Haven: Yale University Press, 2001), p. 4. As Wollstonecraft put it, "The most holy band of society is friendship" (*A Vindication of the Rights of Women*, p. 30).

58. Crain, *American Sympathy*, p. 4. It was therefore male friendship that was of particular interest, since women were not full citizens.

59. See above, note 12.

60. Claudia L. Johnson notes that *Pride and Prejudice* eventuates in the creation of a "band of good friends" related by marriage, with the friendships having come first (*Jane Austen: Women, Politics, and the Novel*, p. 92). See also my article on "Community and Cognition in *Pride and Prejudice*," *ELH* 64 (1997): 518.

61. As well as, in an extended sense, by the ill health and arbitrary tyranny of Mrs. Churchill. As Mr. Woodhouse checks Emma's youthful vitality and Miss Bates Jane's, Mrs. Churchill does Frank's.

62. As a proof-text for the commonplace notion of Highbury as a self-enclosed world, we may note that the Crown's post-horses are kept "more for the convenience of the neighborhood than for any run on the road" (p. 164).

63. Mr. Weston—whose moral imbecility almost matches Mrs. Elton's, as their conversation in chapter 36 demonstrates—is similarly indiscriminate, regarding seemingly everyone as his "old friends" (264), though the temperature of these relationships seems to be more like those of Mr. Woodhouse than of Mrs. Elton.

64. Trilling, "*Mansfield Park*," p. 133; emphasis in the original. Trilling is referring to Mary Crawford and notes that she is "the first brilliant example" of this "distinctively modern type." Each of the last three novels contains such a figure, *Persuasion*'s William Walter Elliot being the final example.

65. Trilling, "*Emma*," p. 57.

66. Most importantly in Duckworth, *Improvement of the Estate*, and Butler, *Jane Austen and the War of Ideas*.

67. This not to say that *Pride and Prejudice* and *Northanger Abbey* are not also playful novels, or that Elizabeth Bennet and Henry Tilney are not every bit as playful as Emma. For *Emma* as a playful novel, see J. M. Q. Davies, "*Emma* as Charade and the Education of the Reader," in Emma, ed. David Monaghan, pp. 77–88; as well as Alastair M. Duckworth, " 'Spillikins, Paper Ships, Riddles, Conundrums, and Cards': Games in Jane Austen's Life and Fiction," in *Bicentenary Essays*, pp. 279–297. Modert also suggests that the novel plays "a hidden calendar game" with the reader, situating many of its events on holy days or holidays but often in ways concealed from immediate view ("Chronology Within the Novels," p. 57).

68. Most of whom, like Marianne, are far more likely to have trouble finding a minute to themselves. For discussions of Emma's loneliness, see James Thompson, "Intimacy in *Emma*," in Emma, ed. David Monaghan, pp. 119–123; and Tanner, *Jane Austen*, p. 203.

69. For a discussion, along different lines, of Emma's friendships with Mrs. Weston, Harriet, and Jane, see Todd, *Women's Friendship in Literature*, pp. 274–301.

70. Todd, *Women's Friendship in Literature*, pp. 284–285. See also above, note 3

71. For a discussion of Emma's thwarted friendship with Jane, see Ruth Perry, "Interrupted Friendships in *Emma*," in Emma, ed. David Monaghan, pp. 127–147. Perry notes that Emma cannot imagine the possibility of friendship based on equality (p. 133). For a similar point, see Thompson, "Intimacy in *Emma*," p. 113.

72. For a different discussion of this passage in the context of English and French cultural stereotypes, see Claudia L. Johnson, *Equivocal Beings*, p. 201. For other discussions of the way the novel pits French against English, see Roberts, *Jane Austen and the French Revolution*, pp. 33–42, and Sales, *Jane Austen and the Representation of Regency England*, p. xx.

73. To my knowledge, the first important English novel after Austen to deal with male-female friendship outside of marriage in any significant way is *Jude the Obscure*, where, in a leading instance of her modernity, a "friend" is precisely what Sue Bridehead wants to be to both Jude and Phillotson, albeit to their continual torment (e.g., Thomas Hardy, *Jude the Obscure* [London: Penguin, 1998], pp. 148, 233, 234).

74. See Bruce Stovel, "Comic Symmetry in *Emma*," in Emma, ed. David Monaghan, pp. 20–34, who remarks that "the action of the novel can be seen as Emma's search for, and triumphant discovery of, a true friend" (p. 25). For a negative view of Emma and Knightley's marriage as involving an incestuous turning inward, see Brown, *Jane Austen's Novels*, p. 15.

75. On *Mansfield Park*, see Ruoff, who remarks that "[b]ecause of their interest in presenting complex and often unlikely experience, Romantic writers were nervous about compartmentalizing either sensation or emotion" ("Sense of a Beginning," p. 184).

76. Nor are these hand-takings the only relevant ones. Emma asks Knightley to "shake hands" in token of their reconciliation after Harriet's refusal of Martin (84), then finds "her hand seized" by Elton during his proposal of marriage (108).

77. See Moretti, *Way of the World*, pp. 3–5, for a discussion of youth as symbolic of

modernity, as expressed especially in the emergence of the *Bildungsroman* as the chief novelistic form in the nineteenth century. "Youth," Moretti writes, "becomes for our modern culture the age which holds the 'meaning of life' " (p. 4). But he also goes on to talk about the inevitable ephemerality of youth, the fact that "[y]outh does not last forever," as essential to the form and meaning of the *Bildungsroman* (p. 6). I am suggesting that in recent decades, with the rise of youth culture to centrality in Western society, and also proleptically in the marriage of Emma and Knightley, youth *is* prolonged forever, as a set of attitudes and practices within adulthood itself.

78. Susan Morgan, *Sisters in Time* (New York: Oxford University Press, 1989), pp. 23–55.

79. Relevant here is Claudia L. Johnson's discussion of Emma as a manly woman and of Knightley as a new kind of man (*Equivocal Beings*, pp. 191–203).

80. For the general statement, see above, note 12. For the specific one, see Claudia L. Johnson, *Equivocal Beings*, who remarks that Knightley's love for Emma is "*fraternal* rather than heterosexual" (p. 201; emphasis in the original).

81. *Friends and Lovers*, p. 17. As does Rousseau, as we have seen, in favor of the first and the exponents of classical-romantic friendship in favor of the second. This prejudice also helps explain why the English, the exponents of the ideal of companionate marriage, have acquired a reputation for sexlessness: by uniting marriage with friendship, that ideal has necessarily been seen as sundering it from sexuality.

CHAPTER 5: *Persuasion*: Widowhood and Waterloo

1. See Julia Prewitt Brown, who notes that "[m]ost of the major characters are literally or figuratively widowed" (*Jane Austen's Novels*, p. 148); Wiltshire, who speaks of the novel as setting Anne against a "continuum of other mourners who freely display their grief" (*Jane Austen and the Body*, p. 156) and regards the adjustment to loss as the novel's major theme (pp. 165ff.); Duckworth, who also discusses the novel's engagement with questions of loss (*Improvement of the Estate*, pp. 190–193); Elaine Showalter, who sees the novel as involving a movement between retrenchment and advancement ("Retrenchment," in *Jane Austen's Business*, pp. 181–191); and especially Mooneyham, in her chapter on "Loss and the Language of Restitution in *Persuasion*," who takes up these and a range of other related issues (*Romance, Language, and Education*, pp. 146–175).

2. Given that both *Mansfield Park* and *Persuasion* deal with loss and deprivation, it is worth delineating the difference between substitution (the way characters deal with them in the earlier novel) and widowhood or mourning (the way they deal with them here). Substitution refuses to acknowledge loss in the first place; the problem with widowhood, as we will see, is that it might never do anything other than acknowledge it. Anne's dilemma, as the novel opens, is that she has never tried to find a substitute for Wentworth (or more properly, has never finished mourning him). For Benwick, Louisa Musgrove does not constitute a substitute for Fanny Harville, since he falls in love with Louisa only after having acknowledged and digested—mourned—the loss of Fanny. (Whether he does so too quickly is a point I take up below.) We may note that the difference between substitution and widowhood accounts for the two novels' differing atmospheres: *Mansfield Park*'s tense unease, *Persuasion*'s melancholy.

3. "Lord Byron's 'dark blue seas' " (129) quotes the first line of the poem, an allusion first traced, according to Wiesenfarth, by Chapman (*"Persuasion*: History and Myth" [p. 168 n. 18]).

4. The climate of critical opinion surrounding the novel has shifted considerably since Litz's judgment that Byron and Scott are present in its pages only as objects of satire (*"Persuasion*: Forms of Estrangement," p. 225). In fact, Adela Pinch has noted recently that *Persuasion* is the novel of Austen's that critics are most likely to discuss in relation to lyric poetry (*Strange Fits of Passion: Epistemologies of Emotion, Hume to Austen* [Stanford: Stanford University Press, 1996], p. 145). Efforts to trace Byronic parallels tend to focus on character types. Wiesenfarth (*"Persuasion*: History and Myth," p. 165) and Waldron (*Jane Austen and the Fiction of Her Time*, p. 146) have both seen Wentworth as a version of the Corsair, while Juliet McMaster sees him as akin to Childe Harold, another "gloomy wanderer o'er the wave" (*Jane Austen the Novelist* [New York: St. Martin's, 1995], p. 146). Waldron (pp. 146–147) also sees Anne as resembling the Giaour, at least at the start of the narrative, a point I will take up below. Knox-Shaw, in a first-rate study of Byronic analogies and echoes, draws a number of such parallels, seeing Wentworth, Anne, and Louisa as reenacting the roles of the Corsair, Medora, and Gulnare (*"Persuasion*, Byron, and the Turkish Tale," pp. 58–65). Interestingly, although Jane Millgate ("Prudential Lovers and Lost Heirs: *Persuasion* and the Presence of Scott," in *Jane Austen's Business*, pp. 109–123) has examined *Persuasion* as a response to Scott's second novel, *Guy Mannering* (itself, in Trumpener's reading [*Bardic Nationalism*, pp. 183–192], a rewriting of *Mansfield Park*), no one, to my knowledge, has traced the connections between *Persuasion* and those works of Scott it explicitly mentions, the verse romances.

5. Of course, loss and its consequences are also central to Wordsworth, as I discussed in chapter 3. Indeed, Mooneyham notes that loss is "the central theme of the Romantics" (*Romance, Language, and Education*, p. 151). Still, it makes sense to discuss the novel in terms of the poets it explicitly mentions.

6. In Peter J. Manning's words, the Giaour's "self-incarceration in a monastery is the emblem of a psychic arrest as total as Hassan's actual death" (*Byron and His Fictions* [Detroit: Wayne State University Press, 1978], p. 37). For Byron's preoccupation with death from the very beginning of his career (*Byron and the Ruins of Paradise*, p. 3), and especially in *The Giaour*, see Gleckner, who describes the world of the poem as one of "love and death, beauty and death, freedom and death, nature and death, man's human and heroic virtues and death" (p. 100). For Byron's handling of loss throughout his work, see Fry, *A Defense of Poetry*, pp. 159–180.

7. "The sad but living cypress glooms / And withers not, though branch and leaf / Are stamped with an eternal grief" (ll. 1148–1150).

8. For a related discussion, see Jerome J. McGann, *Fiery Dust* (Chicago: University of Chicago Press, 1968), pp. 160–164.

9. Trilling, for example, calls it "unconscionable" (*"Mansfield Park*," p. 139).

10. Of this passage Brown remarks that it is "one of the few instances in Jane Austen in which we sense a loss of control" (*Jane Austen's Novels*, p. 133).

11. I will refrain from speculating as to whether Austen, someone well acquainted with the "*Rears*, and *Vices*" of the Royal Navy (*Mansfield Park*, p. 51; emphasis in the original),

meant to suggest that Wentworth, out of sexual frustration over his loss of Anne, did indeed "go to the bottom" on the "Asp."

12. For different readings of the sea in *Persuasion*, see Clark, "Transfiguring the Romantic Sublime in *Persuasion*," pp. 33–35, who sees it as a symbol of the threat of radical change, and Auerbach, *Romantic Imprisonment*, pp. 38–54, who sees it as a symbol of both danger and liberation.

13. For other discussions of the function of memory in *Persuasion*, see Ruoff, "Anne Elliot's Dowry: Reflections on the Ending of *Persuasion*," *Wordsworth Circle* 7 (1976): 342–351; Morgan, *In the Meantime*, pp. 185–188; and Pinch, *Strange Fits of Passion*, pp. 150ff.

14. "Young" is not meant here in the sense I quoted it in the previous paragraph, as the context makes clear: "You must remember, Captain Harville, that your friend may yet be called a young mourner—Only last summer, I understand."

15. Interestingly, the seasonal logic of Benwick's period of bereavement and renewal parallels that of one of Wordsworth's subtlest pictures of mourning, "The Childless Father," whose title character also leaves off mourning after six months. The poet, however, employs the more expected timing, which makes the revival of hope coincide with the coming of spring.

16. Wiltshire speaks of the novel as posing physical change and decay against a narcissistic fantasy of changelessness (*Jane Austen and the Body*, p. 164).

17. Wiltshire remarks on the mechanical rather than renewing nature of Elizabeth's springs in "*Mansfield Park, Emma,* and *Persuasion*," p. 76.

18. See chapter 1, note 15.

19. Most importantly, by Wiltshire in *Jane Austen and the Body*, especially pp. 164ff., but see also Sales, *Jane Austen and the Representation of Regency England*, who discusses the novel in terms of the contemporaneous debate over the status of midwives.

20. Anne's homelessness and eventual finding of a home have been discussed by a number of critics, including Mooneyham (*Romance, Language, and Education*, pp. 158–159) and Brown (*Jane Austen's Novels*, pp. 138–140). For an extended discussion of the idea of hospitality in *Persuasion* in particular and Jane Austen's novels in general, see McMaster, *Jane Austen the Novelist*, pp. 47–58.

21. I am adapting the notion of a winter solstice or symbolic death from Northrop Frye's discussion of the "point of ritual death" through which romance plots typically pass (*Anatomy of Criticism* [Princeton: Princeton University Press, 1957], p. 187 [and see also p. 179]).

22. That last word has only recently become an Americanism, and not entirely even now. The relevant entry in OED II cites several eighteenth- and early-nineteenth-century examples and gives the following note on usage: "In N. Amer. the ordinary name for autumn; in England now rare in literary use, though found in some dialects; *spring and fall, the fall of the year*, are, however, in fairly common use." "Spring and fall," of course, is precisely the usage of most relevance here.

23. I have refrained, for reasons mentioned above, from making this chapter into another discussion of Austen's reception of Wordsworth, but it is certainly suggestive that she gave her hero a name so similar to that of one of the most famous poets of the day, and in a novel where the "richness of the present age" of poetry is explicitly mentioned (121).

24. Brown compares the novel to Shelley's "Ode to the West Wind" in this respect, arguing that both exhibit a "consciousness that spring will come," but that in both "this consciousness is held in check" (*Jane Austen's Novels*, p. 148). "The dominant experience of the novel," she concludes, "is one of loss."

25. Mary begins her letter on February 1 (174) and concludes it the following day (175). The Crofts arrive in Bath on February 3 or thereabouts (175–176). "About a week or ten days after the Crofts arrival"—sometime between February 10 and 15—Anne runs into the Admiral in town (179). A day or two later—February 11–17—she runs into Wentworth (184). It is ten days after that—February 21–27—that Wentworth dashes off his note and that, later in the day, he and Anne take their walk up Union-street (240).

26. Rory Muir, *Britain and the Defeat of Napoleon, 1807–1815* (New Haven: Yale University Press, 1996), p. 344. Wiesenfarth notes that "Jane Austen knew that Napoleon would escape from Elba the very month Anne and Wentworth were engaged" ("*Persuasion*: History and Myth," p. 167), but he does not note how close the coincidence is nor discuss its implications.

27. *Letters*, p. 191 (31 May 1811).

28. *Letters*, p. 235 (11 Oct. 1813). Frank is her brother Francis-William, a captain in the Royal Navy.

29. *Letters*, p. 298 (23 Nov. 1815).

30. *Letters*, p. 327 (24 Jan. 1817).

31. Southam, "Was Jane Austen a Bonapartist?," p. 29.

32. See chapter 1, note 47.

33. The poem proper also contains a complex thematics of resurrection, one that allegorizes Scott's own endeavor—an ancient book is unburied—but that considerations of space prevent me from discussing here.

34. In *The Giaour*:

Thy Heroes, though the general doom
Hath swept the column from their tomb,
A mightier monument command,
The mountains of their native land.—(ll. 130–133)

In *Childe Harold*:

Each hill and dale, each deepening glen and wold
Defies the power which crushed they temples gone

. . . .
The Sun, the soil . . .
Unchanged in all except its foreign Lord—
Preserves alike its bounds and boundless fame.
(II.lxxxviii.7–8, II.lxxxix.1–3)

35. In fact, he is referring to his source for the tale, "the venerable Lord Hailes, as well entitled to be called the restorer of Scottish history, as Bruce the restorer of Scottish monarchy"—a parallel that makes explicit the connection between national political revival and the kind of cultural revival Scott himself was practicing, two forms of "restoration."

36. See Georg Lukács, *The Historical Novel*, trans. Hannah Mitchell and Stanley Mitchell (Lincoln: University of Nebraska Press, 1962), p. 48. As Lukács remarks, this intertwining of the personal and the national continues to be central to Scott's design in the novels: "certain crises in the personal destiny of a number of human beings coincide and interweave within the determining context of an historical crisis . . . the split of the nation into warring parties always runs through the centre of the closest human relationships."

37. Litz sees the novel as involving a shift to modernity in terms of its delineation of character, from the "stable self" to one marked by "dynamic growth and unpredictable change" (" 'A Development of Self': Characters and Personalities in Jane Austen's Fiction," in *Jane Austen's Achievement*, pp. 75–76). For a dissenting view, see Wiltshire, *Jane Austen and the Body*, pp. 157–158, who disputes the idea that the novel registers a social transformation, pointing out that the Elliots will return to Kellynch in seven years. Among others who discuss the function of history in the novel, Wiesenfarth argues that "history provides the realistic context in which Jane Austen works out the myths," like Narcissus and Cinderella, that structure the novel's action (*"Persuasion*: History and Myth," p. 167). Speaking of *Mansfield Park*, Leo Bersani writes that "[i]n 1814, English society is on the threshold of major changes" (*A Future for Astyanax* [New York: Columbia University Press, 1984], p. 75), while Tanner, writing of the same novel, calls the years 1811–1813 "a period of great stability just about to give way to a time of unimagined changes" (*Jane Austen*, p. 144).

38. Strictly speaking, Queen Anne (like Mary II, who was, of course, a mere figurehead) also belonged to the House of Stuart, but she ruled, like William III, by grace of the Revolutionary settlement. Indeed, the fact that she was a Stuart strengthens the parallel between the Elliots and the Tudor-Stuart line, each family including an Elizabeth and a Mary who represent the old order and an Anne who represents the new.

39. Modert notes this discrepancy ("Chronology Within the Novels," p. 58).

40. Two final pieces of coded information, unrelated to the foregoing analysis, that may appear in the passage. Anne is born August 9, the day after Austen started writing the novel. Lady Elliot's maiden name of Stevenson is extremely close to Steventon, the village where Austen was born and raised. As Lady Elliot embodied the home that Anne has lost, so did Steventon surely play something like the same role in Austen's psychic life.

41. Gleckner, *Byron and the Ruins of Paradise*, p. 51.

42. See Lukács, *Historical Novel*, pp. 51–53.

43. For a different view of the influence of Scott's early novels, see Millgate, "Prudential Lovers and Lost Souls," who argues that in the three that were published by the time Austen had finished *Persuasion—Waverley, Guy Mannering*, and *The Antiquary*, the last two of which are set more or less in the present—Scott looks more like a novelist of Scottish manners than of his nation's history.

44. One can understand why the navy in particular might have started being forgotten even during the war's later stages, displaced in the national consciousness by the army. As for after the war, Byron, writing *Don Juan* I in the summer of 1818, notes just such a displacement:

Nelson was once Britannia's god of War,
And still should be so, but the tide is turned;
There's no more to be said of Trafalgar,
'Tis with our hero quietly inurned;
Because the army's grown more popular,
At which the naval people are concerned;
Besides, the Prince is all for the land-service,
Forgetting Duncan, Nelson, Howe, and Jervis. (stanza iv)

45. Tanner sees the naval officers as forming "a potentially new model of an alternative society or community" (*Jane Austen*, p. 228).

46. Avrom Fleishman, *The English Historical Novel* (Baltimore: Johns Hopkins University Press, 1971), p. 77. Litz speaks of a "new natural aristocracy of the navy" ("*Persuasion*: Forms of Estrangement," p. 231).

47. Lionel Trilling, *E.M. Forster* (New York: New Directions, 1965), p. 118. Brown sees the question as applying to all of Austen's novels (*Jane Austen's Novels*, p. 146).

48. Fleishman, *English Historical Novel*, p. 49.

49. Brown claims, for example, that "the ambiguous, autumnal mood of *Persuasion* comes . . . from a full consciousness of the fate of marriage in the century to come" (*Jane Austen's Novels*, p. 150).

50. Muir calls his chapter on the period between Napoleon's abdication and return "The Year of Revelry" and quotes Samuel Romilly, writing in his diary at the news of that return, "The name of Bonaparte is one '—at which the world turns pale' " (*Britain and the Defeat of Napoleon*, p. 345).

51. As Mooneyham says, loss in the novel is a permanent condition, never fully overcome (*Romance, Language, and Education*, p. 147). For a different view, see Auerbach, who sees loss as leading to recovery and enrichment (*Romantic Imprisonment*, p. 38).

52. It is a remarkable meteorological coincidence (or perhaps rather another source of inspiration) that in 1816, the year Austen finished the novel (in August), spring in England was severely delayed. In what became known as "the year without a summer," frost lingered on the heaths until July (Tom Bissel, "A Comet's Tale: On the Science of Apocalypse," *Harper's* Feb. 2003: 35).

53. As Mooneyham puts it, their home becomes "free-floating" (*Romance, Language, and Education*, p. 159).

Bibliography

Abrams, M. H., ed. *English Romantic Poets*. 2nd ed. New York: Oxford University Press, 1975.

———. *Natural Supernaturalism: Tradition and Revolution in Romantic Literature*. New York: Norton, 1971.

———. "Structure and Style in the Greater Romantic Lyric." In Frederick W. Hilles and Harold Bloom, eds., *From Sensibility to Romanticism*, pp. 527–560. New York: Oxford, 1965.

Anderson, Misty G. " 'The Different Sorts of Friendship': Desire in *Mansfield Park*." In Devoney Looser, ed., *Jane Austen and the Discourses of Feminism*, pp. 167–183. New York: St. Martin's, 1995.

Andrews, P. B. S. "The Date of *Pride and Prejudice*." *Notes and Queries* 213 (1968): 338–342.

Aristotle. *Introduction to Aristotle*. Richard McKeon, ed. New York: Modern Library, 1947.

Auerbach, Nina. "Jane Austen and the Romantic Imprisonment." In David Monaghan, ed., *Jane Austen in a Social Context*, pp. 9–27. Totowa, N.J.: Barnes and Noble, 1981.

———. "Jane Austen's Dangerous Charm: Feeling as One Ought About Fanny Price." In Janet Todd, ed., *Jane Austen: New Perspectives*, pp. 208–223. New York: Holmes and Meier, 1983.

———. *Romantic Imprisonment*. New York: Columbia University Press, 1985.

Austen, Jane. *Emma*. London: Penguin, 1996.

———. *Lady Susan/The Watsons/Sanditon*. London: Penguin, 1974.

———. *Mansfield Park*. London: Penguin, 1996.

———. *Northanger Abbey*. London: Penguin, 1995.

———. *Sense and Sensibility*. London: Penguin, 1995.

———. *Persuasion*. London: Penguin, 1965.

———. *Pride and Prejudice*. London: Penguin, 1996.

Austen, Jane, and Charlotte Brontë. *The Juvenilia of Jane Austen and Charlotte Brontë*. London: Penguin, 1986.

Austen-Leigh, J. E. *A Memoir of Jane Austen*. In Jane Austen, *Persuasion*, pp. 273–391. London: Penguin, 1965.

Banfield, Ann. "The Influence of Place: Jane Austen and the Novel of Social Consciousness." In David Monaghan, ed., *Jane Austen in a Social Context*, pp. 28–48. Totowa, N.J.: Barnes and Noble, 1981.

Bate, Jonathan. *Romantic Ecology: Wordsworth and the Environmental Tradition*. London: Routledge, 1991.

Berg, Maxine, and Helen Clifford, eds. *Consumers and Luxury: Consumer Culture in Europe, 1650–1850*. Manchester: Manchester University Press, 1999.

Bersani, Leo. *A Future for Astyanax*. New York: Columbia University Press, 1984.

Bissel, Tom. "A Comet's Tale: On the Science of Apocalypse." *Harper's* Feb. 2003: 33–47.

Bloom, Allan. *Love and Friendship*. New York: Simon and Schuster, 1993.

Bloom, Harold, ed. *Jane Austen*. New York: Chelsea House, 1986.

——, ed. *Jane Austen's* Emma. New York: Chelsea House, 1987

——, ed. *Jane Austen's* Mansfield Park. New York: Chelsea House, 1987.

——. *The Ringers in the Tower*. Chicago: University of Chicago Press, 1971.

——. *The Visionary Company*. Rev. ed. Ithaca: Cornell University Press, 1971.

Bradbrook, Frank W. *Jane Austen and Her Predecessors*. Cambridge: Cambridge University Press, 1967.

Bradley, A. C. "Jane Austen." *A Miscellany*, pp. 32–72. London: Macmillan, 1929.

Brain, Robert. *Friends and Lovers*. New York: Basic Books, 1976.

Brissenden, R. F. "*Mansfield Park*: Freedom and the Family." In John Halperin, ed., *Jane Austen: Bicentenary Essays*, pp. 156–171. Cambridge: Cambridge University Press, 1975.

Brown, Julia Prewitt. *Jane Austen's Novels: Social Change and Literary Form*. Cambridge, Mass.: Harvard University Press, 1979.

Brown, Marshall. "Romanticism and the Enlightenment." In Stuart Curran, ed., *The Cambridge Companion to British Romanticism*, pp. 25–47. Cambridge: Cambridge University Press, 1993.

Brownstein, Rachel M. "*Northanger Abbey, Sense and Sensibility, Pride and Prejudice*." In Edward Copeland and Juliet McMaster, eds., *The Cambridge Companion to Jane Austen*, pp. 32–57. Cambridge: Cambridge University Press, 1997.

Burrows, J. F. *Computation Into Criticism: A Study of Jane Austen's Novels and an Experiment in Method*. Oxford: Clarendon, 1987.

Butler, Marilyn. "Culture's Medium: The Role of the Reviews." In Stuart Curran, ed., *The Cambridge Companion to British Romanticism*, pp. 120–147. Cambridge: Cambridge University Press, 1993.

——. *Jane Austen and the War of Ideas*. Oxford: Clarendon Press, 1975.

——. "Jane Austen's Sense of the Volume." In David Monaghan, ed., *Jane Austen in a Social Context*, pp. 49–65. Totowa, N.J.: Barnes and Noble, 1981.

——. *Romantics, Rebels, and Reactionaries*. New York: Oxford University Press, 1981.

Byron, George Gordon, Lord. *The Poetical Works of Lord Byron*. Reprint 1972. London: John Murray, 1905.

Castle, Terry. "Sister-Sister." *London Review of Books* 3 Aug., 1995, pp. 3–6.

Chapman, R. W. *The Novels of Jane Austen*. 5 vols. Oxford: Clarendon Press, 1923.

Chartier, Roger, ed. *A History of Private Life*, vol. 3. Trans. Arthur Goldhammer. Cambridge, Mass.: Harvard University Press, 1989.

Cicero. *Two Essays on Old Age and Friendship*. Trans. E. S. Shuckburgh. London: Macmillan, 1927.

Clark, Lorrie. "Transfiguring the Romantic Sublime in *Persuasion*." In Juliet McMaster and Bruce Stovel, eds., *Jane Austen's Business*, pp. 30–41. New York: St. Martin's, 1996.

Clayton, Jay. *Romantic Vision and the Novel*. Cambridge: Cambridge University Press, 1987.

Coleridge, Samuel Taylor. *The Works of Samuel Taylor Coleridge*. Ware, Hertfordshire: Wordsworth Editions, 1994.

Copeland, Edward, and Juliet McMaster, eds. *The Cambridge Companion to Jane Austen*. Cambridge: Cambridge University Press, 1997.

Cottom, Daniel. *The Civilized Imagination*. New York: Cambridge University Press, 1985.

Crain, Caleb. *American Sympathy: Men, Friendship, and Literature in the New Nation*. New Haven: Yale University Press, 2001.

Crompton, Louis. *Byron and Greek Love*. Berkeley: University of California Press, 1985.

Curran, Stuart, ed. *The Cambridge Companion to British Romanticism*. Cambridge: Cambridge University Press, 1993.

Davies, J. M. Q. "*Emma* as Charade and the Education of the Reader." In David Monaghan, ed., Emma, pp. 77–88. Houndmills, Basingstoke, Hampshire: Macmillan, 1992.

Deresiewicz, William. "Community and Cognition in *Pride and Prejudice*." *English Literary History* 64 (1997): 503–535.

———. "Conrad's *Lord Jim* and the Transformation of Community." *Raritan* 20 (Fall 2000): 71–105.

Doody, Margaret Anne. "Jane Austen's Reading." In J. David Grey, ed., *The Jane Austen Companion*, pp. 347–363. New York: Macmillan, 1986.

———. "The Short Fiction." In Edward Copeland and Juliet McMaster, eds., *The Cambridge Companion to Jane Austen*, pp. 84–99. Cambridge: Cambridge University Press, 1997.

Duckworth, Alastair M. *The Improvement of the Estate*. Baltimore: Johns Hopkins University Press, 1971.

———. " 'Spillikins, Paper Ships, Riddles, Conundrums, and Cards': Games in Jane Austen's Life and Fiction." In John Halperin, ed., *Jane Austen: Bicentenary Essays*, pp. 279–297. Cambridge: Cambridge University Press, 1975.

Eagleton, Terry. *Figures of Dissent: Critical Essays on Fish, Spivak, Zizek, and Others*. London: Verso, 2003.

Evans, Mary. *Jane Austen and the State*. London: Tavestock Publications, 1987.

Ewen, Frederick. *The Prestige of Schiller in England*. New York: Columbia University Press, 1932.

Faderman, Lillian. *Surpassing the Love of Men*. New York: Morrow, 1981.

Fergus, Jan. *Jane Austen: A Literary Life*. Houndmills, Basingstoke, Hampshire: Macmillan, 1991.

Ferguson, Frances. *Wordsworth: Language as Counter-Spirit*. New Haven: Yale University Press, 1977.

Fleishman, Avrom. *The English Historical Novel*. Baltimore: Johns Hopkins University Press, 1971.

———. *A Reading of* Mansfield Park. Minneapolis: University of Minnesota Press, 1967.

Freud, Sigmund. "Fetishism." In *Sexuality and the Psychology of Love*, pp. 214–219. New York: Macmillan, 1963.

———. *Three Essays on the Theory of Sexuality*. Trans. James Strachey. [No city]: Harper-Collins, 1962.

Fry, Paul H. *A Defense of Poetry*. Stanford: Stanford University Press, 1995.

———. "Georgic Comedy: The Fictive Territory of Emma." In David Monaghan, ed., *Emma*, pp. 165–185. Houndmills, Basingstoke, Hampshire: Macmillan, 1992.

Frye, Northrop. *Anatomy of Criticism*. Princeton: Princeton University Press, 1957.

Galperin, William. *The Historical Austen*. Philadelphia: University of Pennsylvania Press, 2003.

———. "What Happens When Jane Austen and Frances Burney Enter the Romantic Canon?" In Thomas Pfau and Robert F. Gleckner, eds., *Lessons of Romanticism: A Critical Companion*, pp. 376–391. Durham: Duke University Press, 1998.

Gillooly, Eileen. *Smile of Discontent: Humor, Gender, and Nineteenth-Century British Fiction*. Chicago: University of Chicago Press, 1999.

Gilpin, William. *Observations on the River Wye and Several Parts of South Wales, etc., Relative Chiefly to Picturesque Beauty; Made in the Summer of the Year 1770*. 2nd ed. London, 1789.

Gleckner, Robert. *Byron and the Ruins of Paradise*. Baltimore: Johns Hopkins University Press, 1967.

———, ed. *Critical Essays on Lord Byron*. New York: Maxwell Macmillan International, 1991.

Gleckner, Robert, and Gerald Enscoe, eds. *Romanticism: Points of View*. 2nd ed. Englewood Cliffs, N.J.: Prentice-Hall, 1962.

Goldsmith, Oliver. *The Vicar of Wakefield*. London: Oxford University Press, 1967.

Grey, J. David, ed. *The Jane Austen Companion*. New York: Macmillan, 1986.

Grove, Robin. "Austen's Ambiguous Conclusions." In Harold Bloom, ed., *Jane Austen*, pp. 179–190. New York: Chelsea House, 1986.

Hagan, John. "The Closure of *Emma*." In Harold Bloom, ed., *Jane Austen's* Emma, pp. 19–35. New York: Chelsea House, 1987.

Haggerty, George E. *Unnatural Affections: Women and Fiction in the Later Eighteenth Century*. Bloomington: Indiana University Press, 1998.

Halperin, John, ed. *Jane Austen: Bicentenary Essays*. Cambridge: Cambridge University Press, 1975.

———. *The Life of Jane Austen*. Brighton, Sussex: Harvester Press, 1984.

———. "The Worlds of *Emma*: Jane Austen and Cowper." In John Halperin, ed., *Jane Austen: Bicentenary Essays*, pp. 197–206. Cambridge: Cambridge University Press, 1975.

Handler, Richard, and Daniel Segal. *Jane Austen and the Fiction of Culture*. 2nd ed. Lanham, Md.: Rowman and Littlefield, 1999.

Harding, D. W. "Introduction" to *A Memoir of Jane Austen*. In Jane Austen, *Persuasion*, pp. 267–270. London: Penguin, 1965.

Hardy, Barbara. "The Objects in *Mansfield Park*." In John Halperin, ed., *Jane Austen: Bicentenary Essays*, pp. 180–196. Cambridge: Cambridge University Press, 1975.

———. "Properties and Possessions in Jane Austen's Novels." In Juliet McMaster, ed., *Jane Austen's Achievement*, pp. 79–105. London: Macmillan, 1976.

Hardy, Thomas. *Jude the Obscure*. London: Penguin, 1998.

Harmsel, Henrietta Ten. *Jane Austen: A Study in Fictional Conventions*. The Hague: Mouton, 1964.

Harris, Jocelyn. "Jane Austen and the Burden of the (Male) Past: The Case Reexamined." In Devoney Looser, ed., *Jane Austen and the Discourses of Feminism*, pp. 87–100. New York: St. Martin's, 1995.

———. *Jane Austen's Art of Memory*. Cambridge: Cambridge University Press, 1989.

Hartman, Geoffrey. "Nature and the Humanization of Self in Wordsworth." In M. H. Abrams, ed. *English Romantic Poets*, pp. 123–132. 2nd ed. New York: Oxford University Press, 1975.

———. "Wordsworth, Inscription, and Romantic Nature Poetry." In Frederick W. Hilles and Harold Bloom, eds., *From Sensibility to Romanticism*, pp. 389–413. New York: Oxford University Press, 1965.

———. *Wordsworth's Poetry: 1787–1814*. New Haven: Yale University Press, 1964.

Hayden, John O., ed. *Romantic Bards and British Reviewers*. Lincoln: University of Nebraska Press, 1970.

Heydt-Stevenson, Jill. "Liberty, Connection, and Tyranny: The Novels of Jane Austen and the Aesthetic Movement of the Picturesque." In Thomas Pfau and Robert F. Gleckner, ed., *Lessons of Romanticism: A Critical Companion*, pp. 261–279. Durham: Duke University Press, 1998.

Hilles, Frederick W., and Harold Bloom. *From Sensibility to Romanticism*. New York: Oxford University Press, 1965.

Hudson, Glenda A. "Consolidated Communities: Masculine and Feminine Values in Jane Austen's Fiction." In Devoney Looser, ed., *Jane Austen and the Discourses of Feminism*, pp. 101–114. New York: St. Martin's, 1995.

———. *Sibling Love and Incest in Jane Austen's Fiction*. London: Macmillan, 1992.

Hunt, John Dixon. "The Picturesque." In J. David Grey, ed., *The Jane Austen Companion*, pp. 326–329. New York: Macmillan, 1986.

Jacobus, Mary. *Tradition and Experiment in Wordsworth's Lyrical Ballads*. Oxford: Clarendon Press, 1976.

Johnson, Claudia L. *Equivocal Beings: Politics, Gender, and Sentimentality in the 1790's: Wollstonecraft, Radcliffe, Burney, Austen*. Chicago: University of Chicago Press, 1995.

———. *Jane Austen: Women, Politics, and the Novel*. Chicago: University of Chicago Press, 1988.

Johnson, Samuel. *The Yale Edition of the Works of Samuel Johnson*. 16 vols. W. J. Bate, ed. New Haven: Yale University Press, 1969.

Jordan, John E. "The Novelty of *Lyrical Ballads*." In Jonathan Wordsworth, ed., *Bicentenary Wordsworth Studies*, pp. 340–358. Ithaca: Cornell University Press, 1970.

———. *Why the Lyrical Ballads?* Berkeley: University of California Press, 1976.

Kelly, Gary. "Romantic Fiction." In Stuart Curran, ed., *The Cambridge Companion to British Romanticism*, pp. 196–215. Cambridge: Cambridge University Press, 1993.

Kestner, Joseph. "Jane Austen: The Tradition of the English Romantic Novel, 1800–1832." *Wordsworth Circle* 7 (1976): 297–311.

Kiely, Robert. *The Romantic Novel in England.* Cambridge, Mass.: Harvard University Press, 1972.

Kirkham, Margaret. "Feminist Irony and the Priceless Heroine of *Mansfield Park.*" In Harold Bloom, ed., *Jane Austen's* Mansfield Park, pp. 117–133. New York: Chelsea House, 1987.

Knox-Shaw, Peter. "*Persuasion,* Byron, and the Turkish Tale." *Review of English Studies,* n.s. 44 (1993): 47–69.

Kroeber, Karl. *Ecological Literary Criticism: Romantic Imagining and the Biology of the Mind.* New York: Columbia University Press, 1994.

———. "Jane Austen, Romantic." *Wordsworth Circle* 7 (1976): 291–296.

———. *Romantic Landscape Vision.* Madison: University of Wisconsin Press, 1975.

———. *Styles in Fictional Structure: The Art of Jane Austen, Charlotte Brontë, and George Eliot.* Princeton: Princeton University Press, 1971.

Kroeber, Karl, and Gene W. Ruoff, eds. *Romantic Poetry: Recent Revisionary Criticism.* New Brunswick, N.J.: Rutgers University Press, 1993.

Kroeber, Karl, Jerome J. McGann, and Robert Langbaum. "British Romanticism and British Romantic Fiction: A Forum." *Wordsworth Circle* 10 (1979): 139–146.

Lascelles, Mary. *Jane Austen and Her Art.* London: Clarendon Press, 1939.

Lau, Beth. "Jane Austen, *Pride and Prejudice.*" In Duncan Wu, ed., *A Companion to Romanticism,* pp. 219–226. Oxford: Blackwell, 1998.

Leavis, Q. D. "A Critical Theory of Jane Austen's Writing." In *Collected Essays,* 3 vols. Cambridge: Cambridge University Press, 1983, I:61–146.

———. "Jane Austen: Novelist of a Changing Society." *Collected Essays,* 3 vols. Cambridge: Cambridge University Press, 1983, I:26–60.

———. "*Mansfield Park.*" *Collected Essays,* 3 vols. Cambridge: Cambridge University Press, 1983, I:161–171.

Le Faye, Deirdre. "Chronology of Jane Austen's Life." In Edward Copeland and Juliet McMaster, eds., *The Cambridge Companion to Jane Austen,* pp. 1–11. Cambridge: Cambridge University Press, 1997.

———, ed. *Jane Austen's Letters.* Oxford: Oxford University Press, 1995.

Levine, George. *Darwin and the Novelists.* Cambridge, Mass.: Harvard University Press, 1988.

Lewis, C. S. "A Note on Jane Austen." In Ian Watt, ed., *Jane Austen: A Collection of Critical Essays,* pp. 25–34. Englewood Cliffs, N.J.: Prentice-Hall, 1963.

Linkin, Harriet Kramer. "The Current Canon in British Romantics Studies." *College English* 53 (1991): 548–570.

Litvak, Joseph. "Reading Characters: Self, Society, and Text in *Emma.*" In Harold Bloom, ed., *Jane Austen's* Emma, pp. 119–134. New York: Chelsea House, 1987.

Litz, A. Walton. "Chronology of Composition." In J. David Grey, ed., *The Jane Austen Companion,* pp. 47–52. New York: Macmillan, 1986.

———. " 'A Development of Self': Characters and Personalities in Jane Austen's Fiction." In Juliet McMaster, ed., *Jane Austen's Achievement,* pp. 64–78. London: Macmillan, 1976.

———. *Jane Austen: A Study of Her Artistic Development*. New York: Oxford University Press, 1965.

———. "*Persuasion*: Forms of Estrangement." In John Halperin, ed., *Jane Austen: Bicentenary Essays*, pp. 221–232. Cambridge: Cambridge University Press, 1975.

Looser, Devoney, ed. *Jane Austen and the Discourses of Feminism*. New York: St. Martin's, 1995.

Lovejoy, Arthur O. "On the Discrimination of Romanticisms." In M. H. Abrams, ed., *English Romantic Poets*, pp. 3–24. 2nd ed. New York: Oxford University Press, 1975.

Lukács, Georg. *The Historical Novel*. Trans. Hannah Mitchell and Stanley Mitchell. Lincoln: University of Nebraska Press, 1962.

Macfarlane, Alan. Review of *The Family, Sex, and Marriage in England, 1500–1800*. *History and Theory* 18.1 (Feb. 1979): 121–122.

———. *Marriage and Love in England: Modes of Reproduction, 1300–1840*. Oxford: Basil Blackwell, 1986.

McGann, Jerome J. *Fiery Dust*. Chicago: University of Chicago Press, 1968.

———. "On Reading Childe Harold's Pilgrimage." In Robert F. Gleckner, ed., *Critical Essays on Lord Byron*, pp. 33–58. New York: Maxwell Macmillan International, 1991.

———. *The Romantic Ideology: A Critical Investigation*. Chicago: University of Chicago Press, 1983.

McKendrick, Neil, John Brewer, and J. H. Plumb. *The Birth of a Consumer Society: The Commercialization of Eighteenth-Century England*. Bloomington: Indiana University Press, 1982.

McMaster, Juliet, ed. *Jane Austen's Achievement*. London: Macmillan, 1976.

———. *Jane Austen the Novelist*. New York: St. Martin's, 1995.

McMaster, Juliet, and Bruce Stovel, eds. *Jane Austen's Business*. New York: St. Martin's, 1996.

Manning, Peter J. *Byron and His Fictions*. Detroit: Wayne State University Press, 1978.

Marx, Karl, and Friedrich Engels. *The Marx-Engels Reader*. Robert C. Tucker, ed. New York: Norton, 1978.

Matlak, Richard E. "The Men in Wordsworth's Life." *Wordsworth Circle* 9 (1978): 391–397.

Mellor, Anne K. *English Romantic Irony*. Cambridge, Mass.: Harvard University Press, 1980.

———. *Romanticism and Gender*. New York: Routledge, 1993.

Miller, D. A. *Narrative and Its Discontents: Problems of Closure in the Traditional Novel*. Princeton: Princeton University Press, 1981.

Millgate, Jane. "Prudential Lovers and Lost Heirs: *Persuasion* and the Presence of Scott." In Juliet McMaster and Bruce Stovel, eds., *Jane Austen's Business*, pp. 109–123. New York: St. Martin's, 1996.

Modert, Jo. "Chronology Within the Novels." In J. David Grey, ed., *The Jane Austen Companion*, pp. 53–59. New York: Macmillan, 1986.

Moler, Kenneth. *Jane Austen's Art of Allusion*. Lincoln: University of Nebraska Press, 1968.

———. "The Two Voices of Fanny Price." In John Halperin, ed., *Jane Austen: Bicentenary Essays*, pp. 172–179. Cambridge: Cambridge University Press, 1975.

Monaghan, David, ed. *Emma*. Houndmills, Basingstoke, Hampshire: Macmillan, 1992.

———, ed. *Jane Austen in a Social Context*. Totowa, N.J.: Barnes and Noble, 1981.

———. "Structure and Social Vision." In Harold Bloom, ed., *Jane Austen's* Mansfield Park, pp. 83–102. New York: Chelsea House, 1987.

Montaigne, Michel de. *The Complete Essays of Montaigne*. Trans. Donald M. Frame. Stanford: Stanford University Press, 1957.

Mooneyham, Laura G. *Romance, Language, and Education in Jane Austen's Novels*. Houndmills, Basingstoke, Hampshire: Macmillan, 1988.

Moretti, Franco. *The Way of the World: The Bildungsroman in European Culture*. London: Verso, 1987.

Morgan, Susan. *In the Meantime*. Chicago: University of Chicago Press, 1980.

———. "Jane Austen and Romanticism." In J. David Grey, ed., *The Jane Austen Companion*, pp. 364–368. New York: Macmillan, 1986.

———. *Sisters in Time: Imagining Gender in Nineteenth-Century British Fiction*. New York: Oxford University Press, 1989.

Mudrick, Marvin. *Irony as Defense and Discovery*. Princeton: Princeton University Press, 1952.

Muir, Rory. *Britain and the Defeat of Napoleon, 1807–1815*. New Haven: Yale University Press, 1996.

Nardin, Jane. "Jane Austen and the Problem of Leisure." In David Monaghan, ed., *Jane Austen in a Social Context*, pp. 122–142. Totowa, N.J.: Barnes and Noble, 1981.

———. *Those Elegant Decorums*. Albany: State University of New York Press, 1973.

Newton, Judith Lowder. *Women, Power, and Subversion: Social Strategies in British Fiction, 1778–1860*. Athens: University of Georgia Press, 1981.

Page, Norman. "Orders of Merit." In Joel Weinsheimer, ed., *Jane Austen Today*, pp. 92–108. Athens: University of Georgia Press, 1975.

Peckham, Morse. *The Triumph of Romanticism*. Columbia: University of South Carolina Press, 1970.

Perrot, Michelle, ed. *A History of Private Life*, vol. 4. Trans. Arthur Goldhammer. Cambridge, Mass.: Harvard University Press, 1990.

Perry, Ruth. "Interrupted Friendships in *Emma*." In David Monaghan, ed., *Emma*, pp. 127–147. Houndmills, Basingstoke, Hampshire: Macmillan, 1992.

Pfau, Thomas, and Robert F. Gleckner, eds. *Lessons of Romanticism: A Critical Companion*. Durham: Duke University Press, 1998.

Pinch, Adela. *Strange Fits of Passion: Epistemologies of Emotion, Hume to Austen*. Stanford: Stanford University Press, 1996.

Plato. *Symposium*. Trans. Alexander Nehemas and Paul Woodruff. Indianapolis: Hackett, 1989.

Poovey, Mary. *The Proper Lady and the Woman Writer: Ideology as Style in the Works of Mary Wollstonecraft, Mary Shelley, and Jane Austen*. Chicago: University of Chicago Press, 1984.

Price, Martin. "Austen: Manners and Morals." In Harold Bloom, ed., *Jane Austen*, pp. 163–178. New York: Chelsea House, 1986.

Prost, Antoine, and Gérard Vincent, eds. *A History of Private Life*, vol. 5. Trans. Arthur Goldhammer. Cambridge, Mass.: Harvard University Press, 1991.

Richardson, Alan. "The Dangers of Sympathy: Sibling Incest in English Romantic Poetry." *Studies in English Literature, 1500–1900* 25 (1985): 737–754.

Roberts, Warren. *Jane Austen and the French Revolution*. New York: St. Martin's, 1979.

Roth, Barry. *An Annotated Bibliography of Jane Austen Studies, 1973–83*. Charlottesville: University Press of Virginia, 1985.

———. *An Annotated Bibliography of Jane Austen Studies, 1984–94*. Athens: Ohio University Press, 1996.

Roth, Barry, and Joel Weinsheimer. *An Annotated Bibliography of Jane Austen Studies, 1952–1972*. Charlottesville: University Press of Virginia, 1973.

Ruoff, Gene W. "Anne Elliot's Dowry: Reflections on the Ending of *Persuasion*." *Wordsworth Circle* 7 (1976): 342–351.

———. "The Sense of a Beginning: *Mansfield Park* and Romantic Narrative." *Wordsworth Circle* 10 (1979): 174–186.

Sabin, Margery. *English Romanticism and the French Tradition*. Cambridge, Mass.: Harvard University Press, 1976.

Said, Edward W. *Beginnings: Intention and Method*. 2nd ed. New York: Columbia University Press, 1985.

Sales, Roger. *Jane Austen and Representations of Regency England*. London: Routledge, 1994.

Scott, Sir Walter. *Guy Mannering*. Edinburgh: Edinburgh University Press, 1999.

———. *The Poetical Works of Sir Walter Scott*. London: Oxford University Press, 1917.

———. *Waverley*. London: Penguin, 1985.

Sedgwick, Eve. "Jane Austen and the Masturbating Girl." *Critical Inquiry* 17 (1991): 818–837.

Sheets, Paul D. *The Making of Wordsworth's Poetry: 1785–98*. Cambridge, Mass.: Harvard University Press, 1973.

Showalter, Elaine. "Retrenchment." In Juliet McMaster and Bruce Stovel, eds., *Jane Austen's Business*, pp. 181–191. New York: St. Martin's, 1996.

Simpson, David. *Fetishism and Imagination*. Baltimore: Johns Hopkins University Press, 1982.

———. *Wordsworth and the Figurings of the Real*. London: Macmillan, 1982.

Siskin, Clifford. "A Formal Development: Austen, the Novel, and Romanticism." *Centennial Review* 28–29 (1984–1985): 1–28.

Smith, Johanna H. " 'My Only Sister Now': Incest in *Mansfield Park*." *Studies in the Novel* 19 (1987): 1–15.

Southam, B. C., ed. *Jane Austen: The Critical Heritage*. London: Routledge and Kegan Paul, 1968.

———. *Jane Austen's Literary Manuscripts*. London: Oxford, 1964.

———. "Was Jane Austen a Bonapartist?" In *Report for the Period 2000*, pp. 29–37. Alton, Hampshire: The Jane Austen Society, 2000.

Spacks, Patricia. "Muted Discord: Generational Conflict in Jane Austen." In David Monaghan, ed., *Jane Austen in a Social Context*, pp. 159–179. Totowa, N.J.: Barnes and Noble, 1981.

Sperry, Stuart M. "From 'Tintern Abbey' to the 'Intimations Ode': Wordsworth and the Function of Memory." *Wordsworth Circle* 1 (1970): 40–49.

Stewart, Maija. *Domestic Realities and Imperial Fictions*. Athens: University of Georgia Press, 1993.

Stone, Lawrence. *The Family, Sex, and Marriage in England, 1500–1800*. New York: Harper and Row, 1977.

Stovel, Bruce. "Comic Symmetry in *Emma*." In David Monaghan, ed., Emma, pp. 20–34. Houndmills, Basingstoke, Hampshire: Macmillan, 1992.

Sutherland, John. "The Novel." In Duncan Wu, ed., *A Companion to Romanticism*, pp. 333–344. Oxford: Blackwell, 1998.

Swingle, Larry J. "The Perfect Happiness of the Union: Jane Austen's *Emma* and English Romanticism." *Wordsworth Circle* 7 (1976): 312–319.

———. "The Poets, the Novelists, and the English Romantic Situation." *Wordsworth Circle* 10 (1979): 218–228.

———. "The Romantic Emergence." In Karl Kroeber and Gene W. Ruoff, eds. *Romantic Poetry: Recent Revisionary Criticism*, pp. 44–59. New Brunswick, N.J.: Rutgers University Press, 1993.

Tadmor, Naomi. *Family and Friends in Eighteenth-Century England: Household, Kinship, and Patronage*. Cambridge: Cambridge University Press, 2001.

Tanner, Tony. *Jane Austen*. Houndmills, Basingstoke, Hampshire: Macmillan, 1986.

Tave, Stuart M. "Jane Austen and One of Her Contemporaries." In John Halperin, ed., *Jane Austen: Bicentenary Essays*, pp. 61–74. Cambridge: Cambridge University Press, 1975.

———. *Some Words of Jane Austen*. Chicago: University of Chicago Press, 1973.

Thomas, Keith G. "Jane Austen and the Romantic Lyric: *Persuasion* and Coleridge's Conversation Poems." *ELH* 54 (1987): 893–924.

Thompson, James. "Intimacy in *Emma*." In David Monaghan, ed., Emma, pp. 110–126. Houndmills, Basingstoke, Hampshire: Macmillan, 1992.

Thorslev, Peter. "German Romantic Idealism." In Stuart Curran, ed., *The Cambridge Companion to British Romanticism*, pp. 74–94. Cambridge: Cambridge University Press, 1993.

———. "Incest as a Romantic Symbol." *Comparative Literature Studies* 2 (1965): 41–58.

Todd, Janet. *Women's Friendship in Literature*. New York: Columbia University Press, 1980.

———, ed. *Jane Austen: New Perspectives*. New York: Holmes and Meier, 1983.

Tomalin, Clare. *Jane Austen: A Life*. London: Viking, 1997.

Trilling, Lionel. *E.M. Forster*. New York: New Directions, 1965.

———. "*Emma*." *Encounter* 8 (1957): 49–59.

———. "*Mansfield Park*." In Ian Watt, ed., *Jane Austen: A Collection of Critical Essays*, pp. 124–140. Englewood Cliffs, N.J.: Prentice-Hall, 1963.

Trumpener, Katie. *Bardic Nationalism*. Princeton: Princeton University Press, 1997.

Tuite, Clara. *Romantic Austen*. Cambridge: Cambridge University Press, 2002.

Waldron, Mary. *Jane Austen and the Fiction of Her Time*. Cambridge: Cambridge University Press, 1999.

Watt, Ian, ed. *Jane Austen: A Collection of Critical Essays*. Englewood Cliffs, N.J.: Prentice-Hall, 1963.

———. *The Rise of the Novel*. Berkeley: University of California Press, 1957.

Weinsheimer, Joel, ed. *Jane Austen Today*. Athens: University of Georgia Press, 1975.

Wellek, René. "The Concept of Romanticism in Literary History." In Robert Gleckner and Gerald Enscoe, eds., *Romanticism: Points of View*, pp. 181–206. 2nd ed. Englewood Cliffs, N.J.: Prentice-Hall, 1962.

Whalley, George. "Jane Austen: Poet." In Juliet McMaster, ed., *Jane Austen's Achievement*, pp. 106–133. London: Macmillan, 1976.

White, Laura Mooneyham. "Jane Austen and the Marriage Plot: Questions of Persistence." In Devoney Looser, ed., *Jane Austen and the Discourses of Feminism*, pp. 71–86. New York: St. Martin's, 1995.

Wiesenfarth, Joseph. *The Errand of Form: An Assay of Jane Austen's Art*. New York: Fordham University Press, 1967.

———. "*Persuasion*: History and Myth." *Wordsworth Circle* 2 (1971): 160–168.

Wiltshire, John. *Jane Austen and the Body*. Cambridge: Cambridge University Press, 1992.

———. "*Mansfield Park, Emma*, and *Persuasion*." Edward Copeland and Juliet McMaster, eds., *The Cambridge Companion to Jane Austen*, pp. 58–82. Cambridge: Cambridge University Press, 1997.

Wlecke, Albert O. *Wordsworth and the Sublime*. Berkeley: University of California Press, 1973.

Wolfson, Susan J. "Romanticism and Gender." In Duncan Wu, ed., *A Companion to Romanticism*, pp. 387–396. Oxford: Blackwell, 1998.

Wollstonecraft, Mary. *A Vindication of the Rights of Women*. New York: Norton, 1988.

Woodring, Carl. "The New Sublimity of Tintern Abbey." In D. H. Reiman et al., eds., *The Evidence of the Imagination*, pp. 86–100. New York: New York University Press, 1978.

———. *Wordsworth*. Boston: Houghton Mifflin, 1965.

Woolf, Virginia. "Jane Austen." In *The Common Reader*, pp. 134–145. New York: Harcourt Brace, Jovanovich, 1984.

Wordsworth, Jonathan, ed. *Bicentenary Wordsworth Studies*. Ithaca: Cornell University Press, 1970.

Wordsworth, William. *Poems*, vol. 1. London: Penguin, 1977.

Wu, Duncan, ed. *A Companion to Romanticism*. Oxford: Blackwell, 1998.

Yeazell, Ruth Bernard. *Fictions of Modesty*. Chicago: University of Chicago Press, 1991.

Index